Could this be

OUT OF EGYPT!

**Preparing
the Way of the Lord
in Your Life
for History's Final Hour**

CHARLES CRISMIER

elijah books
Richmond, Virginia

Printed in the United States of America

Elijah Books
P.O. Box 70879
Richmond, VA 23255

All Scripture quotations are from the King James Version. The choice of the King James Version was based upon its continued prominence as the most quoted, read, and published version. Emphasis has been added by the use of bold type to highlight portions of the text for particular focus throughout.

ISBN-13: 978-0-9718428-3-0
ISBN-10: 0-9718428-3-3

Get Ready!

The Promised Land was straight ahead. God had a showdown with earth's greatest powerbroker, Pharoah, calling God's son, Israel, out of the bondage of Egypt. But after 40 years in the wilderness, the Lord could never get the spirit of Egypt out of His people. Only two out of 600,000 male descendants of Abraham were allowed into the Promised Land.

Over 400 times from Genesis to Revelation we find the theme "Out of Egypt." The Apostle Paul reminds us that "all these things happened unto [Israel] for our example," written to warn us "upon whom the ends of the world are come" (I Cor. 10:11). Yet, American Christians, poised on the near edge of the Second Coming, are living in the spirit of Egypt as never before.

Here is a chariot ride through history, building end-time trust for end-time trials, preparing the way of the Lord in your life for history's final hour. The Promised Land lies ahead. Get ready!

Ten Reasons You Must Read Out of Egypt

1. Do you long for spiritual fulfillment, yet it seems so difficult to grasp?
2. Do you feel TIRED OF PLAYING CHURCH?
3. Do you have a sense that something is not right in the professing Body of Christ in America, even in the face of apparent success?
4. Do you feel overburdened by buildings and programs?
5. Do you ever wince at the pomp, power, and pride frequently displayed from pulpit to pew?
6. Do you have a troubled spirit about the attitudes that are often displayed in the church's involvement in politics?
7. Do you ever wonder why America and the West has not experienced genuine revival even though we have prayed for it for a generation?
8. Do you feel troubled that national leaders find ethical behavior among Christians to be indistinguishable from the nation as a whole?
9. Do you believe that professing Christians are truly prepared for the Second Coming of Christ?
10. Do you have trouble tying the Old and New Testaments together meaningfully?

An Urgent Message to Every Professing Christian

From Genesis to Revelation, over four hundred times, God used the words "out of Egypt" or similar words, reminding His people of their call to leave Egypt. He took Israel out of Egypt but could never get Egypt out of their hearts. Could this be His *final call*?

Every True Christian Must
Come Out of Egypt!

THE MESSAGE OF THIS BOOK WILL RADICALLY CHANGE YOUR LIFE AND THINKING, just as it has for countless others. It is a message for the end-time church. It will tie together history and themes from the Word of God in ways you may never have dreamed possible.

THIS IS A VERY PERSONAL MESSAGE. But it is also a message to the church at large. It is a cry from the very heart of God to your heart and the heart of His people. It is a cry to pastors and people alike. For all of us must come *out of Egypt* if we would inherit the *Promised Land*.

THIS IS NOT AN EVANGELISTIC MESSAGE but a prophetic call to those who call themselves by the name of the Lord on the near edge of the culmination of history.

- ABRAHAM came OUT OF EGYPT.
- MOSES came OUT OF EGYPT.
- ISRAEL came OUT OF EGYPT.
- JESUS came OUT OF EGYPT.

AND SO MUST WE!

For it is written,
"Out of Egypt have I called my son"
(Matt. 2:15).

Contents

Fornicating with Egypt

Thou hast also committed fornication with the
Egyptians...great of flesh...to provoke me to anger.
—Ezek. 16:26

AMERICA HAS A LUSTFUL FASCINATION with the things of Egypt. Similarly, the Body of Christ (the church) in America is infatuated with the ways of Egypt. Many have succumbed to her seductive ways and fornicated with her pomp, pride, and power.
Throughout biblical history, God was deadly serious in His dealing with the spirit of Egypt. The words of Isaiah echo down the corridors of history:

> Woe to them that go down to Egypt for help; and stay on horses and trust in chariots...they look not to the Holy One of Israel, neither seek the Lord! (Isa. 31:1)

> The spirit of Egypt shall fail...and I will destroy the counsel thereof:...And the Egyptians will I give over into the hand of a cruel lord; and a fierce king will rule over them, saith the Lord, the Lord of hosts (Isa 19: 3–4).

Interestingly, this passage follows Isaiah 18, pronouncing, "Woe to the land shadowing with wings...," which some believe refers to a severely judged America in the end times.

Ultimately, the spirit of Egypt and the pharaohs of her power shall bow to Christ, apparently in His millennial reign: "The Lord shall be known to Egypt.... And the Lord shall smite Egypt: He shall smite Egypt and heal it: and they shall return even to the Lord, and He shall be entreated of them, and shall heal them" (Isa. 19:21–22). But before the soon return of Christ, will those in the American church who are walking in the spirit of Egypt return to the God of Moses, who once led the people out of Egypt? What does that mean for you and for me?

Will the Spirit of Egypt Define the End-Time Apostasy of the Church?

Is the church really walking like an Egyptian? How can we know? Has the Egyptian spirit become inbred into our ways, thinking, and traditions? While professing to have left Egypt, do even our spiritual leaders declare with ancient Aaron, the high priest of Israel, "These be thy gods?" Could the "I Am" be calling His adopted sons out of Egypt one last time before the Second Coming of His only begotten son?

I believe this is an end-time message to the end-time church. It is a message of end-time truths to prepare you for end-time trials. If you profess and confess Jesus Christ as both Savior and Lord, this message is for you, for time is running short. God is calling His people one last time OUT OF EGYPT.

Abraham, father of the faith, came out of Egypt that he might bring forth the "son of promise." Moses, the "great lawgiver," came out of Egypt that he might lead many sons out of Egypt to the "land of promise." God's "son"—the children of Israel—came up out of Egypt to point the nations to the promised "only begotten son." The "only begotten son"—the Christ—came out of Egypt that it might be fulfilled as was spoken by the prophet: "Out of Egypt have I called my son," that He might "lead many sons into [the] glory" of the eternal "promised land" (Heb. 2:40). And Zechariah promised that in the last days, The Lord will again call His people out of Egypt and "the sceptre of Egypt shall depart away" (Zech. 10:10–11).

Are you ready to come out of Egypt? It is Yahweh's FINAL CALL! God is wooing and warning. "Today, if you will hear His voice, harden not your hearts as in the provocation...for they could not enter in because of unbelief" (Heb. 3:7–19). It is time to COME OUT OF EGYPT!

> Behold...I will gather all thy lovers...I will even gather them round about against thee, and I will discover thy nakedness unto them...And I will judge thee, as a woman that breaks wedlock (Ezek. 16:37–38).

A Word for Liberals, Evangelicals,

GOD HAS A CONTROVERSY with those who profess His name in America "because **there is no truth**, nor mercy, **nor knowledge of God** in the land" (Hos. 4:1). "My people," says the Lord, "are **destroyed for lack of knowledge**" (vs. 6). "Hear ye…the Lord's controversy…for I brought thee up out of the land of Egypt, and redeemed thee…" (Mic. 6:2, 4).

We have become a profoundly unbelieving people. Statistics reveal that 92 to 96 percent of us believe *in* God yet few of us truly *believe* God. We have rewritten His Holy Word by editing out those portions that disagree with our will to believe or that do not suit our modern experience. We have become empowered by the spirit of science and have spurned the Spirit of God.

Evangelicals revile liberals for rejecting the resurrection, while liberals rebuke evangelicals for forgetting the poor. Both expressions of unbelief are disdainful to the Father. Yet many evangelicals in both mainline and recognized evangelical denominations and associations reject either by principle or practice the present-day application and operation of God's covenantal commitments to His people, substantially weakening our stand of faith.

Having grown up in that environment, professing to believe the Bible "from cover to cover and the cover, too," I am intimately acquainted with our multifaceted skills to manipulate the clear words of Scripture to conform to preconceived notions and denominational traditions.

We have become adept at excusing, twisting, spiritualizing, misapplying, dispensationalizing, or outright ignoring many of the plain and consistent words, themes, and patterns of Holy Writ that a Holy God intentionally placed in His Holy Word to prepare and protect a holy people for a holy calling. We have turned unbelief into an art form.

While professing to believe the Bible as "the inspired Word" and echoing mantras of "*sola Scriptura*," we often deceive ourselves and our followers by relegating to the dust of antiquity many of the most precious and needed promises of God's covenant, while proclaiming "Jesus Christ the same yesterday, today and forever" (Heb. 13:8). We have, in effect, become skeptics.

It is time to come out of Egypt. Have we not become one in spirit with the ten spies who brought forth what they perceived to be a truthful report of giants in the land, yet God called it an evil report?

Haven't we as leaders, to preserve our personal or denominational positions and pride, prevented our people from "entering the Promised Land?" Will the Lord of the church reiterate to us, "because thou has rejected knowledge, I will also reject thee, that thou shalt be no priest to me"? Or will He decree, "Seeing thou hast forgotten the law of the Lord thy God, I will also forget thy children" (Hos. 4:6)?

Perhaps it is such spiritualized unbelief the apostle Paul had in mind when he advised us as an act of spiritual warfare: "Casting down imaginations, and every high thing that exalteth itself against the knowledge of God," bring "into captivity every thought to the obedience of Christ" (2 Cor. 10:3–5). Our imaginations—our reasoning and thoughts—are very dear to us. We hold them under various labels: doctrinal belief, dispensational position, denominational stance, or personal conviction.

But friends, if our thoughts disagree with God, regardless of how reasonable we may think them to be, have we not arrogated ourselves to a par with the Almighty? Is not our unbelief on the verge of rebellion? And if we persist in such rejection, do we not jeopardize our own entrance to the Promised Land (see Rev. 21:8, Num. 14:26–38)?

In our interpretations and analysis, we have often defied the most elemental rule of interpretation: to take God at His plain, open, and obvious words. This rule applies to both the law of God and the laws of men. Having criticized the judiciary of our land for twisting and morphing clear words of the law of men to suit personal or politically correct fancy, it is now time for pastors, priests, and parishioners who purport to practice the "perfect law of liberty" to repent of theological gymnastics that have taken God's people back into Egypt.

I realize this is straight—yes, even confrontational—talk. But the Lord of the church is calling His people out of Egypt one last time:

- "Today if ye will hear His voice, harden not your hearts..." (Heb. 3:7–8).
- "Take heed, brethren, lest there be in you an evil heart of unbelief..." (Heb. 3:12).
- "To whom sware He that they should not enter His rest, but to them that believed not? So we see that they could not enter in because of unbelief" (Heb. 3:18–19).

Let us therefore fear, lest, a promise being left us of entering into His rest, any of you should seem to come short of it. For unto us was the gospel preached, as well as unto them: but the word preached did not profit them, not being mixed with faith in them that heard it (Heb. 4:1–2).

Have we been preaching the whole gospel? Have you been believing the whole gospel? Or have you preached or believed only the portion you could understand or agree with? Has your group, tradition, or denomination restricted you in any way from either believing or preaching the whole gospel—the entire good news of God's full and complete covenant? If so, are you not, by your tradition, making the Word of God without effect (see Matt. 15:39)? Are you rejecting the very Word of God that you might keep your own traditions (see Mark 7:6–13)? Will you obey God, or men? Will you come out of Egypt? Time is short.

Section One

America: Where Pharaohs Rule

...the Lord, having saved the people out of the land of Egypt,
afterwards destroyed them that believed not. —Jude 5

YOU ARE ABOUT TO EMBARK on an unusual journey. You will follow a motley crew of three million slaves as they exit Egypt on order of Pharaoh who has had a showdown with the God of Abraham, Isaac, and Israel.

This journey may change your viewpoint. It may cause you to reassess ideas, notions, beliefs, and positions. This account reveals why revival tarries in America today, despite a generation of prayer and revival talk. Missing is the revival walk.

This is not intended to be as much a theological treatise as a narrative that interweaves Scripture with our personal and national condition. Hopefully it will unfold themes that are often either ignored, redefined, rejected, or misunderstood.

Unlike material common in today's Christian writing, this is not a collection of stories and anecdotal accounts tied together with a few Scripture passages. Rather, it is a piecing together of a profound and provocative biblical story interlaced throughout the Scriptures from Genesis to Revelation, as a people are formally delivered from the bondage of Egypt but refuse to leave its ways. We begin with America's love affair with Egypt.

America, Where Egypt Vies for Authority

The Washington Monument, a 555-foot, elevated pyramid exalting the procreative power of the Egyptian sun-god, "lords it over" America's capital city, presiding over the Washington Mall and the country's executive, legislative, and judicial branches of government. How did such a monument get erected? Why was its cornerstone, along with those of the capitol itself and our most prominent government buildings, laid in Masonic ritual dedicated to ancient Egyptian mystery religions? Does this have any import for the future of America?

Chapter One

America Loves Egypt

We're all pharaohs here. So go pagan.

AMERICA MAY NOT BE "IN EGYPT," but "Egypt" is deeply ingrained in America! Egypt was the first great world political power. Her ancient lore has lured the world's leading historians and archeologists to the bosom of her temples and tombs.

The Memphis Connection

Memphis, the capital of Egypt in the earliest times, was the greatest of all commercial cities in the land. It was there that Abraham and Sarah sojourned with Lot four thousand years ago. There Joseph was sold as a slave and later ruled as second only to Pharaoh. It was there that Moses threw down the "rod of God" before earth's greatest power broker, and the rod became a hissing snake that swallowed up the writhing rods of Pharaoh's prophets.

This was the place where Pharaoh's pomp and pride was brought to the feet of Hebrew slaves as the cry over the death of the firstborn of all Egypt finally touched the throne. Yet all—Egyptian or Hebrew—who by faith painted the blood of the lamb upon the doorpost, were spared the earthly cost of confrontation between the God who declared "I AM" and the pharaoh who would be god.

The great Nile hosted the congregation of Egyptian gods at Memphis. The worship of Ptah brought Egypt "the Mind of the Universe." Osiris, Lord of the Dead and God of Resurrection, controlled all phases of life.[1] And Apis, the Sacred Bull, inspired Aaron and the Hebrews who had "come out of" Egypt to point to the golden calf and declare, "These be thy gods, O Israel, which brought thee up out of the land of Egypt" (Exod. 32:4).

But Israel was not alone in corrupting herself with the ways and worship of Egypt. The modern city of Memphis on the Mississippi—the American "Nile"—has embraced the ways of that ancient world, now obscured by the sands of time. Heralding the opening of The Great Bridge in April 1892, was the following announcement: "Faithful Followers of His Majesty to Pay Homage to Isis, Goddess of Memphis."

The Great American Pyramid was erected along the Mississippi riverfront at a projected cost exceeding fifty-four million dollars. The thirty-nine-story structure was to bring "a new spirit" to the city, a century after a miniversion of the Egyptian pyramid of Cheops (built for Tennessee's hosting of the World's Fair in 1897) was abandoned. Egyptian inscriptions mark the pavement of downtown Memphis, describing a city fallen under the mystical spell of Egypt with its own secret society, "Mystic Society of the Memphis."

Developers envisioned the "greatest magic show on earth" to ordain The Great American Pyramid. It would be baptized into the "Egyptian Experience" with a $100 million, three-dimensional, holographic display incorporating scenes of clouds, an oasis, winged snakes, beetles, and evil gods of the netherworld.

While the Egyptians dedicated seventeen million dollars to clean up their pyramids and sphinxes, could it be that the I AM again reacted with plagues to the spirit of Egypt and the pomp and prideful idolatry of modern Memphis? In the final decade of the second millennium, with Egypt close to her heart, Memphis on the Mississippi saw an epidemic of bankruptcies, bank failures, business collapses, falling cotton prices, tax hikes, unemployment, and the worst flood of Memphis' history?

A new message of salvation had been proposed in the *Memphis Commercial Appeal*, October 10, 1990:

> The pyramid. Disney on the Nile. The Mid-South Jewel. Modern Memphis' ticket to fame, fortune, salvation and all that [the] pyramid manager is preaching.[2]

If the future of modern Memphis is to be ordered upon the ruins of the capital of ancient Egypt, perhaps the dust of antiquity should be brushed from the words of Isaiah, which read:

> Thus saith the Lord, the labor of Egypt shall be thine…they shall make supplication…saying, Surely God is in thee; and there is none else, there is no God…. They shall be ashamed, and also confounded, all of them: they shall go to confusion together that are makers of idols (Isa. 45:14, 16).

Memphis, warned Isaiah, incarnated the spirit of Egypt:

> The…princes of Noph [Memphis] are deceived; they have also seduced Egypt, even [her leaders]. The Lord hath mingled a perverse spirit in the

midst thereof: and they (the leaders) have caused Egypt to err in every work thereof, as a drunken man staggereth in his vomit (Isa. 19:13–14).

Allocation of a quarter of a million dollars was made to erect a colossal statue of Rameses II guarding the Great American Pyramid in modern Memphis.[3] It was Rameses who withstood God's call through Moses to "Let my people go." It was Rameses who built his treasure cities on the backs of God's chosen people. And it is the spirit of Rameses, reflected in the pomp, pride, and power of modern Memphis, that once more seeks to enslave God's chosen people in the American church into Egyptian bondage.

The prophet Ezekiel made the heart of God clear with blistering words:

I will destroy the idols, and I will cause their images to cease out of Noph [Memphis]. And I will set fire in Egypt: Sin shall have great pain, and No shall be set asunder, and Noph [Memphis] shall have distresses daily (Ezek. 30:13–16).

Perhaps the cry of Hosea to God's people best expresses the end-time heart of God to those who profess his name in America:

Rejoice not, O Israel, for joy, as other people: for thou hast gone a whoring from thy God.... What will you do in the solemn day...? Egypt shall gather them up, Memphis shall bury them: The days of visitation are come.... Israel shall know it: the prophet is a fool, the spiritual man is mad, for the multitude of thine iniquity.... They have deeply corrupted themselves... (Hos. 9:1–9).

Decor Declares the Heart

Recent excursions spanning America's coasts revealed the resurgence of Egyptian influence in residential and business decor. One might expect to see colorful busts of the Pharaohs and their princesses intermixed with crystals and New Age trinketry in southern California. But would one expect to find a proliferation of such symbols in the bastions of tradition on our eastern shores?

In Newport, Rhode Island, Egyptian sphinxes, pyramids, and royal cats are interspersed with religious paraphernalia displayed in clothing stores and novelty shops. Richmond, Virginia, is a city declared by industry to be "a testing ground for America," due to its inbred conservatism and traditional outlook. It was shocking for me to walk into a large shop in Richmond for a haircut and find it replete with every conceivable Egyptian symbol—all displayed in the latest of designer taste, covering walls, windows, and lighted displays. Obelisks, pyramids, and other memorials and Egyptian insignias abound in many upscale furniture stores and decor shops throughout the country.

Perhaps the most telling of all discoveries presented itself on the shelf of a specialty Christmas shop near Williamsburg, Virginia. My wife and I gasped in disbelief as our eyes fastened upon the latest in Christmas ornaments. Here, in the birthplace of America—site of the first representative government in the new world—was a magnificent, gold-plated set of eight "Christmas" ornaments that were highlighted in a regal, royal blue, displaying in all the splendor of the ancient past, Egypt's symbols of worship and adoration. For years many voices have called out to restore Christ to Christmas. Yet it would seem a giant leap from the fantasy of Santa Claus to the finery of Egypt, from reindeer to golden lions, and from the glory of angels to the golden crowns of pharaohs and sphinxes.

It appears that what America thinks in her heart is now increasingly being displayed in her homes and business havens. The New Age universal and cosmic Christ is more "universal" than any of us might think.

Just as the Pharaohs of old expected, by purification and petrification within their pyramids, to sit on the right hand of the god Re, so even professing Christians, spiritually mummified and looking good on Sunday mornings, dance with the spirit of Egypt during the week. Avoiding the symbols of Egypt like the plagues of old, many of us have unwittingly embraced the substance and spirit of Egypt in our thinking and our ways.

Surprising to many, Egypt is deeply rooted in American history. Egyptian thinking has captured the American mind for at least two centuries. Deep in the soul of the nation, a spiritual war has been raging from the birth of the republic.

The long-ignored Egyptian seeds of yesteryear have produced fertile fields of Egyptian ways and thinking today, from the church house to the White House. These seeds were carriers of a potpourri of political, economic, and spiritual patterns and outlooks. As they germinated among the mixed fields of American thought, their fibers have been interwoven into every aspect of American life, producing a hybrid of biblical and pagan ways and thought that have become thoroughly ensconced as tradition.

If we dare to look closely at the fabric of even "Christian" thinking today, we might be horrified to find powerful and often-glittering thread gleaned from the cultural tapestries of ancient Egypt, Greece, and Rome. So strong are those threads that they permeate (and often subtly define) even our theology, the way we "do church," the way we think about ministry, the way we think about time and eternity, the way we determine priorities, the way we look at people, and the way the church spends its resources.

At bottom, these Egyptian threads may even inhibit or prevent us from truly trusting God. That, my friend, could indeed be serious if we really believe in the soon return of Christ. Please be patient as we look at the fabric of our lives together. We can unfold only so much at a time. Our lives are more defined by pagan antiquity than we care to admit, but so, too, can they be redefined by God's ancient call to those who would be called by His memorial name, Yahweh, to come OUT OF EGYPT.

Splendors of Egypt

Phoenix "came of age" with *Splendors of Ancient Egypt* in early 1999, according to a museum director. Spread over seventeen thousand square feet, dramatically lighted galleries presented the blockbuster show depicting the reigns of dozens of Pharaohs who would "feel right at home."[4]

There is "a pent-up desire…to have this kind of product," according to the Phoenix Art Museum. And indeed there is, for in every city it has been presented, "Splendors" has broken museum records in major American cities. Visitors can revel vicariously in Pharaonic splendor while expanding exposure to a new bevy of gods and goddesses, adding to their western repertoire of personal prosperity and bless-me-club mantras that echo from New Age gurus to pastors of New Covenant gospel.

As the movement toward blockbuster displays expands across the United States, museum directors agree that the magic words are *Egypt* and *Impressionism*.[5] But why Egypt? Why the incredible fascination?

The very name "Phoenix" evokes that bird in Egyptian religious mythology that consumed itself in fire, only to be "resurrected" from the ashes. And from Phoenix, the *Splendors* display traversed the country to the birthplace of America: Richmond, Virginia.

My River Is My Own!

Richmond, Virginia, relies historically upon the James River, as ancient Egypt did upon the Nile. As Pharaoh declared, "My river is my own,"[6] so it is said that "the James River is the **soul** of Richmond"[7] and will, in fact, "be the city's future **salvation**."[8]

Even as the Nile was the Egyptian source of life, the James River has been to Richmond "the source of all good things."[9] As there would be no Egypt without the Nile, so the director of the Virginia Historical Society observed, "There would be no Richmond without the James River."[10]

It was May 24, 1607, that the cross of the covenant was planted by Christopher Newport at The Falls at Richmond, signaling the Creator God's dominion over the "promised land" that was to become America, Virginius Dabney records in his book, *Richmond, The Story of a City,* that "a great shout confirmed the planting of the cross, followed by a prayer."[11] Now the spirit of Egypt vies for dominion with a glass pyramid raised to worshipful heights atop Virginia Commonwealth University.

Now an epicenter for Satan's global counterfeit religious unity movement, Richmond stands, per industry standards, "a testing ground" for the nation. Tidewater visitors have called this river city "The Holy City," as thousands of steeples jut to the sky from church buildings and as spired buildings rise above the river, defining an image struggling with its reality.[12] Whose "holy city" is it? Will the God of Moses rule, or will Pharaoh continue declaring "My river is my own"?

A glossy-paged contemporary portrait of Richmond declares, "A River City **Reborn**."[13] The opening chapter is entitled "Phoenix by the River."[14] Will such "rebirth" be incarnated in the mystical rise of the spirit of Egypt as the phoenix bird soars in dominion over America, or will the Spirit of a holy God bring rebirth to a city and nation enamored by the "splendor" of Egypt?

The Dollar of Destiny

You have, undoubtedly, been offered at some time "a penny for your thoughts." With inflation, perhaps the offer should now be raised to a dollar. Dryly humorous as the idea may be, our dollar bill may have both defined and reflected more thought in America than we realize, even within the church.

Although Samuel B. Huntington was actually America's first president following the Declaration of Independence under the First Continental Congress, the image of George Washington graces the face of the bill as our first post-Revolutionary War President. He was also a Freemason. Standing alone, that may not be significant. But when combined with a vast host of historical fact, its significance looms larger.

On the reverse side of the dollar bill are engraved the face and reverse sides of The Great Seal of the United States. Take one from your purse or pocket and look at it for a moment. On the right side the American Eagle declares, "Through many, one." On the left is inscribed an incomplete pyramid of thirteen steps. Above the unfinished pyramid is a crystal cap with the illuminated all-seeing eye poised to complete the unfinished project begun with the original thirteen colonies.

The pyramid of ancient Egypt was a massive expression of man's power and pride, conceived as a mathematically perfect, three-dimensional figure. It was intended to house and protect the body of the deified Pharaoh. Like the ancient Tower of Babel, its shape resembled giant stairs, leading the spirit of the deceased god-king to the heavens to sit at the right hand of Re, the sun-god. As it is written in the *Pyramid Texts*, the gilded-peaked pyramids were a sort of Jacob's ladder, providing passage to and from the realm of the gods.[15] Why was this symbol used on the most widely circulated of all American currency?

Manley P. Hall, considered an expert in Masonic lore, reveals that many of the forefathers of the US government were Masons, and that the United States was established for a particular reason known only to a select and secret body. Using the Great Seal as a signature for this private intent, the unfinished pyramid on our dollar bill represents the task to which the secret body undertook from the beginning. The eagle purportedly represents the phoenix bird rising out of the cold ashes of lifeless creeds to the ancient mysteries once again united under the auspices of "universal wisdom."[16]

The message of this book does not rest upon the truth of this symbolism. Neither is this writing intended to be an exhaustive or even substantial discourse on Freemasonry. Nor is it intended in any way to demean or diminish the memory of George Washington. It is nevertheless a fact that the great Egyptian "master-builders," as they are called, impressed millions of laborers to unite their efforts in order to perpetuate their faith. And similarly, Freemasons believe that building and geometry—the arts of stonemasons—under the watchful eye of Osiris, symbolize the moral foundations of the universe.

Masons Build Pyramids and Capitols

Modern Freemasonry in the English-speaking world began in London in 1717. By 1776, there were 100 American lodges with as many as 5,000 members out of a population of 2.5 million. When George Washington laid the cornerstone of the Capitol in 1793, it was done in the form of a Masonic ceremony, "in the thirteenth year of American independence…and in the year of Masonry, 5,793." Washington wore the traditional Mason's apron, made specially by the wife of a French Mason, none other than the Marquette de Lafayette. And the cornerstones for the majority of the public buildings in our nation's capital were laid in Masonic ritual.[17]

Does it matter that the buildings and monuments of our capital city are dedicated to pagan gods? Were these harmless acts? Why does the elaborate image of the Egyptian sun-god dominate the Arlington, Virginia, headquarters of Scottish Rite Freemasonry—one of more than 13,000 Masonic temples in the United States? What are the mysteries guarded by the Sphinx-like lions that guard their sacred chambers?

Why was a 555-foot-tall monument—an elevated pyramid exalting the procreative power of the Egyptian sun-god (exceeding the height of many of the world's most famous obelisks, including the one near the great pyramid of Cheops in Egypt)—installed to dominate and preside over the Washington Mall and over our Capitol? Why was its cornerstone laid by Robert Mills, a master Mason? And how did such a monument get erected when the original plans of Congress called for a statue of General Washington on a horse?

In the November 1, 1997, issue of *Charisma*, Ron Campbell, in his feature article entitled "Unearthing the Mysteries of Freemasonry," asks a probing question of every professing Christian: "Does any of this affect our lives today?"[18]

Notwithstanding a public persona of service, every Mason's initiation rite requires this oath: "…under no less penalty than to have my throat cut, my tongue taken from the roof of my mouth, my heart plucked from under my left breast, then to be buried in the sands of the sea…my body to be burnt to ashes…so help me God."[19] This is one of the milder oaths to be taken as a man climbs the Masonic ladder to the thirty-third degree.

Masonry's theology is an odd mixture of biblical imagery and Egyptian ideology blended into a religious stew. It lures members, by appealing to the hunger for social acceptance and to the power of secrecy, to a religious conversion—from the light of Christ to the all-seeing eye of Osiris and a pantheon of other deities, and from the Cross to the Pyramid. Could this explain, in part, why despite the words adjoining the Masonic symbol on our dollar bill—IN GOD WE TRUST—that *Time* magazine found it necessary to write a banner headline on its front cover April 5, 1993: "A nation that forgot God," and in the fall of 1993, *Time* declared, "America, 'ONE NATION UNDER **GODS**'?"

Even *Civilization*, the secular magazine for the Library of Congress, reports Freemasonry is enveloped in Egyptian trappings. The compass and square, Egyptian symbols of the master builders of temples and pyramids, are the recognized emblems of Masonry, inscribed throughout this nation. Men initiated into the thirty-second degree of the Freemasons may not be told their classic engraving depicts solar deities: Osiris the sun-god and Isis, the "goddess of a thousand names." One glance at the great Egyptian Hall of the Masonic Temple in Philadelphia exemplifies the profound commitment of United States Freemasons to the spirit of ancient Egypt.

What can explain the historical refusal of America's largest Protestant denomination to rise with one voice against such a pagan influence? Why boycott Disney and wink at Masonry? Do we have only the conscience of a conservative, or do we have the convictions of a Christian? Have the "sacred cows" of India and Egypt wandered into American pastures? When pastors, deacons, and elders have taken their place in the ranks of the Masonic Order, can we still claim to be "under God?" Or are we now "under gods?" When professed "Christian" pastors cast their spiritual lot with Freemason Louis Farrakhan, head of the Nation of Islam, who is this "God" we profess to serve?[20]

Perhaps we need the help of secular observers to sort through the fog of pagan pantheism that enshrouds us. From *Civilization*, published by the Library of Congress, the report is clear:

> The major religious objection to Freemasonry is that it teaches a "natural religion," honoring a generic God who may be approached **without** the sacraments **or faith in Christ. Such universalism offends any church that makes serious exclusive claims about its own way to salvation.**[21]

Is our dollar determining the destiny of America's sons? Has it affected your husband or father? The Library of Congress made no mistake in combining feature articles on Freemasonry and the pagan celebration of the spirit of Egypt in its August-September 1996 issue of *Civilization* featuring the new Las Vegas.

We're All Pharaoh's Here

A short jaunt from Caesar's palace takes you from Rome to Egypt in the "new" Las Vegas. There, thirty million Americans annually pay homage to what the official publication of the Library of Congress describes as "pagan ambiance."

The Luxor Hotel and Casino is the third-largest pyramid in the world. You can stack nine of the monstrous Boeing 747s on top of each other in the atrium alone. American pagans are encouraged to take a Disney-style ride down the simulated Nile, while receiving catechism on ancient Egyptian religion. Then visit King Tut's tomb.

What else would you expect when visiting a hotel named after one of the greatest cities of ancient Egypt? Thebes (now called Luxor) lies three hundred miles south of Memphis. Thebes has preserved noteworthy shrines and temples devoted to the great Egyptian deities, including the sun-god.

The great Luxor pyramid of Las Vegas captures the spirit of a city where the renowned Rameses II could have made himself right at home. One could almost hear an echo across the sands of Vegas from the great Pharaoh's challenge to the prophet: "Who is the Lord that I should obey him?" One can capture the arrogance of yet another Pharaoh declaring of the Nile, "My river is my own." Has not America's renowned musician crooned a new national anthem from the entertainment platforms of sin city: "I'll do it my way"?

What would the prophets of old say to such a city? What warnings would they thunder to thirty million Americans who annually come to worship at the secular shrine? What would they say to born-again Christians who traffic there with the world, or to the author of the *Book of Virtues* reported to have emerged with a gambling purse of sixty thousand dollars?[22]

Where are the prophets today? Are their voices drowned by the cacophony of clanging bells, rolling dice, spinning wheels, and the cries of those who have just gambled away their life savings and their grandchildren's inheritance? Or is the church silent because she is enjoying the pleasures of sin for a season?

Is it any wonder *Civilization* magazine must become the "mouth of a donkey" to a nation that pledges herself "under God." The secular prophets now speak what has become unspeakable from the general cross-section of America's pulpits:

> **Egypt is perfect for Las Vegas**; it's all about glamour, power, hierarchy; very primal, very up-front about death and ecstasy. **None of this Christian trifling over sin** and the wages of same at the Luxor Hotel (**we're all pharaohs here**). *So go pagan.*[23]

And as *Civilization* described it,

> Everywhere you look there are attempts to create a pre-Christian (preguilt) scene. The New Vegas is emphatically more pagan than the Old…Vegas

is designed to get you back beyond the old guilt culture into a culture of imperial pleasure and ease, rife with glory, sensuality and decadence.[24]

The MGM Grand, a great, golden lion in all the splendor of imperial Egypt, opens its unsatiated maw to swallow millions who come within the grasp of its extended paws. All the new hotels are in imperial style. *Civilization* calls to America from its front cover, "Bring the family—and pay for your sins." The official publication of the United States Library of Congress preaches a profound message that should cause "Christian" America to gasp in spiritual anguish.

It is "the simple fact that Las Vegas is becoming an ever-more-pressing metaphor for American life overall."[25]

The Power of the Pyramid

Las Vegas and Memphis are not alone in succumbing to the power of the pyramid. The late twentieth century has spawned more pyramids, not to house dead bodies, but for living bodies with dead spirits.

Cleveland sports a five-story glass pyramid to house the Rock and Roll House of Fame. Galveston erected its Rainforest Pyramid, Grand Rapids its Corporate Development Center, and Long Beach its physical education pyramid. San Francisco's Transamerica Corporation headquarters stands supreme, 48 stories and 853 feet towering twice the height of the Great Pyramid of Khufu. Transamerica customers and stockholders can rest in the corporate motto "The power of the pyramid working for you."[26]

But America's pyramidal trust in the mysterious powers of Egyptian architecture extends far beyond corporate matters. *Newsweek* announced in its November 28, 1994, cover story that America is "In Search of the Sacred." A professor of religion at the University of California noted, "...they sense the need for spirituality, but they do not know where to get it."[27] Now Americans, in hot pursuit of spirituality, are yearning for Egypt.

"Under 2.3 million pounds of granite come meditative incantations," declares *Newsweek*. In the deepest room of the Great Pyramid of Cheops, 345 feet under the entrance, an American mystic and "channeler" guides his flock of initiates from Washington, Hawaii, and Georgia through "experimental mythology" and "the ancient art of emotional healing." An Atlanta mother of five, whose Presbyterian upbringing gave her little solace, says she now needs "more support in my journey." Her pyramid companions "are the most loving people."

Strange, you say? Not at all. No exotic corner of the globe attracts so many Americans searching for transcendence as the land of Moses and the Pharaohs. "While Biblical Israel has the firmest grip on our Judeo-Christian consciousness, many spiritual voyagers find ancient Egypt more magical."

Since the Great Pyramid opened for private after-hours visits in 1990, thousands of mystical seekers have come. The American mystic guides observe, "They feel this is their home."

"It is the architecture of Pharaonic monuments that gives them such power over their mind," academics conclude, "epitomizing a world of order." Americans, said the channeler, are impressed by this "sacred science."[28]

Fascination and Fornication

The spirit of Egypt fascinates the American and Western mind and heart on the leading edge of the third millennium. Our infatuation with her lore, our longing to dance with popular culture, and our search for spirituality—coupled with massive biblical illiteracy, the pride of prosperity, and our anthem of rebellion: "I'll do it my way"—has lead us to bed with all the mystery of Egyptian gods and goddesses, while privately divorcing the God who said, "I AM."

Ours has become a "culture of disbelief." Yet it is not that we believe in nothing. We believe in everything. When a national magazine reports, "In So Many Gods We Trust," it places us squarely in Egypt where gods and goddesses abound. The problem in the church is not that we do not believe IN God. We just do not **believe** Him. We have joined 3 million Israelites who were led out of Egypt in body but remained there in spirit. But for now, *Civilization* laments…

> Las Vegas, we ought to admit, is rising. In the midst of the desert [like Egypt of old], it glows strong and stronger, a flaming bright light of all American darkness.

Since the birth of the Republic, the spirit of Egypt has vied for dominion with the Spirit of God. Which will prevail in this dark hour on the near edge of Christ's Second Coming? The answer lies in the willingness of American Christians to come OUT OF EGYPT.

Chapter Two

Where Pharaohs Ruled

Now the Egyptians are men, and not God; —Isa. 31:3

FASTEN THE SEATBELT OF YOUR CHARIOT. We are going to take a ride back in time from the last great civilization of human history to the first great civilization.

The Joseph-Jesus Connection

The Bible, from Genesis to Revelation, speaks of Egypt. Joseph and Jesus define the kingdoms portrayed between. Joseph was used to save Israel **in** Egypt; Jesus died to deliver His people **from** Egypt. Joseph was **crowned** in Egypt; Jesus was **crucified** in Egypt (Rev. 11:8). Joseph appeared before Potiphar; Jesus appeared before Pontius Pilate. Joseph, by faith, commanded that his bones be removed from death in Egypt, that he might be resurrected **from** the land of promise; Jesus' bones were raised from death out of Egypt that He might be resurrected **to** the Promised Land.

Joseph was raised from a pit to power on earth; Jesus was raised from the pit of hell to power on high. Both were tried and convicted unjustly. Each was rejected by his own. Both forgave their enemies. And both came OUT OF EGYPT.

Egypt: A Primary Biblical Theme

The word *Egypt* appears 611 times in the Bible. In most instances there is a clearly negative connotation. The words *OUT OF EGYPT* or words similar appear over 400 times throughout the Scriptures. It is reasonable to conclude, therefore, that God was seeking and continues to seek to communicate some

28

powerful truth in such repetition. Apparently He did not want the truth to be missed by a cursory reading.

Egypt has played and continues to play a significant role in Israel's history. Once Israel feared Egypt. Today, Egypt fears Israel. Egypt, in the 1967 War, lead an Arab coalition to annihilate Israel. Israel, by a preemptive strike, disarmed the Egyptian air force in just one day, ultimately regaining lost portions of the "Promised Land," including control of Jerusalem for the first time since the Roman destruction in 70 A.D.

Nowhere do we read that Egypt will live in peace with Israel until the Messiah comes to rule and reign as the "Prince of Peace." For now, Israel, I am told, does not even appear as a nation on official Egyptian or Arab maps. A similar war or tension exists between the "Spirit of Egypt" and the "Israel of God" consisting of all—both Jew or Gentile—who truly embrace and believe Jesus Christ as Messiah, the promised Anointed One. We can gain needed insight into this historical battle by looking back over the shoulder of history to the pomp, power, and pride of the ancient civilization known as Egypt.

Where Men Become Gods

The Egyptians—according to Will Durant in his monumental *Story of Civilization*—were the greatest builders in history. But "beneath and above everything in Egypt was religion." Durant observes, "We cannot understand the Egyptian or man—until we study his gods."[1]

The greatest of the gods was the sun. Sometimes it was worshiped as the supreme deity Ra or Re, the father who fertilized Mother Earth. Sometimes it was worshiped as a divine calf. Or the sun was the god Horus, taking the form of a falcon, a symbol of Egyptian religion and loyalty. Ra was always the creator. Isis, Osiris, and Horus "took on the seminal role of Holy Trinity."[2]

Durant describes Egyptian piety as so exuberant that "the Egyptians worshiped not merely the source, but almost every form of life."[3] Plants became sacred. More popular were animal gods. One can readily see a similar trend in modern America's increasing worship of Mother Earth. Rabbits, frogs, spiders, and insects increasingly appear in jeweled and ceramic forms to suit the taste of modern earth-bent consumers. Religious environmentalism abounds.

The goat and the bull were especially sacred to the Egyptians as representing sexual creative power. Signs of sex worship appear frequently in figures depicted on temple sculptures with erect sexual organs. America's celluloid and tabloid depictions reveal similar worship.

"At last the gods became human—or rather, men became gods." The "personal gods of Egypt were merely superior men and women, made in heroic mould [a celebrity faith of power, prestige, and pretty faces]. Men became objects of worship, yet were "composed of bone and muscle, flesh and blood; they hungered and ate, thirsted and drank, loved and mated, hated and killed, grew old and died."[4]

Mother of God

The "reimagining God" conference led by United Methodist, Episcopal, and Presbyterian women in America brought nothing new to the historical temple of goddess worship. What may have been new—at least in America—was the introduction of goddess worship to monotheistic Christianity. Ancient Egypt nurtured the maternal tenderness of Isis, the Great Mother. As the loyal wife (and sister) of Osiris, she symbolized the mysterious power that produced the earth and every living thing. Although Osiris was "god of the beneficent Nile," whose death and resurrection were celebrated yearly, Isis was even considered greater than he, for she conquered death through love. To Egypt she was "the original priority and independence of the female principle in creation…." The Egyptians worshiped her with fondness and piety, and they raised up jeweled images to her as the Mother of God.[5]

The Protestant convergence of gender-neuterizing of Scripture, the feminization of God, and worship of Mother Earth through the high priests of hyperextended environmentalism (with a fevered Roman Catholic revival of the theology of Mary as co-redemtrix with Christ)[6] reveals a nation not "under God" but under gods, wallowing soul-deep in the Spirit of Egypt.

Priests, Not of Purity, but of Power

It is a land bloated with religious words, symbols, and rituals and obese with religious information. It is a land abounding with temples of worship—350,000 identified to be "Christian." It is a people abounding with Bibles—more per capita than any other nation on earth. It is an economy saturated with "Christian" books, "Christian" music, and "Christianese."

A clergy-class rules and reigns over a population, 90 percent of which claim to believe in God; 80 percent of which claim to be "Christian"; 45 percent of which claim to be born again. The prophets and priests deliver their daily or weekly diet of spiritual salve and religious good-feelings from pulpits of positive thinking, directed more by prevailing winds than by prevailing prayer.

The nation is America—Egypt on the Mississippi or on the James, on the Colorado or on the Snake. Moralisms on Sunday refuse to pay moral dividends on Monday. Truth is whatever lures thousands and raises millions for the expanding coffers of the kingdoms of priests in divine competition, erecting monuments to their memory and devising programs for their promotion. Irrelevant is the fact that 91 percent of the population regularly tells lies,[7] that the divorce rate among fundamentalist Christians exceeds (by 7 percent) that of the population as a whole,[8] that the priests divorce their spouses at a rate equal to their congregations.[9] Of remote reflection to popular religion is the daring reality of an illegitimacy rate rapidly approaching 50 percent, fostered by frolicking fornicators whose pastors and priests dare not mention sexual forfeit of the Promised Land, for fear of damaging delicate feelings and thereby cutting off the flow of funds to temple coffers (see 1 Cor. 6:9).

Similarly, *The Story of Civilization* reveals:

> Egyptian religion had little to say about morality; the priests were busier selling charms, mumbling incantations, and performing magic rites than inculcating ethical precepts. Charms blessed by the clergy would overcome all impediments to the soul's salvation. Emphasis was rather on religious rhetoric and rites rather than on righteous living. Theirs was a formula faith that might be marketed to "secure even the Devil himself into Paradise."[10]

The connection between morality and religion tended to be forgotten in the land of majestic pyramids and monuments to personal power and self-praise. The road to eternal bliss was connected more to religious forms and traditions and required generosity to the priests than to a holy or moral life. In the words of a great Egyptologist: "Thus the earliest moral development which we can trace in the ancient East was suddenly arrested, or at least checked, by the detestable devices of a corrupted priesthood eager for gain."[11]

Let My People Go!

God is seeking to deliver His people from the Egyptian system that substitutes religion for relationship and power for purity.

For four hundred years, the Hebrew people were oppressed as slaves in the land of Pathros, just as Yahweh had promised faithful Abraham: "Know of a surety that thy seed shall be a stranger in a land that is not theirs, and shall serve them, and they shall afflict them four hundred years" (Gen. 15:13).

No sooner did the "father of the faithful" receive the covenant of an "heir of promise" (Abraham's faith being counted by God as righteousness), than he compromised the covenant by fleshly fulfillment in the "spirit of Egypt" with Hagar, a daughter of Egypt. Compassionate as we might be to Abraham's failure, world history—to this most recent moment—reveals the devastating consequences of Abraham's choice to fornicate with the "spirit of Egypt." Abraham's seed became afflicted long before they physically entered Egypt, due to Abraham's spiritual dalliance with Egypt. Doing God's work man's way will always be combustibly dangerous, no matter how good it may first appear.

Abraham fathered Isaac and Ishmael. Although frequently out of view in the past, the sons of Ishmael will ultimately make a secret alliance for a last-stand revolt against the sons of Isaac, to exterminate the "son of promise" (see Ezek. 38). The warriors of Ishmael and the Islamic confederacy will be virtually annihilated on the mountains of Israel.

Isaac, the "son of promise," brought forth Jacob and Esau. Esau sold his birthright for a mess of pottage. Jacob wrestled, as a prince with God, and God changed his name to Israel. Esau fathered the Edomites who refused to trust God and who continually distressed Israel.

Israel had twelve sons—the "children of Israel." Joseph was betrayed by ten of his brothers and sold into Egypt. A sore famine arose in Canaan, and the aging Israel sent his sons to Egypt for food. The covenant-keeping God of Abraham, Isaac, and Israel provided a means of temporal salvation through Joseph, the brother rejected by his own. Raised by divine favor to second in command only to Pharaoh, Joseph ruled Egypt and masterminded the plan to save Egypt and surrounding neighbors from seven years of devastating famine.

At Joseph's command, Israel brought his sons, the "children of Israel," into Egypt to sojourn there. They prospered and multiplied and "waxed exceedingly mighty" (Exod. 1:7). But there arose a new king over Egypt "which knew not Joseph" (Exod. 1:8). That king, fearing the children of Israel, "set over them taskmasters to afflict them." They became slaves, and on their blistered backs were built the treasure cities Pithom and Raamses for Pharaoh (Exod. 1:11). Bitterness with hard bondage was Israel's lot. But God did not forget His covenant with Abraham, Isaac and Israel.

> The children of Israel sighed by reason of the bondage, and they cried, and their cry came up unto God by reason of bondage. And God heard their groaning, and God remembered His covenant with Abraham, with Isaac, and with Jacob (Exod. 2:23–24).

> And the Lord said, I have surely seen the affliction of my people which are in Egypt…And I am come down to deliver them out of the hand of the Egyptians, and to bring them out of the land unto a good land…" (Exod. 3:7–8).

So God raised up a deliverer, one raised in Pharaoh's own house: Moses. Banished from the halls of influence and the seat of prominence, stripped of the scepter of power, the man drawn from the River of Egypt, carrying only a shepherds rod, cried, "Let my people go!" to the greatest powerbroker on earth—the Pharaoh of Egypt.

The God who declared himself the "I AM" to Moses over three thousand years ago continues to cry through His prophets to the political and spiritual powerbrokers of earth, "Let My people go!" Moses, the "meekest of men," yet the "great deliverer," led Israel out of Egypt, but he could never get Egypt out of Israel. Bondage or not, they loved what they could taste and touch. "Cater to our 'felt needs,'" they cried.

The God who through His prophets trumpeted, "Let My people go!" cries out today to His own people, "Let go! Let go of Egypt." Do you hear His voice? Can you hear His voice?

Pharaohs and Priests

Who was the Pharaoh of the Exodus? This has been the subject of much conjecture. Some have concluded that Thutmose III was the Pharaoh confronted by Moses. First Kings 6:1 tells us that Solomon began building the temple in the 480th year after the Exodus. If Solomon ascended the throne about 965 B.C., the temple was begun in the fourth year of his reign—about 962 B.C. This would place the Exodus at 1442 B.C. Thutmose III died in 1441 B.C.

Thutmose III was a great builder according to Egyptian records. An interesting tablet from his day shows Semitic captives at work building him a temple. The "king who knew not Joseph" could then be this Pharaoh.

Most indications, however, seem to point to a later date for the Exodus. Exodus 1:11 tells us the Israelites were compelled to construct treasure cities of Pithum and Rameses. Archaeologist Edouard Naville discovered that Pithum was indeed a store-city, with treasure chambers separated by eight-foot brick walls. Some of the bricks were molded with straw and others not.

According to inscriptions, Pithum was built by Rameses, who reigned about two hundred years after Thutmose III. If Rameses II was the Pharaoh of the Exodus, the children of Israel may have worked under his rulership about ten years before fleeing in about 1290 B.C. That would mean the Israelites entered Egypt around 1720 B.C. when the Hyksos dynasty first conquered Egypt.

The prevailing view is that Rameses II was the Pharaoh who stubbornly refused to let the Hebrews go, despite ten ravaging plagues that culminated with the death of all the firstborn of Egypt. Merenptah, the son of Rameses II, left on record the first and only inscription so far found in Egypt that contains the name "Israel." It is on a large black granite stela found in the Merenptah mortuary temple at Thebes.[12]

The profile of Rameses II well matches the pompous profile of the Pharaoh of the Exodus, who declared, "Who is the Lord that I should obey him?" He gave fashionable expression to the cult of the *self* so prevalent in modern America.

Rameses II appeared to rule well. He rewarded himself with several hundred wives. He left one hundred sons and fifty daughters. He married several of his own daughters so that they too might be blessed by his splendid seed. He built so lavishly that half of all surviving edifices of Egypt are ascribed to his reign. He blessed Egypt with colossal monuments to and of himself throughout the land.

Not satisfied with the massive temple at Luxor, he added to it. No wonder Las Vegas chose "The Luxor" as the name for its new Egyptian hotel. He built a canal from the Nile to the Red Sea. Commerce flourished. He raised a vast shrine to himself, the Ramesseum. His entire reign could be described as "pride incarnate" until his death at age ninety. His has been described as one of the most remarkable reigns in all history.

Despite his pomp and power, "only one human power in Egypt had excelled his, and that was the clergy." The lion's share of taxes from conquered provinces went to the temple and priests. The religious system reached its pinnacle under Rameses III. As Egypt seemingly exulted in her prosperity, the clergy-class grasped for its moment in the sun. At that time, they possessed

- 107,000 slaves (one-thirtieth of the entire population of Egypt)
- 750,000 acres (one-seventh of all arable land)
- 500,000 head of cattle
- Tax-exempt revenues from 169 towns
- 185,000 sacks of corn annually
- 32,000 kilograms of gold
- 1,000,000 kilograms of silver

According to Durant, "More and more the people starved in order that the gods might eat."[13] In the reign of the last Ramessid king, the high priest usurped the throne and ruled as openly supreme.[14]

The empire became a stagnant theocracy in which architecture, temple buildings, and superstition flourished while every other element of national life decayed. Omens were manipulated to give a divine sanction to every decision of the clergy.[15] Does anyone see the poignant parallels between the pomp of ancient Egypt and the pride of modern America?

Egypt became basted in the juice of her own pride and prosperity. She faded and rotted away from the inside. She "lost her trade, her gold, her power, her art, at last even her pride; one by one her rivals crept down upon her soil, harassed and conquered her; and laid her waste."[16]

Dead Civilization, Living Spirit

In 30 B.C., Egypt became a province of Rome and disappeared from history.[17] Is America also destined to disappear from history, perhaps as a province of a united Europe, a "resurrected Rome?" Does your pride and trust in national power prevent you from even considering such a possibility? Are you continuing to grasp for the pomp and prosperity of modern America—the leeks, onions, and garlic of Egypt—while a people once "under God" deteriorate from pulpit to pew and from the church house to the White House?

Like America, "Egypt was perceived by its neighbors as an invincible empire...."[18] Yet its greatest temple, the Ramesseum, is "in an advanced state of ruin today."[19] "Egyptian civilization underwent an irreversible process of disintegration when it could not resist the rise of Christianity."[20] But as Durant in his weighty *Story of Civilization* concludes, "...**the sands have destroyed only the body of ancient Egypt; its spirit survives....**"[21]

It is the spirit of ancient Egypt that now threatens the soul of America and the heart of the Christian Church on the near edge of Christ's Second Coming.

Chapter Three

Time Is Running Out

The greatest peril of perilous times is deception.
The granddaddy of all deceptions is the "Spirit of Egypt."

THE RIVERS OF HISTORY are converging into one surging maelstrom, churning everything in its path as it inexorably advances to the Second Coming of Jesus Christ.

The Prophetic Time Clock

Just fifty years ago, a nation that was not, became a nation in one day. It was fulfillment of the prophet Isaiah's own incredulous prophecy-in-a-question (Isa. 66:8): "Shall the earth be made to bring forth in one day? Or shall a nation be born at once?" The prophet then asked, "Who hath heard such a thing?" Unheard of? Yes. But now an historical fact, for on May 14, 1948, Israel was reborn as a nation.

It was the first time in history that a nation had vanished for two thousand years and was resurrected that "the desert shall blossom as a rose" (Isa. 35:1). And it started the prophetic time clock ticking, the countdown to the end of time.

The Antichrist Spirit

Daniel tells us of another nation or empire that shall rise from obscurity, a revived Roman Empire (Dan. 7: 23–25). It shall be ruled by one who shall "speak great words against the Most High," governed by the world's greatest powerbroker who is ruled by and is the incarnation of the spirit of antichrist. But the saints, under the rule of the Most High, shall finally reign (see Dan. 7:27), even as Christ Himself comes to rule and reign from Jerusalem, the

"City of God" (or Mount Zion) over the remaining nations of the earth (see Zech. 14:16).

Now consider this. In that day when Christ rules from Jerusalem, whosoever of "all the families of the earth" refuses to come to Jerusalem to worship and submit to Christ and His Spirit "shall have no rain." God could have left His message with those words, but He did not. For Zechariah went on to specifically single out "the family of Egypt," declaring, "And if the family of Egypt go not up, and come not, that have no rain; there shall be the plague..." (Zech. 14:18). We know that rain is frequently used as a reference to the presence of God's Spirit.

Why did God, through the prophet, consider it necessary or even important to single out "the family of Egypt?" Is that not a kind of discrimination or reverse "respecting of persons" or nations? But He did not stop there. He continues to drive home a message: "This shall be the punishment of all nations that come not to keep the feast of tabernacles" (Zech. 14:19).

The prophet singled out Egypt because Egypt represents—and has always represented—something in God's heart, something beyond mere geographic confines as one of the nations of the earth. Rather than represent the Spirit of God, it symbolizes the spirit of this age, the spirit of man in control, the spirit of rebellion against the Most High, and ultimately the spirit of antichrist. It is a spirit that holds sway in the nations of the earth. It dominates the leaders and the economic and political brokers of our world. And I regret to say, the spirit of Egypt has a vice grip on the land of my birth—the United States of America, from the church House to the White House, including the school house, and very likely your house.

Egypt and the End-Time Church

The tentacles of the spirit of Egypt are insidious. They masquerade in many forms, some blatant, others subtle. Often coming under a religious cloak, they gently intertwine themselves in and around our lives, squeezing out trust, cutting of the oxygen of faith and moral truth, tearing at our robe of righteousness, and leaving us spiritually naked, mentally tangled and deceived, emotionally and physically destroyed.

The Lord who will judge the nations spoke of an end-time church so infected—the church at Laodicea: "I know thy works, that thou art neither cold nor hot. So then, because thou art lukewarm, and neither cold nor hot, **I will spew you out of my mouth** (Rev. 3:15–22). I do not know about you, but I do not want the Lord of the church to find me so contaminated and unpalatable that He spits me out.

If you are with me, then we need to hear what Jesus says: "Because thou sayest, I am rich, and increased with goods, and have need of nothing; and knowest not that thou art wretched, and miserable, and poor, and blind, and naked" (Rev. 3:17).

Jesus offers us His advice to avert divine regurgitation:

I counsel thee to buy of me gold tried in the fire, that thou mayest be rich, and white raiment, and that thou mayest be clothed, and **that the shame of thy nakedness do not appear**; and anoint thine eyes with eye-salve that thou mayest see (Rev. 3:18).

If we were seeing clearly, the Lord would not counsel, "...anoint thine eyes...that thou mayest see," would He?

Now think with me. In America, we have 350,000 "Christian" congregations, over two thousand "Christian" radio stations, hundreds of "Christian" television stations, and more Bibles per capita than any nation on earth. We have freedom of worship and freedom of speech. Polls consistently tells us that at least 90 percent of all Americans believe in God, 80 percent profess to be Christian, 45 percent claim to be born-again Christians, yet 78 percent believe we have a severe national moral crisis. How can these statistics be reconciled? Is there an explanation?

The Nature of Blindness

The explanation is clear if we can bear to admit it. We do not see! As Christians, we protest loud and long to the nation how clearly we see. We are proud of how well we see and do not hesitate to trumpet that message through the horn of conservative politics. But in truth, we do not see. The unbelievers know we do not see, because our own lives and attitudes do not consistently reflect what we profess. They see the widening gap between our walk and our talk.

Perhaps George Gallup's observation at the massive Christian bookseller's convention in 1995 gives us an entry-level clue on our blindness. "We are a nation of biblical illiterates," he declared. But it is more than information about the Bible or from the Bible that we need. We need transformation. Something serious has infected our soul and spirit that is revealing itself in our outward ways.

The unfortunate nature of blindness is that we do not know what we cannot see. If we admit blindness, there is hope that one who sees, or who sees more clearly at the moment, might assist us in dealing with the truths and facts of the real world. But to claim we see, when the facts scream to the contrary, is the height of either pride or foolishness.

Yet is that not where we stand in the church in America? Perhaps our spiritual pride has blinded us that we cannot see. Have we become "the blind leading the blind?" Jesus warned the religious leaders of His day, because "ye say, We see; therefore your sin remains" (John 9:41). And He went on to say, "If the light that is in thee be darkness, how great is that darkness" (Matt.

6:23). We cannot be the "light of the world" if the light that is in us is darkness. So where does that leave us?

Deceived and Don't Know It

The unfortunate nature of deception is that it is deceptive. When Jesus was asked by His disciples as to the sign of His second coming and of the end of the world, his first response was, "Take heed that no man deceive you" (Matt. 24:4). He also warned that many would be deceived (Matt. 24:5).

Satan is known by many names, but one of those is "the deceiver." Deception is his principal weapon. If he destroys through deception, we may never know until it is too late. That is why those who claim to be followers of Christ are warned repeatedly to be on guard. Consider these, among many, warnings:

- **Jesus:** "Take heed lest any man deceive you" (Mark 13:5).
- **Jesus:** "Beware of false prophets…" (Matt. 7:15).
- **Paul:** "Evil men and seducers shall wax worse and worse, deceiving and being deceived. But continue thou…" (2 Tim. 3:13–14).
- **Paul:** "…the day of Christ is at hand. Let no man deceive you by any means: for that day shall not come, except there come a falling away first…" (2 Thess. 2:2–3).

Please note carefully. Paul said there would come an apostasy or a "falling away." He is addressing professing Christians. We cannot "fall away" from a place or position if we have never been there, can we? That means that all professing believers—including pastors, board members, deacons, bishops, broadcasters, parachurch leaders—are in the class of persons being warned. And as has been said, "To be forewarned is to be fore-armed."

But most of us, in the deepest recesses of our minds and hearts, do not really believe that *we* could be deceived, do we? Somebody else, sure! But not me. And that is precisely why deception is so deadly.

Let me translate this practically so that we can see in stark reality how deceptive deception truly is. On May 26, 1996, the *Los Angeles Times* came out with a huge article dealing with America's moral decline. Are you prepared for this? They reported that 78 percent of all Americans believe the country is in severe moral decline. That, we can agree with, I am sure. But here is the shocker. The same article revealed that 96 percent of our country's citizens believe they are doing "a good or excellent job" in teaching their children moral values. And only 11 percent of our fellow citizens believe their own life—their ways, behavior, values, and morals—have contributed in any way to America's moral decline. Conclusion: At best, 89 percent of Americans are deceived.

We are so monumentally steeped in the deceptive spirit of Egypt that we cannot even recognize it when it slaps us in the face. Since at least 45 percent of Americans claim to be born again, it would appear that, at minimum, 75 percent of all those who claim to be born again have no clue or conviction that their own moral or spiritual condition may be in need of a course correction.

Even as I write, I am so overwhelmed by the vastness of our national deception, especially among us, my Christian brothers and sisters, that it causes a purportedly rational mind to ponder if even God can break through such a cloud of deception. Our hope and confidence is that He **is** God. Our problem is that we are not, that we do not really like His intervention, except as it affects THEM or the other guy.

Is it any wonder that we have not seen real revival in our land after a generation of crying out to God to heal our land on our annual National Day of Prayer? Is it surprising that after years of national solemn assemblies, the Lord of the church has been unable to pierce the veil of blindness that has wrapped itself as a shroud around His people?

My dear friends and countrymen, we are massively deceived, yet we do not know it. And I must admit, it is most difficult to write such a message, for I am one with you. We battle the deceiver together. Our greatest struggle is to be freed from the spirit of Egypt.

Perilous Times, Perilous Spirit

Many of us refuse to listen to or look at the avalanche of news cascading upon us, revealing daily fulfillment of each and every prophecy foretold that would immediately precede our Lord's return and the end of the age. The less prepared we are, the more frightening it seems. Many key leaders of the church in America have unabashedly declared on my daily radio broadcast, *VIEWPOINT*, that they believe vast numbers—indeed the majority—of professing Christians in this nation are utterly and totally unprepared for what lies ahead. God is lawful, just, and merciful. It is His pattern to provide "due process" to His people. When people are unprepared, God makes every effort to woo and warn them. That is precisely the purpose of this epistle to you. Paul advised:

This know also, that in the last days perilous times shall come (2 Tim. 3:1).

The greatest peril of perilous times is deception. And the granddaddy of all deceptions is the "spirit of Egypt." The spirit of Egypt is the fleshing out and incarnation of the deceiver's question to Eve back in the Garden: "Hath God said?" (Gen. 3:1).

In effect, Satan has marketed the wares of his false or antichrist kingdom as a counterfeit or alternative to the true Kingdom of God. He deals in spiritual sleight-of-hand. His method is a kind of bait-and-switch. And he has framed his marketing plan well since World War II. Interestingly, the conclusion of World

War II ushered in the rebirth of Israel, which began the final countdown of the prophetic clock. It should therefore come as no surprise that deception has increased dramatically in the past two generations.

Time is running out! From Genesis to Revelation, God has been calling His people OUT OF EGYPT. We are poised on what appears to be history's final hour, and He still waits. Will you come out?

A Word for Leaders, Pastors, Prelates, and Presidents

When thou art come into the land which the Lord thy God giveth thee…and shall say, I will set up a king over me…he shall not multiply horses to himself, **nor cause the people to return to Egypt**…. Ye shall henceforth return no more that way" (Deut. 17:14–16).

WARNING!

Do NOT read chapters 4–6 until you have sincerely prayed that God would open your heart and mind to its message.

Chapter Four

Doing Church in Egypt

*Is belief in God killing America? Do not answer too quickly.
Israel believed in God but God refused to allow Israel's
entrance to the Promised Land.*

PREPARE FOR COSMIC WAR! It is a war that is and will be waged in your mind and heart. It is the ultimate battle for power and authority. This battle, while waged in the heavenly realm, will be won or lost in the mind and heart of each man , each woman, one at a time.

The God who created the universe by and through Christ (through whom all things consist) has declared and demonstrated His unsurpassed power and authority. As the psalmist so aptly stated, "The heavens declare the glory of God; and the firmament showeth His handiwork" (Ps. 19:1). It is the eternal power unrivaled and unquestioned with only one exception: Satan.

Satan, also known as Lucifer, is a created being, who once was the most glorious of all the angels. He said in his heart:

> I will ascend into heaven, I will exalt my throne above the stars of God: I will be like the most High (Isa. 14:13–14).

God then likens Pharaoh unto Satan, directing Ezekiel to write (in chapter 31):

- Verse 2: "Speak unto Pharaoh king of Egypt, and to his multitude; Whom art thou like in thy greatness?"
- Verse 16: "I made nations to shake at the sound of his fall, when I cast him down to hell with them that descend to the pit."

- Verse 17: "They also went down into hell with him...that dwelt under his shadow in the midst of the heathen."
- Verse 18: "This is Pharaoh and all his multitude, saith the Lord God."

Satan and Pharaoh are best buddies. If you are a friend of Pharaoh, his friends are your friends. A new amusement park in Redlands, California, declares itself "Pharaoh's Lost Kingdom." Replete with sphinxes crowned by the ever-present serpent, it competes—American style—with the lore of Egypt. But one need not go to entertainment centers to revel in the spirit of Egypt. It lurks about in the pulpits and pews of America.

Chest-Deep in EGYPT

From conservative politics to the church-growth movement, the American church is chest-deep in the spirit of Egypt. The Israelites may have come out of Egypt in body, but the American church is infatuated with the "leeks, onions, and garlic" of the Land of Pathros.

Our rhetoric is the power of God. But our reliance is on the power of politics. Our talk is of salvation in Christ. But our walk is of salvation by Congress. Souls to be saved have become enemies to be destroyed. Hubris reigns supreme. Humility somehow no longer fits. Many of us have, I fear, unwittingly made the great power exchange and reek, both to God and to an observing world, of Egyptian leeks and onions. Egyptian "garlic" stains our testimony. We long for the ways of Egypt. They seem so much more convenient, a shortcut to power. Oh, what a tangled web we weave when we become so willingly deceived.

The problem is not with politics, but with people. The problem with the rich young ruler was not his money, but his trust (see Mark 10:24). I, too, have twice run for public office. But a Congress full of Christians operating in the spirit of Egypt cannot save America. We will merely elect "Pharaohs" and rule with a fist of bondage. We cannot bring a nation to her repentant knees by political power, but by purity. We cannot restore truth without godly trust. We cannot restore righteousness in the White House, without right living in the church house and in our own house.

In the early days of the conservative revolution, we humbly joined with King David, proclaiming, "Some trust in chariots, and some in horses: but we will remember the name of the Lord our God" (Ps. 20:7). Now we trust in Pentium computers, mailing lists, and the power of the people. We have become more interested in recruiting voters than in recruiting disciples. If righteousness alone exalts a nation, what can we expect of electing representatives from the cross-section of unrepentant Christians who act as functional or biblical illiterates? After a generation of praying the scripture 2 Chronicles 7:14—"If **my** people...will humble themselves..." we still point the finger of judgment at THEM, while ignoring God's warning that "judgment must begin at the house of God" (1 Pet. 4:17).

My brothers and sisters. Is it not time to come out of Egypt? Where is our trust? Like the Jews awaiting the first coming of Messiah, many look any day for Christ to come riding on a white stallion into Washington, DC, with fire in His eyes and a flaming sword, with the word *conservative* engraved thereon. Others pine for a silver-tongued leader, strong in compassion but sanitized of truth.

During this same period since our nation's bicentennial, the church-growth movement has burgeoned into a megabusiness. We are obsessed with keeping up with Pastor Jones' church, driven by the ministry of envy. Many became disillusioned with the words "church growth," changing the rubric to "church health." But as Shakespeare noted, "What's in a name? That which we call a rose / By any other name would smell as sweet."

Jesus said, "I'll build my church; you make disciples." But we have gone into massive debt "building churches," while leaving a nation radically undiscipled. How long can the God of Abraham countenance this massive and rebellious defection to the spirit of Egypt without raising up a Moses to cry, "Let my people go!"?

In His still, small voice, the God of mercy yet reminds, "Not by might, nor by power, but by *my* spirit" (Zech. 4:6). The choice is yours. But here is a simple message to guide us out of the tangled web of Egypt, a message from the one who once led God's people out of the house of bondage. You can find it in Hebrews 11:24–27.

By Faith Moses...	Application
• Refused to be called the son of Pharaoh's daughter;	• He refused to claim or align himself with the perks of power.
• Chose rather to suffer affliction with the people of God than to enjoy the pleasures of sin for a season;	• He chose to do things God's way even if it meant enduring that which he might have avoided by being invested with Egyptian power.
• Esteemed the reproach of Christ greater riches than the treasures of Egypt;	• He valued the eternal over the temporal; the power of the cross over the power of congress.
• Forsook Egypt, Not fearing... For he endured...	• He feared God, following the Divine model, while rejecting the cultural mandate.

Perhaps we can see why God chose Moses, described as the "meekest" of men. Interestingly, the Captain of our salvation described Himself as "meek" (see Matt. 11:29), and we are told that the King of kings, in His earthly role, came "meek, and sitting upon an ass" (see Matt. 21:5). Not much resemblance to the last twenty-five years of Evangelical power politics, is it?

The culture wars are not our biggest problem. They only raise the biggest money for our ministries. The conservative-versus-liberal battle presents solemn symptoms in the White House and school house—symptoms of spiritual wars raging in the church house and perhaps in your house. What WE (conservatives) are today, THEY (liberals) were thirty years ago. It is a war that takes no prisoners. It is the spirit of Egypt vs. the Spirit of God. Will you be a casualty? Or will you come OUT OF EGYPT while there is yet time?

Yes, let us **serve** in public office. Yes, let us speak in the public forum. Yes, let us be involved in the marketplace of ideas and be salt in our communities, but let it be with the power of Christ living in and through us, rather than the power of the Congress ruling over us.

PREPARE FOR WAR! Those are not idle words. Perhaps you already have some understanding of the cosmic battle being waged. You and I are engaged in the war of the ages but must prepare for the battle of a lifetime. It will be a battle for your very life...for your mind and heart...for your eternal destiny.

More Serious Than Culture Wars

This war in which we are engaged is not the "culture war." The culture wars raging around us merely represent the flack from a much more serious war—the war of the ages, a no-holds-barred, take-no-prisoner war that may determine where you, your children, and grandchildren spend eternity.

You say, "Well, I am a Christian. That question is settled." That may be true. But I have it on good authority that vast numbers of professing Christians will not meet their intended eternal destiny for a variety of reasons. Jesus warned, "Many will say to me in that day, Lord, Lord, have we not prophesied in thy name? And in thy name cast out devils? And in thy name done many wonderful works? And then I will profess unto them, I never knew you: depart from me ye that work iniquity" (Matt. 7:22–23).

Jesus went on to say that it is not just doers of iniquity who will not get a ticket through the pearly gates. Listen carefully to His words from Matt. 7:21: "Not everyone that saith unto me, Lord, Lord, shall enter the Kingdom of Heaven, but he that **doeth the will** of my Father which is in Heaven."

Now that is tough talk. It may not even match your theology. But then much of what we pass in the name of inerrant Scripture and Bible-believing theology today is far removed from what God has really said. Why is that? And how did it happen?

Who Is in Authority?

Bottom line: it is a matter of authority. Who is in authority? Gradually over the years, people have modified their beliefs and ways, conforming to culture rather than to Christ. Many have been more interested in being politically correct or denominationally correct than in being biblically correct. And by no means have we wanted to offend anyone. So God's truth has been relativized, trivialized, and sometimes even pulverized to conform to our tastes and traditions.

God's authority in our lives or nation has not been eradicated or undermined overnight. There have been significant historical assaults on belief, such as Darwin's theory of evolution. But generally, God's authority in our lives has been undermined by the erosion of small choices. We have made choices—one at a time—that have shifted our authority base away from God.

If we are honest with ourselves, the problems we moan and groan about in the culture wars are consequences or symptoms of lost battles over the years in the spiritual war. The evangelical Christians of today look nearly identical, in cultural ways and beliefs, to the "world" of just thirty years ago, with a dose of religious tradition and jargon tossed on for good measure. In truth, our unbelief, disbelief, or disobedience as Christians today is laying the foundation for an unprecedented vacuum of faith and obedience in the next generation.

In America, there is a very strong link between shattered values in the church house and fractured character in the White House or school house. It has been somewhat of a red-herring for Christians to vehemently call for hell's fire to fall on homosexuals and abortionists (abominations such as these sins are) when fundamentalist Christians, notwithstanding God's unmitigated expression of hatred for divorce, now leave their spouses faster than the nation as a whole and pastors break their marriage vows at a rate equaling their congregation, all revealed by the premier edition of the *Barna Report*.

Perhaps America is now revealing in Technicolor the psalmist's observation: "…all the foundations of the earth are out of course" (Ps. 82:5). But he also inquired, "If the foundations be destroyed, what can the righteous do? (Ps. 11:3). So who are the righteous? If professing Christians, with impunity and en mass, refuse to do as God says, are they righteous? Or have even we who call ourselves "righteous" gradually shifted our authority to another father—the father of lies?

A Lordship Crisis

At root, America's crisis is not a moral crisis but a lordship crisis. The root of the word *lordship* is *lord*. And who is lord, is determined by who is in authority.

Honestly now, who is truly in authority in your life? Would twelve reasonable men sitting as jury, upon hearing or seeing the evidence, form the same conclusion you now so much desire? Could you get a unanimous verdict declaring, "Jesus is Lord!" in your life? Could you convince the jury beyond a reasonable doubt? If not, how could you convince God? Take a moment. Let the magnitude of these questions settle in. Do you need to pray?

It has been said, "If Jesus is not Lord **of** all, He is not Lord **at** all." Americans have an especially hard time with authority, even Christian Americans. Our inbred hyperindividualism has convinced us that we are the captain of our soul and the final arbiter of what will be true. Our international reputation as a rebellious people is translated poignantly in our new "national anthem"—"I'll do it my way!" So where does that leave American Christians on the road into or out of Egypt?

The War of the Ages

Power and authority are everything to God. Everything! Yes, God is love. Yes, He is truth. Yes, He has many wonderful attributes. But when all is said and done, He is God. He has a kingdom over which Christ is king. And He does not want you or I to forget it. But the deceiver does. As the apostle Paul so aptly phrased it, the destroyer wants you and me to **know** God but not glorify Him **as** God (see Rom. 1:21).

You see, Satan believes in God. He knows Him very well. The devils also believe, and unlike most American Christians, they even tremble (James 2:19). God expects us to tremble in His presence. David, a man after His own heart, cried out, "The Lord reigneth; let the people tremble" (Ps. 99:1). God said, "...to this man will I look, even to him that...trembleth at my word" (Isa. 66:2).

The deceiver wants us to have a "user-friendly" God. *Time* magazine, April 5, 1993, declared on its front cover that America is "a nation that forgot God." Inside, the feature article of this particular magazine describes us as "looking for a custom-made God—one made in our own image," as we search from church to church to satisfy our fancy. From all appearances, Satan is winning the war of the ages for power and authority, even in American churches. For if he can get us to believe **IN** God but not believe Him **AS** God, he has won. It would appear, strange as it may seem, that belief **IN** God is killing America, for 90 percent of us profess to so believe.

It is at this point that deception is greatest. For if we only religiously believe **IN** God without both **BELIEVING** and **OBEYING** Him **AS** God, we remain in Egypt and we are disqualified from the Promised Land, notwithstanding all of our religious confessions, protestations, or traditions to the contrary. John set the test for our professed *love* of God as God; love is revealed by our obedience to what God says (see 1 John 5:2–3). James confirmed this when he declared that a mere confession of faith—a confession without accompanying works—is dead (see James 2:14–26).

Jesus left no doubt on the issue. "He that hath my commandments, and keepeth them, he it is that loveth me" (John 14:21). Without obedience, Jesus is not Lord, and God is not God in your life. Then if God is not your God, who is? Yes, we are saved by grace through faith, but as the great hymn reminds us, we must obey, "for there's no other way / To be happy in Jesus, / But to **TRUST AND OBEY**" (empahsis added).

Perhaps now you can more clearly understand the true nature of the War of the Ages and the massive deception Jesus and the apostles warned of at the end of the age. Things will all look very religious. The Antichrist will even have a miracle-working prophet (Rev. 13:11–15). Obedience to God and His Word will be the defining line.

You and I will be tested continually. It will be our choices on the seemingly little things that will chart our course and determine who will be Lord. Jesus encourages us eight times in His final word to us in Revelation, "To him that overcometh…"

Overcoming is not accomplished merely by flailing against powers of the netherworld but by overcoming the adversary's assault on the space between our ears and in our hearts. We must resist at all costs the tempter's subtle marketing of the spirit of Egypt to a people whose ears itch and whose palates crave the leeks and onions of Egypt. We cannot "do church in Egypt" while laying claim to the Promised Land.

Chapter Five

The Great Power Exchange

Who is the Lord that I should obey His voice? —Exodus 5:2

YOU MAY RECALL that when Jesus, the only begotten Son of God, came to earth, He spoke "as one having authority and not as the scribes" (Matt. 7:29). His was a delegated authority from the Father while on earth. He testified that the Father has "...given Him authority to execute judgment also, because He is [the] Son of man" (John 5:26–27). (NOTE: The definite article *the* is not in the original text.)

Contrary to many Christians' belief, Jesus' authority on earth was not primarily because He was the Son of God but because He was, as He frequently said Himself, "the son of man" (e.g., John 5:27; 6:63). He was truly God, yet truly man.

Jesus came as the "second" and last Adam to restore God's authority in the earth. Adam had committed treason against the Kingdom of God by rebelling against God's authority and submitting to Satan's authority. It took only one choice. He wanted fellowship with God, but he also liked what another authority figure, the deceiver, had to offer. Adam rebelled, but Eve was deceived (1 Tim. 2:14). That is precisely why Satan's undermining of the home and the husband's leadership is so devastating.

The combined forces of the radical feminist movement with the legitimizing of divorce have opened our women, our children, and an entire nation to unprecedented deception. And the Destroyer is bowled over with laughter at our swallowing his bait, hook, line, and sinker, all in the name of compassion and personal rights.

The spirit of Egypt now perpetuates the cycle even in the church. Satan need not act further to destroy our families. We've believed his offer of exchange of authority, denying what God said about marriage, divorce, and the roles of men and women. We now carry on the deceiver's work for him, yes even from pulpit to pew, and often in the name of Christ. We may not be in Egypt, but Egypt is deeply engrained in us. America's fathers have lost authority because they and/or their wives rebelled against the Heavenly Father's authority. When asked, "Hath God said…?" they respond, "Yes, but…"

The temporal penalty (in our families and in our nation) for this exchange of spiritual authority resulted in a shift of earthly authority. God warned His people that if they rebelled against His authority, children would become their oppressors, and women would rule over them (Isa. 3:4, 12). But the eternal consequences are beyond all description. Having opened our sons and daughters to the destroyer's deception, listening to the clarion call of culture ruled by the spirit of Egypt while despising the claims of Christ, have we not become co-conspirators with the deceiver to consign our own children to his kingdom? Certainly they can and must make their own choice, but have we not rendered their choice infinitely more difficult?

You may be thinking, *This is too tough for me! God would not allow that to happen to my children.* But He would. He is so kind and so just that He will let both you and them make decisions and reap the consequences thereof. For it is written,

> Be not deceived; God is not mocked: for whatsoever a man soweth, that shall he also reap. For he that soweth to this flesh shall of the flesh reap corruption (Gal. 6:7–8).

Jesus watched a very fine young man who had kept the commandments from his youth walk away sorrowfully because he could not, or would not seek FIRST the Kingdom of God (see Mark 10:17–27). He was a "good" man, very religious. Jesus did not dispute that. But he was deceived. His trust was displaced.

Let us not continue to open our children to the deceiver's devices by tearing apart God's front-line plan of protection in our homes, while we selfishly embrace the offerings of Egypt. But rather, "Let us not be weary in well doing: for in due season we shall reap if we faint not" (Gal. 6:9).

The Great Contenders

Jesus came as the "second" and last Adam to restore authority and offer redemption. But in order to deliver sinners who "through fear of death were all their lifetime subject to bondage" and to "destroy him that had the power of death, that is, the devil" (Heb. 2:14–15), he did not take on "the nature of angels" but rather "the seed of Abraham" (Heb. 2:16).

The Son of God became the "son of man." And in so doing, he not only was tempted and suffered as a man (see Heb. 2:18), but He also refused to claim the perks or rights of being God (see Phil. 2:6–7). He restored the pattern of Kingdom power and authority by humbling Himself as a man and became obedient, even to death (see Phil. 2:7–8). Notice, it was because of Jesus' humility and obedience that He received power and authority:

> Wherefore God also hath highly exalted Him and given Him a name that is above every name: That at the name of Jesus every knee should bow…and that every tongue should confess that Jesus Christ is Lord… (Phil. 2:9–11).

Jesus refused to usurp authority or power. He received it by delegation. Jesus confessed, "I can of my own self do nothing" (John 5:30). And everyone who heard Jesus could tell the difference between the natural authority issuing from His submissive spirit and the authority of the leading figures of the religion of the day, whose authority was based solely in power and position.

The scribes and Pharisees embodied the spirit of Egypt. Jesus revealed the Spirit of the Heavenly Father. Is it any wonder, then, that Jesus cried out in rebuke to the Pharisees: "Ye are of your father the devil, and the lusts of your father ye do" (John 8:44).

Contrast with me, now, the ways of Jesus with the ways of the usurper. Jesus "thought it not robbery [something to be sought after or grasped at] to be equal with God; but made Himself of no reputation; and took on Him the form of a servant…" (Phil. 2:6–7). Satan, the deceiver, declared, "I will ascend unto heaven, I will exalt my throne above the stars of God:… I will be like the Most High" (Isa. 14:12–14).

These are the two great contenders. One gains authority through humility, the other through hubris. One gains power through purity, the other through pomp and pride. One will ascend to the right hand of God to judge the earth; the other will be "brought down to hell" (Isa. 14:15).

If you are struggling to see where we are going, please be patient. I believe it will all come together.

Spirit of Egypt, Seat of Satan's Authority

Egypt was the only nation to be reckoned with three thousand years ago when Joseph was elevated to second in command under Pharaoh. Jacob, Abraham's grandson and Joseph's father, was renamed "Israel." And he and his other eleven sons sojourned into Egypt because of the brutal famine throughout the Middle East.

The sons of Israel were blessed in Egypt's land of Goshen due to God's preservation through the hand of Joseph under the authority of the Pharaoh. They multiplied and prospered.

But after Joseph's death, there arose a king "who knew not Joseph" (Exod. 1:8). He did not fear God but man—especially the children descended from Israel. And so he enslaved them, making their lives "bitter with hard bondage" (Exod. 1:13–14). He built on their beaten backs treasure cities of Pithom and Rameses. After escaping extermination with all newborn baby boys of his race, a Hebrew named Moses was raised in Pharaoh's own house. And though raised by Pharaoh's daughter in the palace, Moses slew an Egyptian who was brutally expressing the power-based mind of Egypt. Moses was banished to the desert and dwelt forty years in Midian.

It came to pass that the power-mongering king of Egypt died, and the children of Israel cried out by reason of their bondage. And God heard their groaning. God remembered His covenant with Abraham, who had looked for a city with foundations whose builder and maker was God (see Heb. 11:8–10), and had respect unto the children of Israel (see Exod. 2:23–25). And He sent Moses to confront the spirit of Egypt as a deliverer under the direct authority of God Himself, declaring, "Israel is my son, even my firstborn: Let my son go, that he may serve me…" (Exod. 4:22–23).

But Pharaoh responded in character of the spirit of Egypt and retorted,

> **Who is the Lord that I should obey His voice** to let Israel go? I know not the Lord, neither will I let Israel go (Exod. 5:2).

And so the lines were drawn in the sands of time, **the Spirit of Egypt vs. the Spirit of God**. Those lines remain drawn spiritually to this day. You and I are daily confronted with that question, "Who is the Lord that I should obey His voice?" Pharaoh's stubborn pride and rebellious heart revealed the spirit of his nation to which God brought plagues and judgment, a memorial engraved in history of man's arrogant confrontation with God.

It has been said that the only thing we learn from history is that we do not learn from history. And Egypt never learned. Her pomp, pride, and power prevailed until she was brought low. Egypt became a symbol of man's power and ways vs. God's power and ways. The way of the kingdom of Egypt was hubris; the way of the Kingdom of God is humility. The key to entering the spirit of Egypt was pride and position, while entrance to the Kingdom of God is purity and submission. Fear and intimidation drives the spirit of Egypt. Faith moves the Kingdom of God. Self-reliance fuels "Egyptian" faith. Obedience reveals and releases the God kind of faith.

What will God be moved to bring upon America in response to your daily measure of obedience, as you answer the question, "Who is the Lord that I should obey His voice?" Your response may determine whether Christ will be crucified again in Egypt.

Chapter Six

Crucified in Egypt

It can be dangerous to resist the spirit of Egypt.
And the most dangerous place is not in the
world but in the church...

LOOK BACK WITH ME for a moment over the shoulder of history. Do you remember our friend, Joseph? He had ten brothers who could not stand the sight of him. Theirs was serious sibling rivalry! Their father's name had been changed from Jacob, meaning "supplanter" or "deceiver" to Israel, or "Prince with God" (see Gen. 32:28).

Stephen, the first martyr of the church, declared to the religious leaders of his day, who were about to stone him, a dark secret of their heritage they did not care to hear. Stephen made no effort to be politically correct or to respect their tradition, for disclosing this secret was essential to conveying the whole truth. It would reveal the "Egyptian heart" of the majority of Jewish priests.

Envy: The Engine of Egypt

Look for a moment at Acts 7:9. Stephen simply declared in his condensed spiritual history of the Jews, "...the patriarchs, **moved with envy**, sold Joseph into Egypt." Now why would Stephen make such a negative statement when his life was on the line? Because it was necessary and unmitigated spiritual truth! The very same spirit that had been in the revered forefathers, the patriarchs—out of whose loins had come the twelve tribes of Israel and who had sold Joseph into slavery—was in the present respected leaders of God's chosen people; it was the spirit of envy.

Now since Stephen, an unknown, had demonstrated such faith and power that, as a result, disciples multiplied greatly (see Acts 6:5–8), the surrounding religious leaders had to suborn perjury, stirring up the people around so as to make a case for why Stephen would dare to resist the existing spirit of Egypt that rendered powerless the worship of the day (see Acts 6:9–15). We are told that Stephen was "full of the Holy Ghost and wisdom" (Acts 6:3). But Stephen, shooting straight for the heart of the matter, declared,

> Ye stiffnecked and uncircumcised in heart and ears, **ye do always resist the Holy Ghost:** as your fathers did, so do ye (Acts 7:51).

What was Stephen saying? He was insightfully noting that, just as our fathers "in their hearts turned back again into Egypt," so have you (Acts 7:39). In fact, he declared, in essence, "Not only are you playing religious games in the spirit of Egypt, but also your fathers persecuted and killed all of the prophets whom God sent to show the coming of the Messiah, who was to come out of Egypt (Hos. 11:1), and now you have betrayed and killed Him, too" (Acts 7:51–52).

They could not stand spiritual truth! We have difficulty doing much better. Theirs was a spiritual leadership rooted in position and power. The whole gang of upstanding, culturally accepted ministers, rabbis, priests, etc. "…cried out with a loud voice, and stopped their ears, and ran upon him **with one accord**, and cast him out of the city, and stoned him" (Acts 7:57–58). Can you imagine such a sight? As an aside, please take notice: Stephen did not plead his constitutional rights. He "kneeled down, and cried…lay not this sin to their charge" (Acts 7:60).

Consider this also. The Holy Spirit came upon the disciples to empower them to do the work of the Kingdom of God when they were **in one accord** (see Acts 2:1). We have already seen that Stephen was "full of the Holy Ghost." Of what spirit, then, were the predominating group of religious leaders of God's chosen people who rabidly stopped their ears and stoned Stephen? Just as the Holy Spirit works in us when we are in one accord, so the spirit of Egypt empowers and sustains those who come in one accord in religious garb to stifle the true Spirit of God.

The Spirit of Egypt Can Be Dangerous

Let me warn you now. It can be dangerous to resist the spirit of Egypt. And the most dangerous place is not in the world but in the church where it is camouflaged with religious trappings and a spiritual cloak. Just ask the disciples and the apostle Paul.

Peter and John were beaten in Jerusalem because the "high priest and all that were with him…the Sadducees, were **filled with indignation**" (Acts 5:17–42). The Greek word translated here as "indignation" is *jealousy*.

At Thessalonica, the Jews **which believed not,** "**moved with envy,**" gathered "certain lewd fellows of the baser sort" and set all the city in an uproar, undermining Paul's teaching. They assaulted Jason's house where they gathered and arrested him (Acts 17:1–9).

You may ask, "Why are you saying these things? I want to feel good about everything and everybody. I do not want to make waves. Shouldn't things be all at peace, nice and tranquil?" That answer could itself require a book, but simply stated, the answer is no. We have been peddled and marketed a brand of Christianity in America these last two generations that is not "the whole truth and nothing but the truth." It has been as much of the truth as many of our leaders thought would "sell" or could bring in larger crowds or maximize fund-raising for programs, projects, and buildings.

My friends, time is running short. The things that are about to take place on planet earth, yes even in America, would cause you to faint if you really knew. Jesus warned that in the period leading to history's final hour, men's hearts will fail them for fear. Our faith is anemic. We have been resting on our "blessed assurances," but much of what passes in the name of Christ in this country has drunk deeply of the spirit of Egypt.

Envy Crucified Christ

We must turn our attention now to the Lord of the church. If Paul, Stephen, Peter, and John were confronted with the envy of Egypt in the New Testament, and the patriarchs tried to dispose of Joseph with envy in the Old Testament, would not Jesus, who links both testaments, have explicitly encountered this dramatic divide? Absolutely!

Matthew 27:18 records, "...the chief priests and elders of the people took counsel against Jesus to put Him to death." Please note again, it is almost always the religious leaders of what **seem to be** God's people, who conspire, in the spirit of Egypt, to prevent either voice or victory to the Spirit of God. It upsets their ministry and control. At the very beginning of Jesus' ministry, however, the entire synagogue "was filled with wrath, and rose up, and thrust Him out of the city...to the brow of a hill...that they might cast Him down headlong" (Luke 4:28–29).

Why was that? Because Israel never left Egypt in their hearts! Yes, they were religious. Yes, they believed **IN** God. But they did not **BELIEVE** God! They wanted the best of God and of Egypt, too, and would brook no one who dared to stand fully on the whole Word of God and believe it, if such a one refused to make room for Egyptian power, pride, and programmed tradition. Think about it. All Jesus had done was to quote Isaiah 61:1 and to dare to believe it. Of course He rebuked them for their Egyptian spirit of unbelief, contrasting it with a Syrian and a Sidonnian, whom Israel despised yet who, nevertheless, dared to believe (see Luke 4:16–29).

We see the identical pattern leading to Christ's crucifixion that we saw with persecution of the apostles, Paul, Stephen, and the selling of Joseph into Egypt. Pilate, a secular and crusty Roman governor, saw through the religious dress of the priests, pastors, and elders, so he presented them with an absurd choice: "Whom will ye that I release unto you? Barabbas, or Jesus which is called Christ" (Matt. 27:17).

Why did Pilate present such a seemingly ridiculous choice to seemingly intelligent people? Barabbas was a murderer (see Mark 15:7). With Jesus, Pilate could find no fault (see Matt. 27:23–24). The reason is stated in two of the four gospels: "For he knew that **for envy** they had delivered him" (Matt. 27:18; Mark 15:10). So the priests, pastors and elders "persuaded the multitude that they should ask for Barabbas, and destroy Jesus" (Matt. 27:20).

You may think, "Well that was just the Jews." Not so. Would you dismiss the rest of Scripture that way? Would you say that the Sermon on the Mount was just for Jews and about Jews and their heart motivations? No. And neither was this vignette of spiritual conflict between the spirit of Egypt (driven by the engine of envy) versus the Spirit of God (incarnated in Christ) just about Jews. Satan, through the deceptive spirit of Egypt and its battering ram of envy, sought to once and for all destroy the Anointed One who came to break the bondage of Egypt. It should be increasingly clear why God warned, "Thou shalt not covet." It is particularly applicable in ministry.

Although it has revealed itself worldwide throughout the ages, that same spirit of envy is rampant in the Body of Christ—the church—in America. A call for clear and unswerving obedience to the Word frequently triggers amazingly vitriolic response from pastor, elder, and parishioner who feel their place of power or position threatened or their tidy kingdom challenged. Turf wars abound. Build-a-church-like-mine seminars are big business and fuel the envy frenzy as America's evangelicals strive to clone the culture rather than become like Christ.

Envy crucified Jesus! Envy is the engine of the spirit of Egypt, rooted deeply in man's lust for power. That is why the deceiver's use of it is so simple, so pervasive, and even so deceptive. And it is especially ruthless when it becomes religious.

Envy is born of the union of pride and greed. It is nurtured by SELFishness, it is preserved by fear, it breeds anger, and its ends are achieved through manipulation, control, intimidation, and finally murder—yes, even of God's chosen servants and saints. It countenances no opposition. History bears witness.

Where Was Jesus Crucified?

If envy crucified Jesus, and envy is rooted deeply in the spirit of Egypt, what might this have to do with where Jesus was crucified?

What we are about to see is one of the most puzzling yet profound passages in all of Holy Writ. Look with me at Revelation 11:8. John tells us in chapter 1, verse 1, that this is "The Revelation of Jesus Christ, which God gave unto him…." That is as authoritative as you can get.

A little background is in order here. Jesus tells us through John, in Revelation 11, that two great witnesses will testify and perform miracles, prophesying to the world for three-and-one-half years during the "seventieth week" of Daniel. They will be hated throughout the world. They will have power to stop rain, to bring plagues, and to turn the waters to blood. After three-and-one-half years, God's protective hand will be withdrawn. The witnesses will be killed, and the whole earth will have a party of unprecedented proportions for three-and-one-half days. Suddenly, these prophets will stand resurrected on their feet to the great fear of the inhabitants of the earth, but they will ascend quickly to heaven while their enemies look on, dumbfounded.

With that background, we look at Revelation 11:8. This is worthy of all the attention you can muster.

> ...their dead bodies shall lie in the **street** of the great **city**, which spiritually is called **Sodom** and **Egypt, where** also **our Lord was crucified** (Rev. 11:8).

God, by His Holy Spirit, used this passage to prompt the entire message of this book. The message itself does not rise or fall with this passage. Rather, the Holy Spirit utilized this passage as a key to unlock a more complete understanding of the entire Word from Genesis to Revelation. Our exploration will be both exciting and challenging, and I look forward to taking you on this journey, but for now, let us focus with particularity on Revelation 11:8.

Key words have been emphasized. Virtually everything about the verse is puzzling and, in some respects, seemingly contradictory.

First, we are told in the gospels that Jesus was crucified on Golgotha, which was outside the city of Jerusalem but close enough to drag a heavy cross (see Matt. 27:33). But here we are told He was crucified in Sodom **and** Egypt. Is this clear evidence of the Bible contradicting itself, or is something of greater and more profound understanding intended? Next, we see that their bodies will lie in the "street" of that "city." Note that both words are singular, yet referring to at least two specified "cities," without even considering Jerusalem.

Finally, we note that the "city" is a "great" city, and that its "spiritual" names, or the manner in which the city in its earthly presentation looks to God, is as Sodom and Egypt. Yet Egypt itself is not a city, but rather a nation. What can all this mean?

They All Died in Egypt

The Book of Jude is a single chapter, and interestingly, it speaks of both Egypt and Sodom very explicitly within a span of only four verses. Jude's entire purpose is to "exhort you that ye should earnestly contend for the faith which was once delivered to the saints" (vs 3). His first focus is on Egypt:

> I will therefore put you in remembrance, though ye once knew this, how **the Lord having saved the people out of the land of Egypt, afterward destroyed them that believed not** (Jude 5).

PLEASE NOTE: These were the chosen people, the children of Israel, whom the Lord "once saved." Afterward, having been "once saved," they were destroyed. Why? Because they "believed not." The American Christian version of *belief* and the biblical version of *belief* are not usually the same. The American cultural translation is "mental assent" or to "accept as an historical fact."

But God's use of the word *belief* is much different. It requires "taking wholly at God's Word," regardless of how it squares with culture, tradition, circumstances, or feelings. For that reason, only two adult men out of an entire nation of more than 600,000 adult Israelite men were allowed to enter the Promised Land (see Num. 14:29–30; 26:63–65).

Only Joshua and Caleb were permitted to enter. Why? Because they had "another spirit" (Num. 14:24). Obviously Joshua and Caleb had the Spirit of the Lord. So what spirit did the other 600,000 once-saved Israelite men possess? They joined in agreement, "Let us make a captain; and let us return to Egypt" (Num. 14:4). "Would God that we had died in the land of Egypt," they lamented (Num. 14:2).

The true faith-walk of taking God at His Word was too tough for them. It was easier to conform to Egypt. And God said, "…as ye have spoken in mine ears, so will I do to you" (Num. 14:28). None of them actually went back to Egypt. They all died in the wilderness.

Yet, in God's eyes, they all died in Egypt. Even the pastors and priests were denied entrance to the Promised Land, for they, too, wallowed in the spirit of Egypt.

I fear that millions of professing Christians in America will have the same fate, for we are baptized thoroughly in the spirit of Egypt. What is worse, we do not even know it, because the pastors of the flock are more interested in preserving feelings than in promoting faith. They avoid truth to protect toes. They fear man more than God. They do not know the God who is a "consuming fire," who spoke once in flames to those gathered at the foot of Sinai, and who will speak again by fire in the last days (see Exod. 19:18; Heb. 12:29; Rev. 20:9–15).

NOTE TO PASTORS: If "the shoe" does not fit, do not put it on! But do not blindly deny that it fits until you have gingerly tried it in humble inquiry before the Spirit of God. We have turned unbelief into a chorus that can be sung even to an Evangelical mantra.

Unlocking the MYSTERY OF EGYPT

So how can we unlock this seeming mystery of Egypt "where also our Lord was crucified?" Returning to Jude, we must conclude that Egypt represents a spirit of unbelief. It is a religious spirit that believes **IN** God but refuses to **BELIEVE** God, always preferring to adopt or adapt other more comfortable ways and guidelines than those God has set forth. The spirit of Egypt continually cloaks responses to "Hath God said?" in religious jargon and hybrid composites of cultural norms, religious tradition, and common sense, giving a glowing religious aura to "Yes, but…" responses that never seem to agree straight-on with God's Word. God calls it rebellion. And rebellion is manipulation, as the sin of witchcraft (see 1 Sam. 15:23).

Deception results from deceit. Liberals, Evangelicals and Charismatics alike have become masters of personal and mass deceit, and I might say, we virtually revel in it. After all, it is comfortable. We keep the peace, and no one gets his feelings hurt. Feelings reign supreme, and faith takes short shrift. What really matters is power, perks, and prominence.

This may seem tough, but it does not come close to Jude's scathing critique. Is this not why we are told to judge ourselves? Is it not better to face it now when we can make course correction? Or would we prefer to cruise on in blissful oblivion only to hear the irremediable truth on Judgment Day? If you think this is uncomfortable to read, just imagine how it feels to be compelled of the Spirit to write it!

Now let us look briefly at Sodom. Jude tells us that Sodom and Gomorrah were destroyed for "…giving themselves over to fornication; and going after strange flesh…" (vs. 7). Note that when the Scriptures refer to Sodom and Gomorrah, they invariably refer to behavior as opposed to belief. Rebellious behavior is abomination to God and will not get by the bar of divine justice on Judgment Day. But what few seem to teach or recognize is that God puts "the fearful and unbelieving" at the top of His list of those who will join in the lake of fire (Rev. 21:8).

This brand of unbelief is not just the atheist or agnostic kind but the kind America specializes in and cultivates—the kind that believes IN God but refuses to BELIEVE Him. Let me remind you that at least 90 percent of Americans believe IN God, and 80 percent claim to be Christians. Consider also that the divorce rate among fundamentalist Christians is now greater than the nation as a whole. Obviously we do not believe God either, or at least take generous exception to His Word when it comes to areas in which we choose to dance with Egypt.

Returning now to Revelation 11:8, we can (in light of the vast number of references to Egypt throughout the Scripture, including those reviewed) reasonably conclude that:

1. Egypt represents a deceptive spirit of religious unbelief, relying upon power rather than purity;
2. Sodom represents behavioral rebellion against God;
3. Jerusalem, as the actual physical location of Jesus' crucifixion, and as the religious capital of Israel, was so perverted with the spirit of Egypt with its religious veneer over an underlying system of power,

politics, religious position, and refusal to believe and truly trust God, coupled with the normalization of practices condemned in Sodom, that as far as God is concerned, Jesus was crucified in Sodom and Egypt.

Earthly Decision Determines Eternal Destiny

The question then remains: What are the implications of this truth for each of us on the edge of eternity? How does this theme tie together with other major biblical themes, and how should we respond?

One thing is certain. Each of us must come OUT OF EGYPT! It is an essential for entering the Promised Land. So essential is it, that Joseph, being second in command to Pharaoh himself and having been forced to live and operate in the realm of Egypt all of his adult life, "By faith…when he died, made mention of the departing of the children of Israel; and gave commandment concerning his bones" (Heb. 11:22).

Joseph declared to the patriarchs of Israel, his own brothers, "God will surely visit you and bring you out of this land to the land which He swore to Abraham…" (Gen. 50:24). He took an oath of his brothers to carry out even his bones. "So Joseph died…and they embalmed him, and he was put in a coffin in Egypt" (Gen. 50:25–26). Yet in spirit, he had already left, trusting in the promise of God. He did not want even his bones to remain in Egypt, as a witness to future generations.

And so God pleads with you and me, "Come out of her, my people." "Come out from among them and be ye separate…and I will be a Father unto you, and ye shall be my sons and daughters" (2 Cor. 6:16–18). It has been his call from Genesis to Revelation; and He still waits. He is making one final call to the end-time church. He calls pastors and parishioners alike. The Lord promises those who come out shall be overcomers and "shall inherit all things;

Why God Is Against Egypt

I am God...and I will not enter into the city. —Hos. 11:9

The Lord's voice crieth unto the city...—Mic. 6:9

*God is not ashamed to be called their God, for He has
prepared for them a city. —Heb. 11:16*

THE FIRST CITY WAS BUILT by Cain (see Gen. 4:17). Cain was "hidden from God's face," having left "the presence of the Lord" (Gen. 4:16). Cain's sacrifice was "religious" but not of faith (see Heb. 11:4).

The spirit of the city of man has majored on religion but repudiated true faith ever since that first city. It will continue to do so until the New Jerusalem, the City of God, comes down from heaven.

In the following three chapters we will probe deeply into the "spirit of the city." We will discover the end-time raging battle of cities that is being fought on the soil of your heart.

Chapter Seven

Spirit of the City:
Part One

Have "We the People" become the "I AM"
of American "churchianity"?

WE HAVE TAKEN A SIGNIFICANT JOURNEY through "Egypt" as expressed in our culture. Sometimes the spirit of Egypt in our society appears superficial on the surface. Some may feel too much has been made of individual items, such as decor. But it is the aggregate secular impression, whether serious or seemingly superficial, coupled with the more profound and precise spiritual applications and implications, that requires a closer look. That investigation begins with the "spirit of the city."

Before we launch into this unusual search, would you, as an American Christian, humbly bow your head and ask the Lord's guidance and wisdom as we pursue this together.

Pray with Me

Father, we are so grateful to You that we live in this nation where we have freedom to worship You, to study Your Word, to gather together as believers for the uplifting and encouragement of each other, for ministering to each other, for receiving Your Truth. We are grateful that the freedom we enjoy is more than firecrackers. It is more than just political liberation. It is the liberation of our spirit, for whomever the Son sets free, is free indeed.

You have encouraged us to pray for our leaders, that we might live a quiet and peaceable life, that we, in turn, can be more effective servants for You, and walk in the joy of the Lord, which is our strength. We commit to do that, as You give us guidance. We ask now, however, that You would give each of us eyes to see and ears to hear, and a heart to understand and receive Your Word to see if, while proclaiming liberty, we have unwittingly walked into a deceptive trap, enslaving us in the spirit of Egypt. Deliver us, we pray. In Jesus' name. Amen.

The Deceptive Trap

We are embarking on a journey through the Scriptures that may at times shock you. At other times it may sober you. But ultimately it may save you from perhaps the most heinous and deceptive trap the enemy has devised since the beginning of time, one by which he seeks to prevent those who seem to profess the name of Christ from reaching the Promised Land. It is a bondage that enslaves people from pulpit to pew. It is no respecter of persons.

The word *exodus* means "to come out of, to remove yourself from." That is exactly what happened to the children of Israel. Israel came out of Egypt, but God could not get "Egypt" out of Israel.

The story of the Exodus—the coming out from Egypt—did not stop in the final chapter of the Book of Exodus. As a matter of fact, the story of the Exodus continues throughout the entire Pentateuch (i.e., the first five books of the Bible). We see it being rephrased, reiterated, in each of those books, each with a different focus.

In these books we see focus on God's living law, revealing how God's children were to walk in the law by faith. The Word of God was to live in them and through them and was to be written on the tablets of their heart. That is not something that was instituted in the Book of Hebrews. That "My people shall have My Word written on the tablets of their heart" was written in the Book of Deuteronomy (6:4–6), and it is all part of the Exodus.

Instead of focusing on a limited book study, we are going to focus on how the Exodus theme runs throughout the Word of God. We are going to tie together many of the major spiritual themes of the Bible, all under the banner: OUT OF EGYPT. When we are through, you will have an applied understanding of the Scriptures in a way, perhaps, you never dreamed possible. The journey may be bumpy at times, so you will need to fasten your spiritual seatbelt. This journey begins with a conviction that God has called each one of us out of Egypt. We are first going to look at what that means under the heading, "The Spirit of the City."

The Liberator

You may want your Bible with you as we go on this journey. I am a lawyer by trade, having spent twenty years in the private practice of law. I have also pastored for many years and have taught God's Word publicly for twenty years. As a lawyer, I was accustomed to looking to primary sources to support the propositions that I wished to convey and impress upon the court. That is equally as important for any who purport to practice God's law or teach His Word.

If I were to use secondary sources that write **about** the law, such as legal encyclopedias or digests that attempt to draw together many areas of the laws and to synthesize it in digestible portions, the court would not receive that with the same degree of convincing authority as if I went directly to the law itself. The actual law is composed of the legislative acts of our various legislative bodies—whether a state legislature or the Congress—or of case law, what we call "stare decisis," which means basically that the courts are doing some legislation for us.

In any event, I quoted primary authorities when I created my points and authorities to support a legal proposition before the court. Likewise, it is very comfortable for me to go to THE authority when I want to understand what God's Word has to say. You can use commentaries. You can use Bible dictionaries. You can use all kinds of helps. But if you want to really know what the Bible has to say, the Bible is its best interpreter. The Holy Spirit was given to be our teacher. So it is up to us to become students. The Holy Spirit will be our tour guide. He also is the "liberator" for "where the Spirit of the Lord is, there is liberty" (2 Cor. 3:17).

If you become a student, see yourself as a student, operate as a student, and have the heart and mind of a student, you desire to absorb everything that God has in His Word for you. You long to understand the completeness of it, not just as raw information, but so it becomes your very life. Then you will be able to be taught by the Holy Spirit. The Word will become a living reality. You will begin to love the law of the Lord your God, and it will live in your heart.

The New Testament and the Old Testament will then become a cohesive whole. It will all be tied together and will live in you and through you. You will say, like Jeremiah, "Thy words were found, and I did eat them; and thy word was unto me the joy and rejoicing of mine heart: for I am called by thy name, O Lord God of hosts" (Jer. 15:16). You have God's "last name." You have been surnamed by God. You will come to that place in your own heart where you will know that you have been surnamed by God. That is an exciting place to be. And we are going to talk about that a few chapters from now when we discuss walking in the "Spirit of Adoption."

I Am against Thee, Pharaoh King of Egypt...

We are going to begin our journey "out of Egypt" by examining the "spirit of the city". Turn in your Bible to Ezekiel 29. You say, "I thought we were going to talk about Exodus." We are. Do you know that in the Word of God, Egypt is referred to over six hundred times? Over six hundred times! And in approximately four hundred of those times, the basic reference to Egypt is the phrase, "out of Egypt."

In most instances, the word *Egypt* is used in a very negative manner with a seriously negative application. If you were an English teacher and you were going to write an essay, would you continue to use the same phrase over and over and over again? No. That is considered bad English. It is bad usage and bad form, because we think it is boring. It is not good writing style.

But what does God do when He wants to get a point across? He repeats Himself so that we will be blessedly bored. He wants us to get His point, so He says it over and over and over and over again. A classic example can be found in Genesis 1, where it is recorded, "And God said…and God said…and God said…," and "it was…and it was…and it was." God did not say, "Let there be light, let there be water, let there be division of the firmament, let there be trees, let there be grass, let there be animals, let there be people. And everything that God said, was." He chose not to say it that way. Rather, He said, "And God said…and God said…and God said…" He is trying to get a point across, to put us on notice that when God speaks, things happen.

Throughout the Bible we find "out of Egypt…out of Egypt…out of Egypt." God is trying to tell His people something—that He wants them to come out of Egypt. But what does that mean? What does it mean to come out of Egypt? In Ezekiel 29, God speaks through the prophet Ezekiel:

> Son of man, set thy face against Pharaoh king of Egypt, and prophesy against him, and against all Egypt (Ezek. 29:2).

God instructs Ezekiel to prophesy not just against the king, but against everything the king stands for. Egypt stands for something, not just a country. It represents something of great consequence in God's heart, in Gods' eyes. God thunders to Ezekiel,

> Speak and say, Thus saith the Lord God: Behold I am against thee, Pharaoh king of Egypt…which hath said, My river is mine own, and I have made it for myself (Ezek. 29:3).

Immediately you get the sense of what Egypt is all about from God's viewpoint. In God's eyes the spirit of Egypt is the spirit of a city and the spirit of a man, which says, "I can do it myself; I have done it myself, and I will do it myself."

> And all the inhabitants of Egypt shall know that I am the Lord, because they have been a staff of reed to the house of Israel (Ezek. 29:6).

What is a staff of reed? Can you imagine trying to use a skinny, old, wavering reed to support yourself? You try to stick that thing on the ground and it shakes and it bends and it breaks and it pierces your hand. That is exactly what Ezekiel says Egypt has been to God's people: a staff of reed.

When they took hold of thee by thy hand, thou didst break, and rend all their shoulder; and when they leaned upon thee, thou brakest, and madest all their loins to be at a stand (Ezek. 29:7).

It threw them all out of kilter. Every time God's kids, the Israelites, to whom God also refers as His son, went to lean on Egypt, they were thrown all out of kilter. They needed a spiritual chiropractor.

And I will bring again the captivity of Egypt, and will cause them to return into the land of Pathros, into the land of their habitation; and they shall be there a base kingdom [not an exalted kingdom]. It shall be the basest of the kingdoms; neither shall it exalt itself any more above the nations: for I will diminish them, that they shall no more rule over the nations. And it [Egypt] **shall be no more the confidence of the house of Israel…**" (Ezek. 29:14–16).

Do you see why God is against Egypt? We are not talking about the country, as such. We are talking about what it represents in the kingdom of God, in the heart and the mind of God. Ezekiel says, "…it shall be no more the confidence of the house of Israel." What does that mean? Who is the house of Israel? It is God's kids. We are the house of Israel. Did you know that? In Romans 9:6–8 we are told, "…they are not all Israel which are of Israel." And again Paul tells us, "But he is a Jew, which is one inwardly, and circumcision is that of the heart, in the spirit, and not in the letter" (Rom. 2:28–29). So "we" are Israel. You are part of the spiritual "house of Israel" if you have repented of sin and confessed and embraced Jesus Christ as Lord and Messiah. While the church does not replace Israel in every prophecy, it stands with Israel in most of the spiritually directed promises and warnings of Scripture.

And God's Word declares, "Egypt shall be no more the confidence of the house of Israel." What is my confidence as part of the house of Israel? Where is your confidence? God is not talking to the sinners out there. We cannot exculpate ourselves of responsibility to listen to what God is saying here, because this message is not a message to the unbeliever. It is a message to the professing believer. It is a message to those who claim to be God's kids.

There is very little of God's Word that is directed toward those whom we classify as the heathen. It is almost entirely directed toward God's own children. The only portions of the Word that are directed toward the heathen are those parts that deal with the salvation of the soul, to acknowledge that God is who He is. Beyond that point, Hebrews 11:6 declares, "Without faith it is impossible to please Him, for he that cometh to God must [not only] believe that He is, [but] that He is a rewarder of them that diligently seek Him." This message is directed to those who claim to be believers. It is not speaking to those who merely acknowledge that God **is**, but to those who believe and are convinced in heart that He is a rewarder of all who diligently seek Him. Do you believe that God is a rewarder of you, as you diligently seek Him? Do you diligently seek Him? Look with me at Ezekiel 30:6:

> Thus saith the Lord; They also that uphold Egypt shall fall.

God is speaking here to those who want to uphold the spirit of Egypt, or the spirit of the city, as we are going to come to see:

> ...and the pride of her power shall come down... (Ezek. 30:6).

Pomp and Power

What is the basic sin of all mankind? It is pride. And unbelief is an expression of pride. Unbelief is pride because it says "I will only believe what I am going to believe. I will only believe what I can see, what I can do. And I will do it myself." That is the spirit of pride and the spirit of unbelief, which is the essence of sin. It is me. Mine. Ours. That is the spirit of Egypt. That is the spirit of the city. "I will do it myself." "I will exalt myself." "I will believe what I will believe." "I am that I am."

God lambastes the spirit of Egypt, declaring, "I shall break there the yokes of Egypt; and the pomp of her strength shall cease" (Ezek. 30:18). When you think of that word *pomp*, what does it bring to mind? Pride. Pomp and power and pride. Is that not what the political strengths in our nations and our cities are all about? Is that not what our governmental structures are all about? We exalt the pomp of their power.

> And I will scatter the Egyptians among the nations, and will disperse them among the countries (Ezek. 30:23).

This language sounds vaguely similar to God's confrontation with Nimrod in Genesis 11. Remember, we are still talking about coming "out of Egypt" here, so bear with me. You may wonder where we are headed. But if you will stay with me, I think you will find the whole Word tied together as to what the Book of Exodus is really all about.

Genesis 11 presents a very familiar story about the tower of Babel:

> And they said, Go to, **let us build us a city** and a tower, whose top may reach unto heaven; and let us make us a name, lest we be scattered abroad upon the face of the whole earth (Gen. 11:4).

Who was scattered? What did God say He was going to do to the Egyptians in Ezekiel 30:23 because they had the "us without God" syndrome? He was going to scatter them.

Now these people at Babel thought they were going to grab the reins of life, they were going to be in control, and they were not going to be scattered. They were going to build their own way to heaven. They were in unity. And so they confidently said, "...let us build us a city." If we gather together, there is power in numbers. But isn't that an expression of the spirit of humanism?

We talk a lot about humanism. But what is it? Humanism, boiled down, is the philosophy and spirit that says, "We can do it if **we** just get our heads together, because **we** are intelligent people." **The power of positive thinking has subtly replaced the conviction of biblical believing.**

> And the Lord came down to see the **city** and the tower which the children of men built. And the Lord said, Behold, the people is one, and they have all one language; and this they begin to do: and now nothing will be restrained from them, which they have imagined to do. Go to, let us go down, and there confound their language, that they may not understand one another's speech. So the Lord scattered them abroad from thence upon the face of all the earth: and they left off to build the city (Gen. 11:5–8).

What was it about the city that concerned God? Why did God come down and confound their language? God was distressed because of the spirit attached to their purpose and their motivation in forming their city. That spirit was displayed as they exalted themselves to fulfill the place that God wanted to fulfill in their lives. They were going to look to themselves to be their own ruler. They were going to make it to heaven on their own. They were going to build a city. And if they could get enough intelligent people together to be in agreement, they thought they could do it. And God said, "I am going to show you. No way!"

God repeats that theme again in Ezekiel 30:23. He threatens to scatter the Egyptians across the face of the earth. He is not concerned only with the people of Egypt. He is talking about all those who think they can reach heaven or be their own God. He is concerned with those who engage in religious observances, go to church, and create forms of religiosity, but who never really accept and live in the power of God.

In the last days, we are told, many people will have a form of godliness, but they will deny the power thereof (see 2 Tim. 3:5). The difference between form and power is the difference between religion and true faith in God. Religion does not please God. Only faith pleases God. And that is the difference between the "spirit of the city" and the spirit that God desires for His people. It is the difference between Egypt and the Promised Land.

A Problem for the Least and the Greatest

God has been trying to get this message across to His people since day one. Unfortunately, every once in a while we get a little glimpse of it, and then go right back into Egypt.

Jeremiah was confronted with the same issue. In Jeremiah 41:18 we find God's people deathly afraid of the Chaldeans. Now jump to chapter 42.

> Then all the captains of the forces, and Johanan the son of Kareah, and Jezaniah the son of Hoshaiah, and all the people from the least even unto the greatest, came near... (Jer. 42:1).

Let us get the picture. Jeremiah is describing all of God's kids—their leaders first and then all the people of Judah. They all came to Jeremiah. Jeremiah had the Word of the Lord. He was the source of God's Word to the people of Judah. He was the voice of the Lord. And so the people addressed him as such:

> And said unto Jeremiah the prophet, Let, we beseech thee, our supplication be accepted before thee, and pray for us unto the Lord thy God... (Jer. 42:2).

How many times have you heard a member of a church go to a pastor or an elder and say, "Pray for me to the Lord thy God"? Pray for me. Well, that is a noble thing to do, isn't it? We are supposed to do that. In fact, James gives us direction: "Is any sick among you? Let him call for the elders of the church; and let them pray over him, anointing him with oil in the name of the Lord; and the prayer of faith shall save the sick, and the Lord shall raise him up..." (James 5:14–15a). There is nothing wrong with that. We are supposed to be willing, humble of spirit, and ask for prayer.

But let us look at what is behind the people's request here. They continue their petition, explaining what appears to be their motivation:

> That the Lord thy God may shew us the way wherein we may walk, and the thing that we may do (Jer. 42:3).

That sounds good, doesn't it? It sounds so spiritual. Who could possibly object? How many times have you heard someone say, "Let us pray for God's will," about a given situation? Anything wrong with that? Is that not what they were doing here? That is what it says. "Pray for us unto the Lord thy God...that He may show us the way wherein we may walk." In other words, they were praying that God would show them His will about this given situation with the Chaldeans, of whom they were afraid.

> Then Jeremiah the prophet said unto them, I have heard you; behold, I will pray unto the Lord your God according to your words; and it shall come to pass, that whatsoever thing the Lord shall answer you, I will declare it unto you; Then they said to Jeremiah, The Lord be a true and faithful witness

between us, if we do not even according to all things for which the Lord thy God shall send thee to us. Whether it be good, or whether it be evil, we will obey the voice of the Lord our God...And it came to pass after ten days, that the word of the Lord came unto Jeremiah. Then called he Johanan the son of Kareah, and all the captains of the forces which were with him, and all the people from the least even to the greatest. And he said unto them, Thus saith the Lord, the God of Israel, unto whom ye sent me to present your supplication before Him; If ye will still abide in this land, then will I build you, and not pull you down, and I will plant you, and not pluck you up: for I repent me of the evil that I have done unto you. Be not afraid of the king of Babylon, of whom ye are afraid; be not afraid... (Jer. 42:4–11).

Obviously the people were afraid of the king of Babylon. What is the opposite of fear? Faith. And what do we find in the absence of faith? Fear. If you have fear, you do not have faith. If you have faith, you do not have fear. For Paul exhorts, "God hath not given us the spirit of fear: but of power, and of love and of a sound mind" (2 Tim. 1:7).

Here we find that God's people were operating in fear, which means that they were not operating in faith. They asked Jeremiah to pray on their behalf to get the word of the Lord regarding the Chaldeans, of whom they were afraid. Here was Jeremiah's answer: "Be not afraid of the king of Babylon." Babylon is political power. Babylon is a representative city, an emblem of human power structure. "Do not be afraid of the king of Babylon." Do not fear men and their systems and structures.

Then Jeremiah continued:

But if ye say, We will not dwell in this land [in other words, we are going to go somewhere else because we are afraid of the king of Babylon] neither obey the voice of the Lord your God, **Saying, No; but we will go into the land of Egypt,** where we shall see no war, nor hear the sound of the trumpet, nor have hunger of bread; and there will we dwell (vss. 13–14).

Who Will Protect? Who Will Provide?

Think for a moment. Jeremiah basically recited that for which all people are looking. What are the basic needs of people? We have to eat; we need physical sustenance. We want protection; we want to live in peace. Is that not what you are looking for? All people have these needs. But who or what do you and I truly trust to meet these needs?

Jeremiah disclosed the word of the Lord. "Even though you are afraid of those Chaldeans," he said, in essence, "and even though they seem stronger than you, and they have been whipping everybody around you, if you run in fear and you look to yourself and you look to the ways of men to protect you from those Babylonians, the very same things that you are trying to protect against—that is, war and famine—will come upon you."

> **...If ye wholly set your faces to enter into Egypt**, and go to sojourn there; Then it shall come to pass, that the sword, which you feared, shall overtake you there in the land of Egypt, and the famine, whereof ye are afraid, shall follow close after you there in Egypt; and there ye shall die (Jer. 42:15–16).

God is trying to present a choice to His people. This choice extends continuously from the Book of Exodus all the way through the Book of Revelation. And we are going to see that choice unfolded in the chapters that follow. It is the ultimate choice faced by all humanity. Will you believe God? God is not interested in whether you or I believe **IN** Him. Even the devil believes and trembles. Rather, He yearns for us to **believe** Him. The test for whether we believe Him is whether or not we trust Him. And the test for trust is whether we truly take God at His Word, regardless of the testimony of our senses or the ways of our culture.

Moses put it this way, "I set before you life and death...." And then he gave a subtle hint as to what he would like us to choose. He says, "Choose life." Why? "That both thou and thy seed may live" (Deut. 30:19). Life is the epitome of living under the protective umbrella of believing God, of believing that God is our sustainer. He is our provider. He will provide all our needs. He will be our protector. He will be our help. He will be our healer. He will be our strength. He will be our ultimate salvation.

The spirit of Egypt, or the spirit of the city says, "I will look somewhere else, anywhere else but God, to find my protection. I will look to bombs. I will look to airplanes. I will look to rockets. I will look to my doctor. I will look to my banker. I will look to the economy. I will look to the US government. I will look to Social Security. I will look to the Republican or Democratic party. I will look to anything other than God." That is the spirit of Egypt. The issue is not money or planes or doctors. The issue is trust.

That brings it down to home where we live, doesn't it? It may sound a bit harsh, but we are talking about a general attitude and life orientation here that God is trying to convey in His Word. It is a hard message. It does not come easy. I can understand much about this because I lived much of my life in the spirit of Egypt. It is a war of the spirit we will fight increasingly to the end of the age.

I grew up in the church. I had all the right training. I nearly majored in religion in a church-related college. My father was a pastor. I had all the religious heritage, all the Bible training. And I do not criticize any of them. Indeed I am grateful! I do not say they perpetrated anything on me. But for me, though I received Jesus Christ as my Savior and confessed Him as Lord of my life, I was unwittingly walking and living largely in the spirit of Egypt. I trusted myself and human ways of doing things. I did not truly trust God in the ongoing issues of life, other than I believed my salvation was assured, that I would go to heaven someday.

But the Word of God is not designed just to get us to heaven. It is designed to get us there in a world of triumph. If I get a little excited, please forgive me! I just want to get the message across.

God wants you to enter the Promised Land in victory. He despises religious whining, and He deplores unbelief in a religious cloak.

Playing Pretend...Religiously!

So, what happened to Jeremiah's people? They prayed a prayer, just like we pray: "Lord, show me your will." And they said, "We will do everything the Lord tells us to do."

Jeremiah responded, "I will take you at your word and ask God as you have requested. And I will tell you what God says."

Jeremiah then took them to task in chapter 42: "...certainly I have admonished you this day. For you dissembled in your hearts..." In other words, Jeremiah lamented that they had played religious games. "You did not tell me the truth. Just because you **said** you wanted to know God's will does not mean you really did." Does the way Jeremiah responded seem unfair? Were not those folk just like you and me and the majority of professing Christians today? Don't we want to hear only what we want to hear? Listen to Jeremiah:

For **ye dissembled in your hearts**, when ye sent me unto the Lord your God, saying, Pray for us unto the Lord our God; and according unto all that the Lord our God shall say, so declare unto us, and we will do it. And now I have this day declared it to you; but **you have not obeyed** the voice of the Lord your God, nor any thing for the which He hath sent me unto you. Now **therefore know certainly that ye shall die**... (Jer. 42:20–22).

And it came to pass that when Jeremiah had made an end of speaking unto all the people all the words of the Lord...Then spake Azariah the son of Hoshaiah, and Johanan the son of Kareah, and all the proud men, saying unto Jeremiah, Thou speakest falsly; the Lord our God hath not sent thee to say, Go not into Egypt to sojourn there:... (Jer. 43:1–2).

The people AND THEIR LEADERS thought, *God did not say that! How could He possibly say something like that, especially when the Chaldeans are over here and they are stronger than we are? He could not have said something like that. After all, Egypt is a pretty fine place. They are strong. They have food down there. And we could be protected. God would not say something like that.*

But Baruch the son of Neriah setteth thee on against us, for to deliver us into the hand of the Chaldeans, that they might put us to death, and carry us away captives into Babylon. **So they came into the land of Egypt: for they obeyed not the voice of the Lord** (Jer. 43:3, 7).

They went into Egypt. They chose to go back to Egypt, they AND THEIR LEADERS. Yet it all sounded so religious, so spiritual.

Can Cities Become Gods?

We have discussed this idea that Egypt can be equated with the "spirit of the city" in the eyes of God. Let us look at what God says through Jeremiah with respect to that particular matter.

> …Cursed be the man that obeyeth not the words of this covenant, which I commanded your fathers in the day that I brought them forth out of the land of Egypt, from the iron furnace, saying, Obey my voice, and do them, according to all which I commanded you: so shall ye be my people, and I will be your God (Jer. 11:3–4).

There is a choice. God is saying the choice is either "go into Egypt," or "come out of Egypt, and then I will be your God and you will be my people." But you cannot be God's man or woman and have Him be your God if you are in Egypt, living in the spirit of Egypt. You just cannot do it. God said, "Come ye out and be separate."

> Then the Lord said unto me, Proclaim all these words in the cities of Judah, and in the streets of Jerusalem, saying, Hear ye the words of this covenant, and do them, For I earnestly protested unto your fathers in the day that **I brought them up out of the land of Egypt**, even unto this day, rising early and protesting, saying, Obey my voice. **Yet they obeyed not**, nor inclined their ear, but walked every one in the imagination of their evil heart: therefore I will bring upon them all the words of this covenant, which I commanded them to do; but they did them not. **For according to the number of thy cities were thy gods, O Judah…** (Jer. 11:6–13).

What is God trying to say here? Is He creating an equation, saying that if they had twenty-five cities, therefore they had twenty-five gods, and conclude with a factual statement that there were twenty-five gods in Israel? No! He is trying to show us that there is something about humans trying to gather together to form a power enclave, which we call a city, for their mutual support, their mutual protection, their mutual health, their mutual welfare—financially, physically, mentally, emotionally, spiritually, or whatever. There is something about people gathering together in that spirit that greatly risks creating a god.

It is the god of the city. The god of Egypt. The god of self. It is human-ism. It is men claiming to be able to be what God wants to be to them. Remember, God is speaking to Israel, His own kids. This message is not to the heathen. God is talking to His own kids. They had gathered themselves together in the spirit of Egypt. They were operating in the spirit of sin, pride, pomp, selfishness—Egypt. Despite their protestations and religious rhetoric to the contrary, they were not trusting God. Therefore, God could not bless them. They had made themselves gods in the spirit of the city. According to the number of their cities were their gods.

"I Am" vs. "We the People"

Zephaniah 2 speaks to this critical problem. Zephaniah, the prophet of the Lord, recited a whole list of nations or cities or groups of people that God repeatedly discusses throughout His Word. You will find them as you are reading through your Bible. They should be familiar to you. In verse 8, Zephaniah states, "I have heard the reproach of Moab [the Moabites], and the revilings of the children of Ammon [the Ammo-nites]...." In verse 9 he talks of Sodom and Ammon and Gomorrah. He lumps them all together. Then, in verse 12, he speaks of the Ethiopians; in verse 13, of Assyria, Nineveh. All of these were power centers in that day. The people knew what those things meant. They knew these were great cities.

Nineveh was one of those great cities. Jonah was sent to that "great city, Nineveh," to call her to repentance because her people were so evil. Then Jonah got upset when they did repent, because he wanted to see the justice of God wreak havoc upon them. And God had to take him to task.

There were other such cities, or powers. We will later see how Baby-lon was one of those key cities. We will see how the Book of Revelation speaks of that great city, Babylon, engorged on the blood of the prophets. Yet the message speaks not of a mere city called Babylon. It speaks of the spirit of the city. It is the spirit of Egypt.

Zephaniah observed in verse 15, "This is the rejoicing city..." How can he say **the** rejoicing city" when he just mentioned all these other cities and groups of people or power centers? Which one is "the"? "They dwelt carelessly," continued Zephaniah.

That they "dwelt carelessly" means they did not deal or dwell or live by trusting God. They dwelt carelessly. They believed IN God, but they did not BELIEVE Him. Their ways reflected it; their attitudes, their trust, their behavior all revealed a religious spirit without a trusting relationship.

They were rejoicing in their own strength. They dwelt carelessly. It was the spirit of the city "that said in her heart, **I am**" (Zeph. 2:15).

"What is Your name, God? What shall I tell the people when they ask who sent me?" cried Moses. Do you remember God's strange answer? He said, "You tell them, 'I AM.'" What does that mean? I am what?

- I am Jehovah Jireh, the Lord thy provider.
- I am Jehovah Rapha, the Lord thy healer.
- I am Jehovah, the Lord thy savior.
- I am Jehovah.
- I am.

Whom do you trust? Is it the city? Is it the great metropolis of Los Angeles, New York City, Chicago, the hills of Kentucky, or wherever you may live? Who or what do you really depend upon? Do you look to your government, to your city, to religion and religious forms, to your denomination? Do you look to your doctor, your banker, or anything else rather than God to meet your needs? Have "We the People" in America become the "I AM" of American "churchianity"?

Who is your "I am"? Are you operating in the spirit of the city in Egypt, or have you come out of Egypt? Are you walking in faith under the I AM? Do not answer too quickly!

Only TWO Entered the Promised Land

We are going to explore this a little further. It is so hard to adjust our minds and hearts to these questions. They threaten the comfort of religious traditionalism. They probe deeply below the religious veneer that camouflages our fundamental problems—problems with genuine trust. The issue is simple , but answers are not simplistic. We must adjust our hearts and our minds to seriously deal with this issue of trust. And in the process, we will interweave the whole of Scripture to reveal the spirit of Egypt in all its secular grandeur, cloaked in religious trappings.

If this still seems a bit esoteric to you, do not be discouraged. Perhaps you just grasped a little kernel but could not seem to make all the needed connections. Do not give up! This is perhaps the most important matter you could consider in preparing to avoid Satan's end-time deception. It is a matter of trust. And the deceiver will do anything, appearing even as an "angel of light," to get you to shift your true trust. Remember, nearly three million people left Egypt, but only two accountable adults who left Egypt entered the Promised Land.

Before We Move On, Would You Pray This Prayer?

Lord, I thank You that Your Word will not return void, but it will accomplish what You please, and prosper in the thing whereto You sent it, and will live in my heart. And Father, I commit myself today. I will leave Egypt. I want to trust You completely. I do not want to be trapped in the spirit of the city of man. Please forgive me for my own unbelief. Forgive me for substituting religious forms for true faith.

From this day on, where I have been operating in the spirit of the city, where I have gone back into Egypt, where I have not been trusting You and have not walked by faith, I repent. I want to trust You. I want to truly trust You to provide all of my needs. That is my heart's desire. Open my eyes, my mind, and my heart to see Your truth and to walk in it. In Jesus name. Amen.

Chapter Eight

Spirit of the City: Part Two

The city says "I am" and God says "I AM."
Who is right in your life?

VIRTUALLY EVERY SIGNIFICANT THEME in the Bible can be traced to or subsumed under the overarching theme, "Out of Egypt." The whole story of salvation proceeds from the theme, "Out of Egypt," as we will see shortly. Egypt is more than a country. It represents a profound principle—a way of living—that is extremely distasteful to God.

As mentioned earlier, the Word of God refers to "Egypt" over six hundred times. The phrase "out of Egypt" or similar phrasing is used approximately four hundred times in the Scriptures. If you were teaching your children and you had to repeat yourself, you would say, "How many times have I told you?" You try to get across your heart and mind by telling them over and over again. We say, "The third time is the charm." But God reminds us over four hundred times, "Come out of Egypt."

In this chapter, we look further into the topic "The Spirit of the City." The *city* is an encompassing word for "the spirit of political power, of collective power." It is the mentality that says, *If we can only just get ourselves together in agreement, we are smart enough, we have enough intelligence, we can do it on our own. We can even get to heaven on our own.* We have seen the "spirit of the city" first displayed in Genesis 11, at the tower of Babel. The people said, "Let us build us a city and a tower, whose top shall reach unto heaven" (Gen. 11:4). God came down and confounded their languages so that they could not be in agreement. God recognized the power in agreement, in agreement contrary to the Word of God and contrary to His purposes.

There is power in agreement. Jesus confirmed that power in Matthew 18:19, stating, "That if two of you shall agree on earth as touching any thing that they shall ask, it shall be done for them of my Father...." And God said, "...nothing shall be restrained from them, which they have imagined to do" (Gen. 11:6). He had to come down and destroy their agreement so that they could not continue to operate in this power mode to usurp the power of the Almighty God. We call it humanism today. God calls it the spirit of the city. The spirit of Egypt. The spirit of Babylon. The spirit of Tyre. The spirit of Sodom and of Gomorrah.

Thy City or My City?

Our investigation of the "spirit of the city" continues in Daniel 9:

> In the first year of Darius the son of Ahasuerus, of the seed of the Medes, which was made king over the realm of the Chaldeans; In the first year of his reign I Daniel understood by the books the number of the years, whereof the word of the Lord came to Jeremiah, the prophet, that he would accomplish seventy years in the desolations of Jerusalem (Dan. 9:1–2).

Daniel, looking at the words of Jeremiah, discovered that God's people were going to be in Babylon seventy years. He also discovered why they were going to be in Babylon seventy years. When he realized why they were in Babylon and had been taken captive, he reported:

> And I set my face unto the Lord God, to seek by prayer and supplications, with fasting, and sackcloth, and ashes: And I prayed unto the Lord my God, and made my confession, and said, O Lord, the great and dreadful God, keeping the covenant and mercy to them that love Him, and to them that keep His commandments; We have sinned...O Lord, to us belongeth confusion of face, to our kings, to our princes, and to our fathers, because we have sinned against thee (Dan. 9:3–8).

The whole religious structure, the whole of God's people, he says, have sinned against God. That is the reason they are in captivity. How did they get into captivity? Does this relate to Egypt? Egypt is "the spirit of bondage." Paul tells us in Romans 8, "For ye have not received the spirit of bondage again to fear; but ye have received the Spirit of adoption..." (Rom. 8:15). Egypt always represents bondage. And Daniel continued revealing Israel's breach of the Spirit of adoption and consequent curse despite God's deliverance from Egypt.

> Neither have we obeyed...Yea, all Israel have transgressed thy law...therefore the curse is poured upon us...As it is written in the law of Moses, all this evil is come upon us...And now, O Lord our God, that hast brought thy people forth out of the land of Egypt with a mighty hand...O Lord, according to

all thy righteousness, I beseech thee, let thine anger and thy fury be turned away [the same kind of prayer that Moses had to pray when God said He would destroy the people in Exodus 32]…because for our sins, and for the iniquities of our fathers, Jerusalem and thy people are become a reproach to all that are about us. O my God, incline thine ear, and hear; open thine eyes, **and behold our desolations, and the city which is called by thy name**… (Dan. 9:10–18).

"The city which is called by thy name." What does that mean? Remember, we are still talking about coming "out of Egypt, the spirit of the city." Here Daniel was referring to a different kind of city. On the one hand, he talked about the attitude and the heart of the children of Israel that had brought them into captivity, or bondage. He remembered, "You brought us out of Egypt with a mighty hand." Then he spoke of God, focusing on a city that is called by His name. Obviously, Egypt was not that city. Neither were the children of Israel living in the ways of the city of God, or the city called by His name. That is why Daniel found it necessary for God to bring His people back into focus on "the city which is called by thy name."

Then, Daniel cried out:

O Lord, hear; O Lord forgive; O Lord, hearken and do; defer not, for thine own sake, O my God; **for thy city and thy people are called by thy name** (Dan. 9:19).

The Great City Will Burn

In the heart of God, there is a city called by His name. And it is a different kind of city with a different spirit than the city that is characterized by Egypt.

Look with me at Revelation 18. We are going to tie the whole Word of God together on this theme. We are still laying a foundation. Right now we are laying an attitude and heart foundation to discover where this idea of Egypt fits in the whole scheme of God's Word.

And [the angel] cried mightily with a strong voice, saying, Babylon the great is fallen… (Rev. 18:2).

And you say, "I thought we were talking about Egypt. Now you are talking about Babylon." That is right. God uses several different cities or power bases—Egypt, Babylon, Sodom, Gomorrah, Tyre—to illustrate the same theme in His Word. All of these represent the same overarching theme. Egypt predominates over all the others. But here the reference is to Babylon:

For all nations have drunk of the wine of the wrath of her fornication, and the kings of the earth have committed fornication with her, and the merchants of the earth are waxed rich through the abundance of her delicacies (Rev. 18:3).

Jesus is talking about a way of life.

> And I heard another voice from heaven, saying, Come out of her, my people...How much [Babylon] hath glorified herself...she saith in her heart, I sit a queen, and am no widow, and shall see no sorrow (Rev. 18:4, 7).

The City that Says "I Am"

Now we must return to Zephaniah 2:15. This is where we ended in the previous chapter. Here we have a series of cities and countries that are linked together by God as illustrative of the spirit of the city. It speaks of Assyria. It talks about Nineveh. It refers to Gomorrah. Then the prophet said, in verse 15, "This is **the** rejoicing city...." How could Zephaniah say "the"—a definite article—when he had just listed half a dozen cities or countries? That does not make any sense, unless you understand that God is speaking of a general principle, a spirit.

Return in your mind again to the Book of Exodus. God called Moses as a deliverer, and Moses complained, "How can I lead these people out of Egypt? What shall I tell them when they ask me who their God is? What is His name?" And God responded, "You tell them, I AM has sent you." Isn't this fascinating? Zephaniah spoke of that rejoicing city, the spirit of the city, that says "in her heart, **I am.**" I AM. That is the spirit of humanism. It is the spirit of man against God. It is the spirit of antichrist. It is the spirit that says, "I will control my world, my life. If we just get our knowledge together and if we just pool our resources, we can work it out. We can make it happen. I will do it MY way!"

Now let us return to Revelation 18:

- "...for she saith in her heart, I sit a queen, and am no widow, and shall see no sorrow" (vs. 7).
- "The merchants of these things, which were made rich by her, shall stand afar off for the fear of her torment, weeping and wailing, And saying, Alas, alas, that great city..." (vss. 15–16).
- "And cried when they saw the smoke of her burning, saying, What city is like unto this great city?" (vs. 18).

They had all of their hopes wrapped in the spirit of the city. That is where men are prone to wrap up their hopes.

- "...Alas, alas, that great city, wherein were made rich all that had ships in the sea by reason of her costliness!..." (vs. 19).
- "And in her [remember, it is talking about Babylon] was found the blood of prophets, and of saints, and of all that were slain upon the earth" (vs. 24).

A City That Kills Prophets…and You

Now we do not have record of more than a few of prophets involved with Babylon. Daniel was one of them. Jeremiah was another.

We do not have a record that Daniel was killed in Babylon or that he was a martyr. The Scriptures do not bear record that any prophet was actually killed in Babylon as a martyr. So what is Jesus talking about in Revelation? He tells us that the blood of prophets and saints is to be found in Babylon. Then he boldly declares, "…and of all that were slain upon the earth." He is talking about God's children who are slain for their faith upon the earth.

Does that mean that all of those who are recorded in *Fox's Book of Martyrs* were slain in Babylon? Obviously not! Few known martyrs met their demise in Babylon. So what is John's meaning here as he reveals Jesus' message? Obviously he is not talking about a city called Babylon. He is referring to the spirit of a city. He is talking about a way of life, a people that look at life from the point of view that they are in control and God is not in control. The writer envisions a people who trust anything and everything other than God. They are deeply religious but refuse to trust God or take Him at His Word. Persecution of true faith comes from the spirit of Babylon. The spirit of Babylon and the spirit of Egypt are the same spirit.

We are talking about the spirit of the city. We are talking about coming out of Egypt. And we see, in Revelation 18:4, God not-so-subtly clears His holy throat, demanding, "Come out of her, my people." Why is God instructing **His** people to come **out** of her if **His** people were not **in** her? It is obvious that God is not here concerned about everyone. God's concern is focused on His kids—those who profess to be members of His family.

Being a parent and having your own children does not mean you are not concerned about other people's children. But you are not concerned for others' children to the extent that you become a father and mother to them. You are concerned about them to the extent you can help them. But to the extent they will not be helped, you back away.

Your primary responsibility of care, love, affection, and provision is to your own children. The same is true with God. And He is talking to His children—the people called Israel and the people who call themselves His church. He is saying, "You come out from Babylon. You come out from Egypt." Whether or not we can see it, God understands that we are there in Egypt, living in that life focus and style. And He warns, "Come out because you do not belong there. I cannot bless you there." **If the spirit of the city kills prophets, it will kill you too!**

Cities in Conflict

John concluded giving Jesus' words about Babylon in Revelation 18. Now Revelation 21 gives us an amazing contrast:

And I saw a new heaven and a new earth: for the first heaven and the first earth were passed away: and there was no more sea. **And I John saw the holy city**, new Jerusalem, coming down from God out of heaven, prepared as a bride adorned for her husband, And I heard a great voice out of heaven saying, Behold, the tabernacle of God [the living place of God] is with men, and He will dwell with them, and they shall be His people, and God Himself shall be with them, and be their God (vss. 1–3).

Here is a new city—the city of God, the new Jerusalem. This is where God yearns for us to live. But there is a condition. We must come out of Egypt. We must come out of Babylon. Only then can we enter the holy city, because it is a city with different foundations, a city whose builder and maker is God and not men (see Heb. 11:10). It is a completely different city. It has a radically different spirit. And it is interesting that God repeatedly uses this theme of cities. Continuing with verses 22–23, we read,

And I saw no temple therein: for the Lord God Almighty and the Lamb are the temple of it. And **the city had no need of the sun**, neither of the moon, to shine in it: for the glory of God did lighten it, and the lamb is the light thereof.

I must regretfully advise you that on this earth, at this time, the new Jerusalem has not come. We are living in the city. Jesus told us, "I want you to be in the world, but not of it." That is merely a rephrasing of our discussion regarding the spirit of the city. We are **in it**, but must not be **of it**.

Who will be the light of that city? Your city? What is the light of this city? We used to sing that lovely little chorus, "Jesus is the Light, Light of the World." But it is not entirely biblical. Jesus is not the light of this city. Jesus declared, "**As long as** I am in the world, I am the light of the world" (John 9:5). Guess what? Jesus came to bring light to the world (John 12:46), but Jesus ascended back to the Father nearly two thousand years ago. That is why He said He would send the Holy Spirit. And He told you and me in Matthew 5,

Ye are the light of the world. A city that is set on an hill cannot be hid. Neither do men light a candle, and put it under a bushel, but on a candlestick; and it giveth light unto all that are in the house. Let **your light** so shine before men, that they may see your good works... (vss. 14–16).

Therefore, in this city, before we get to the new Jerusalem, you and I are its only light if we are Christ-ones, true Christians. Jesus **was** the light when He was here, by His own testimony (see John 9:5), but He ascended to the Father and left us here in this city. He then deputized us to reflect His light: "As the

82

Father sent me, even so send I you." Therefore, you and I—to the extent that we are not in participation with the Egyptian or Babylonian spirit of this city, but rather living in this city as a sojourner—are the light of the world.

Now that is not arrogance. That is owning up to what God tells me about myself as His child. To the extent that I will not own up to that, I am living in the spirit of Egypt. I am living in the spirit of religion. I am living in the spirit of false humility, which is pride. And that is the spirit of humanism. Remember, it is the spirit of religion. It may sound good. It may match your traditional thinking. But it is the spirit of Sodom, Egypt, Gomorrah, and Babylon, that crucified the "light of the world." The city of God is in mortal conflict with the religious spirit of the city of man. Jesus reminded all who would be His true disciples, "They shall put you out of the synagogue: yea, the time cometh, that whosoever killeth you will think that he doeth God a service" (John 16:2). **The more profoundly religious our disbelief, the more profoundly dangerous it is to true belief.**

John made it clear in Revelation 21:7, "He that overcometh shall inherit all things...."

Overcome What?

Not everyone will inherit all things. Not everyone who says, "Lord, Lord," will inherit the Kingdom. Only he that overcometh. Jesus lists those who will not be among the overcomers. I want you to look at the first two on the list: "But the fearful and the unbelieving..." (Rev. 21:7–8). John, declaring the "Revelation of Jesus Christ," went on to list the kinds of things we normally think of as evil: "the abominable, and murderers, and whoremongers, and sorcerers, and idolaters, and all liars, shall have their part in the lake which burneth with fire..." But the first two on the list are the **fearful** and the **unbelieving**.

What does God mean by "the fearful and unbelieving"? Whom is God addressing? Follow me to Hebrews 3:7–19. As we read these verses, we are so tempted to believe God is talking about somebody else. We conclude, "He must be talking about somebody who does not attend church." No. God's Word is directed primarily toward those who do attend church. More precisely, it is spoken to those who have come to the place in their life where they have acknowledged that God is—even that Jesus is the Son of God, that He died and rose again for their sins—but they are still living in the spirit of Egypt, the spirit of the city.

God's Word calls out, "Today, if ye will hear his voice." The Book of Hebrews was written to Christians, to the Hebrew Christians, and it warns:

> Wherefore as the Holy Ghost saith, Today if ye will hear His voice, Harden not your hearts, as in the provocation, in the day of temptation in the wilderness:...Wherefore I was grieved with that generation, and said, They do always err in their heart; and they have not known my ways.... Take heed,

brethren, lest there be in any of you [talking to Christians] an evil heart of unbelief, in departing from the living God. But exhort one another daily, while it is called Today; lest any of you be hardened through the deceitfulness of sin [which is unbelief].... So **we see that they** [meaning God's kids in Numbers 13 and 14] **could not enter in** [the city of God, the Promised Land, the new Jerusalem symbolized in the Old Testament] **because of unbelief** (vss. 7–8, 10, 12–13, 19).

Egyptian Reports

Who could not enter in because of unbelief? God's kids. Is that not what He said? In fact, He decreed in Numbers 13 and 14 that every adult He delivered from Egypt would die in the wilderness, except for two.

How many of God's professing children in the church are in the wilderness because they are operating in fear and unbelief—in the spirit of the city, in the spirit of Babylon, trusting themselves to man's way of doing things. Their trust is in their doctors, their lawyers, their politicians, their merchants, their chief, or whoever else stands tall in their estimation. Anybody but God. The church in twenty-first-century America is nearly paralyzed by the spirit of science. Our faith is frustrated by addiction to sense knowledge.

And we find, in Numbers 13 and 14, that God's people murmured and complained. They said, "...there be giants in the land, and we be not able to overcome them. We are like grasshoppers in their eyes." And they whined, "Would to God we had died in the land of Egypt. At least there we had some food. At least there we did not have to face giants." That is the spirit of the city. It is the spirit of flesh. It is revealed in "grasshopper vision" and in thoughts, such as *Let us just be comfortable, get together and pool our resources here and let the chips fall where they may.* This kind of spirit will never get out there on the cutting edge of faith. It is fear and unbelief. It is an abomination, a stench in God's nostrils.

God called the report of those ten spies who came back from the Promised Land an "evil report" (Num. 13:32). Their report was truthful and factual, yet God called it an evil report. Why? Because it was a report that, in its very gut, said, "We do not believe God." It was an "Egyptian" report.

The Democratic Majority Is a Dead Majority

Now look at Numbers 14. We are about to see two people who were remarkably different from those around them. Moses wrote, "Doubtless ye [the ten spies and an entire nation who followed them] shall not come into the land...save Caleb the son of Jephunneh, and Joshua the son of Nun" (Num. 14:30). Now of the children who were not of accountable age, who had not come to the place where they could understand the difference between belief and unbelief, God said they would not suffer the penalty. They would not be prevented from entering the Promised Land. But all who had the ability to understand the difference between faith and nonfaith—fear and faith, belief or unbelief, taking God at His word or not taking God at His word—those would not reach the Promised Land.

Verse 24 reveals why: "But my servant Caleb, because he had another spirit with him…" Remember, we are talking about the spirit of the city. It is the spirit of "doing it my way," as opposed to God's way. Notice that faith is not a democratic matter! Notice that God is not concerned about numbers? He is concerned about faith. Without faith it is impossible to please Him (see Heb. 11:6). Numbers do not necessarily carry the day with God. God is not impressed even if the heads of all America's denominations join in affirming your unbelief. Only two men of an entire nation of accountable adults—yes, even of God's "chosen people"—inherited the Promised Land. This has profound implication for us standing on the near edge of Christ's Second Coming.

It is said that there were six hundred thousand Israelite men who came out of Egypt. So there must have been over one million adults, including women. Yet we see only two men, out of all the adults of that entire nation that claimed to be God's kids, who got the blessing. Only two men had "another spirit". Every other adult had the spirit of Egypt. Even though God had taken them out of Egypt with a mighty hand, they kept running right back in. They said, "Would to God we had died in the land of Egypt."

We see then that for God's children there is a choice. The choice is Egypt or non-Egypt: the spirit of the city of man, or the spirit of the city of God. We can make the choice. "Straight is the gate, and narrow is the way, which leadeth unto life, and few there be that find it" (Matt. 7:14). **The democratic majority, with all its spiritual trappings, is still a dead majority.**

Please listen to me carefully! Do not dismiss this lightly! Democracy is the rule of the people. It is said to be the most dangerous of all government forms, yet the best we have. Why is that? A people truly submitted to God and His authority will trust Him and conduct themselves in humility and obedience before Him.

But when "we the people" combine ourselves for common cause outside God's absolute authority, then democracy becomes the ultimate expression of rebellion against God. Unfettered democracy becomes the incarnation of the spirit of the Antichrist.

As democracy now sweeps across our earth, embraced by ungodly yet religious people, it may smell like freedom. But it carries the shackles of ultimate bondage. It is ushering in the Antichrist. And American "Christians" are being swallowed by that spirit, totally oblivious to its eternal consequences.

Who Is "The Israel of God"?

We must, then, establish the true identity of God's kids, His children. Who is Israel, in God's eyes? Who is the Israel that God refers to over and over in Scripture? Is it the nation of Israel that we read about in the newspapers? Is it a geographical region? We must answer that question in our hearts.

Hosea 7, verse 10, tells us, "The pride of Israel testifieth to his face…" Pride of a nation reveals its exaltation against God. It reveals the spirit of the city. It is the spirit of Egypt and Babylon. Continuing in verse 11, "…they call to Egypt, they go to Assyria." Israel continually wants to cry out for Egypt and go to Assyria or any other power other than God. Hosea penned God's lament in verses 13 and 14, "…though I have redeemed them, yet they have spoken lies against me. And they have not cried unto me with their heart." It is a matter of the heart. "They have not cried unto me with their heart." God is talking about people who claim to be God's people, but who have not cried unto Him with their heart. His concern is not the rhetoric of their mind, but the cry of their heart.

Amos 3:1 continues the theme, "The Lord hath spoken against you, O children of Israel, against the whole family which I brought up from the land of Egypt…" There it is again: "out of Egypt." God is talking to Israel now, and He says, "You only have I known of all the families of the earth…" They are His children. And He is talking only to His children, not to the whole world. Only to His children, He says,

> You only have I known of all the families of the earth: therefore I will punish you for all your iniquities… (Amos 3:2).

Just as we are told in Hebrews, "whom the Lord loveth, He chasteneth" as a son (Heb. 10:6). Israel, He said, was His firstborn son. So God is going to chasten His people because they are not walking, in their heart, according to His ways. Then God asks,

> **Can two walk together, except they be agreed?** (Amos 3:3)

Can you walk with your Father unless you are walking in His ways? How can you say that you walk with your Father when you do not trust Him? How can you say that you walk with your Father when, if all the chips are down, you trust your doctor, your lawyer, your medicine man, your chief, or the government more than you do your heavenly Father? Who do you trust? Where is your trust? Are you living in the spirit of Egypt or are you living in the spirit of the new Jerusalem?

Then, in Romans 9, we have the direct question posed: Who is God really talking about when He speaks of Israel in His Word? Paul asks, "Who are Israelites; to whom pertaineth the adoption…?" (Rom. 9:4). In other words, "To whom pertains the rights, privileges, and blessings I have promised you as sons and daughters of God?" To whom pertains "…the glory, and the covenants, and the giving of the law, and the service of God, and the promises." Who is Israel? Then Paul responded:

> Not as though the word of God hath taken none effect. For they are not all Israel, which are of Israel (Rom. 9:6).

What an enigmatic statement! "They are not all Israel, which are of Israel." Then who in the world is Israel? What kind of gobbledygook is this? Either they are Israel, or they are not Israel. Yet he says they are not all Israel which are of Israel. So, who is the "Israel of God"?

> **But he is a Jew [or an Israelite], which is one inwardly; and circumcision is that of the heart, in the spirit...** (Rom. 2:29).

PLEASE NOTE CAREFULLY

There are two broad classifications of promises relating to "Israel." We have been discussing matters of the heart and spirit. It is those the apostle Paul addresses. The Church "stands in the shoes" of Israel with regard to such promises. But there are end-time promises directed specifically to Israel, both geographically and nationally. These remain to be fulfilled as to Israel only. Thus, the Church does NOT replace Israel as to covenants "running with the land" or directed to the land. As to the rest, "All the promises of God are yes and Amen in Christ Jesus" (2 Cor. 1:20).

Foreskins and Faith

Again, as a reminder, we are talking about coming out of Egypt. You see, the Israelites to whom the promises were made were not the people who were Israelites by birth. They were not those who walked out of Egypt in the flesh, but who were Israelites "by promise" or by faith. And my Bible reveals that at the point at which they were facing giants as an obstacle to entering the Promised Land, there were only two true Israelites (other than Moses). Only two Israelites, in God's eyes. One was a man named Joshua, and the other was Caleb. They had a different spirit. The rest had Israelite bodies but Egyptian minds and hearts.

Deuteronomy 10:12–21 ties the testaments together. Contrary to popular opinion, God's character and operation was not "law" in the Old Testament but "grace." God has always been operating in grace since time began. His character never changes. God has always said that the just shall live by faith. Was not Abraham, our father, justified by faith when he offered Isaac, his son, upon the altar (see James 2:21)? That was before the law was even given; therefore, it has always been God's plan that the just shall live by faith. And God always has intended that the just shall live by coming out of Egypt. Moses wrote in Deuteronomy 10:

> Only the Lord had a delight in thy fathers to love them, and He chose their seed after them, even you above all people…Circumcise therefore the foreskins of your heart, and be no more stiffnecked (Deut. 10:15–16).

To whom was Moses addressing these words? He was speaking to those who are "Israel" in the eyes of God. This ties directly with Romans 2:29 and Romans 9:6, where we are told that "they are not all Israel which be Israel." But they are Israel (or Jews) who are inwardly such, not circumcised in the flesh, but circumcised in the heart. God demands that we cut away enslavement to fleshly feelings and our bondage to the powerbrokers of this age, and that we ruthlessly cast our trust on Him and His Word. We must "circumcise the foreskins of our heart."

God Is Pro-Choice

You and I are faced with a profound choice. We must come out from the spirit of Egypt, from the spirit of the city, from the spirit of Babylon, from the spirit of humanism, from the spirit of "doing it my way" and having confidence in men.

> For in Christ neither circumcision availeth anything, nor uncircumcision, but a new creature (Gal. 6:15).

When God speaks of old things passing away and all things becoming new, He speaks about a matter of spirit. He is talking about a spirit, about an attitude toward life and living, and about who you trust. Listen to the apostle Paul:

> And as many as walk according to this rule, peace be on them, and mercy, and **upon the Israel of God** (Gal. 6:16).

Now is that not a strange phrase—"upon the Israel of God"? What other Israel is there? There is the Israel by birth and there is the Israel by faith. Two Israels. The Israel that God is talking about here in His Word is you and me—if and when we are walking by faith, trusting Him in every area and arena of life. Are you? Do not respond too quickly. For our entire culture compels us back into Egypt.

In the next chapter we will see how God called His son out of Egypt before His son was even born and how in these last days God is again calling His people out of Egypt. Then we will begin to make specific applications in God's Word, tying the entire Scripture together. This is an essential part of the gospel. Leave Egypt. Enter the land of promise.

> Be ye not unequally yoked together with unbelievers [those who have a form of godliness but deny the power thereof because of unbelief]…Wherefore come out from among them, and be ye separate, saith the Lord…And [I] will be a Father unto you, and ye shall be my sons and daughters, saith the Lord Almighty (2 Cor. 6:14–18).

Chapter Nine

Spirit of the City:
Part Three

*How is God going to bring His children out of Egypt if
we are not in Egypt? Many of us like to walk with faithful
Abraham, but pitch out tents toward Sodom with Lot.*

THE WORD PHRASE "OUT OF EGYPT" and words akin thereto, are used approximately four hundred times from Genesis to Revelation. When God repeats Himself that many times, He is doing it for a purpose. He is trying to get the attention of His kids. And this fact is repeated here again to drive this truth deeper into our hearts.

We have visited Galatians 6, where Paul talked about the "Israel of God" (vs. 16). Why would Paul, a Jew, speak of "the Israel of God" if there was not another Israel? So there are two Israels. There is the Israel by birth, and there is the Israel by adoption, or the "new birth." For those of us who will truly walk by faith—the faith of Abraham—we then are part of the Israel that was Abraham's grandson, the Israel of promise.

In this chapter, we will delve into this provocative matter a bit further. We are going to complete our three-part introduction focusing on the subtopic "The Spirit of the City" or the spirit of Egypt. What is the spirit of Egypt? What is the spirit of the city that God has called His "Israel of promise" to leave?

We have seen Zephaniah's version of the spirit of the city, the spirit of Egypt. In Zephaniah 2:15, the prophet described a group of cities, or political powers, then used the phrase "the city" in the singular form, referring to a spirit that is characteristic of the city in general, the city as God sees it. God calls it the spirit of the city. He calls it the spirit of Egypt. He calls it the spirit of Babylon. And Zephaniah tells us that the city "says in her heart, **I am**…"

We have also seen that God gave those very words to His servant Moses, when Moses inquired of God, "Whom shall I tell the people hath sent me to take them out of Egypt?" And God responded, "You tell them, I AM sent you." The city says, "I am," and God says, "I AM." The haunting question persists. To which city do we belong?

We have also understood that God is not speaking primarily to those we think of as unbelievers, that is, those who are outside the church. Rather, God is concerned that those who profess to be inside His church come out of Egypt. We heard the writer to the Hebrew Christian church warn, "Take heed brethren, lest in any of you should be found the same example of unbelief" as was found in the children of Israel. They who had just crossed the Red Sea, exiting out from Egypt, murmured and complained when they saw giants in the land, and cried, "Would to God that we had died in the land of Egypt." They wanted to go back. So God gave them their heart's desire: "Indeed as you have spoken, so shall it be done unto you." And, except the two spies who expressed faith, every last one of Israel's accountable adults died physically in the wilderness, and yet, from God's spiritual frame of reference, they all died in the land of Egypt.

God said, "You shall not enter the land I have promised." So the question remains to be answered: Will you and I enter the land that God has promised? Will we enter His rest by truly trusting Him? Or will we die in the spirit of the city, in the spirit of Egypt?

Faith's Father Left Egypt

We have seen that the choice God is giving is a choice for professing believers. Now we will see how God has actually called His Son, His very own Son, out of Egypt, out of the spirit of the city. We are going to tie it all together from Genesis to Revelation. We begin our journey in Genesis 13:

And Abraham went up out of Egypt... (vs. 1).

Notice the timing. Abraham "came out" before the children of Israel ever went into Egypt. This is a curious thing. Abraham went up out of Egypt. If he came up out of Egypt, how did he get into Egypt? Here is the answer:

And there was a famine in the land; [that is, the land where Abraham was] and **Abram went down into Egypt** to sojourn there; **for the famine was grevious in the land** (Gen. 12:10).

Now I want to ask you, "How did the children of Israel happen to go into Egypt?" Exactly the same way. There was a famine in the land. And how do God's kids go down into Egypt today? By famine in the land! Isn't that right? Famine in the land. What is the land? The land is the spirit…the heart (see Mark 4:15). There is famine in the heart and spirit that leads God's children into Egypt. You cannot come up out of Egypt unless you are there. And Abraham was there. Abraham went up out of Egypt.

You will notice that God uses the phrases, "down into Egypt" and "up out of Egypt." That should give us a little clue. *Up* almost always signifies "for the betterment," does it not? *Down* signifies "for the worse." So there is much we can gain if we just take the time to look at God's Word. God does not use His Words lightly. Remember, "Every word of God is pure." He said, "My Word shall not return void." So He chooses His words carefully.

> And Abraham said unto Lot, Let there be no strife, I pray thee, between me and thee… (Gen. 13:8).

Now I want you to know that Lot was related to Abraham, just like you and I are related to those among us in the church. Joshua and Caleb were related to the rest of the children of Israel at the time they came out of Egypt and were asked to spy out the land of Canaan. Remember, there were only two men who inherited the promise of God. Two men out of an entire nation of God's children who had "a different spirit." They were God's kids. Joshua and Caleb were the children of Israel. Only two men got the promise of God. Just two! Yet they were all related.

Faith is not a democratic process. Neither is faith transferred by bloodline. God has not obligated Himself to fulfill His promise just because people acknowledge that God *is*. He is not impressed merely with a raised hand, a checked response card, or church membership. In fact, James got very sarcastic on this point: "Who do you think you are that you think you should get something because you believe God is? Even the devil believes and trembles" (James 2:19, paraphrased). Hebrews 11:6 exhorts, "…he that cometh to God must [not only] believe that [God] **is**, [but] that He is a rewarder of them that diligently seek Him." The issue is not whether God **did** reward in Bible days, but whether He **does** reward today. God's concern is not whether He is the "I AM" but whether He is **your** "I AM." Is He your everything? Is He everything you need? Again, do not be too quick to answer in the affirmative, for **many of us like to walk with faithful Abraham but have pitched our tents toward Sodom with brother Lot.**

Lot Chose Sodom—Like Egypt

Let us return to Abraham and his nephew Lot. They were related by flesh but not by faith. They were of the same blood but not of the same spirit. A closer look reveals a stark contrast between these men.

Just as Joshua and Caleb had a "different spirit" from all the other escapees from Egypt, so Abraham's spirit differed radically from Lot's. Listen to the Divine viewpoint on Lot as Abraham opened the conversation in Genesis 13:

Let there be no strife, I pray thee, between me and thee, and between my herdmen and thy herdmen; for we be brethren. Is not the whole land before thee?
Separate thyself, I pray thee, from me: if thou wilt take the left hand, then I
will go to the right; or if thou depart to the right hand, then I will go to the left.
And Lot lifted up his eyes, and behold all the plain of Jordan, that it was well
watered everywhere, before the Lord destroyed Sodom and Gomorrah, even as
the garden of the Lord, **like the land of Egypt**... (vss. 8–10).

You see, Egypt appears to be well watered. It has always appeared to be
well watered and it continues to appear to be well watered to all who will
look to the land of Egypt. The land of Egypt has always appeared to be well
watered to any person who will look to man's way of doing things, to the man
who trusts the arm of flesh.

Even so today we have the spirit of humanism, which is the spirit of Egypt.
It is the spirit of the city where man says, "If I can just get enough coopera-
tion with enough people, we have enough intelligence, enough smarts and
enough going for us that we can make it all happen. We can produce revival
by collective effort...a little unity...some better strategy. We can even build
a tower and make our way to heaven. And by the way, God, if we ever need
Your help, we'll let You know."

Abram dwelled in the land of Canaan, and Lot dwelled in the cities of the
plain, and pitched his tent **toward Sodom** (vs. 12).

In Which Direction Is Your Tent Pitched?

Remember, Lot and Abraham were related. They were kin, just like you
and I in the church are brothers and sisters in the Lord. But Lot pitched his
tent toward Sodom, and Abraham pitched his tent toward Canaan. A choice.
In which direction is your tent pitched? Give serious consideration to this
question, for Lot models the prevailing mind of American Christians on the
edge of the third millennium.

Notice! Lot went for the city. What is the city? It is a spirit. It is the spirit
of Egypt. It is the spirit of humanism. It is the spirit of Antichrist. It is the
aggregation of man's best efforts to meet his own needs, protect himself, and
govern his destiny.

"And the Lord said to Abram, after that Lot was separated from him..."
Note the word *after*. God spoke **after** Lot was separated from Abram. What
did the Lord say to Abraham **after** Lot was separated from him? After the
spirit of unbelief left and the unequal yoke was broken, what happened?

And the Lord said unto Abram, after that Lot was separated from him, Lift
up now thine eyes, and look from the place where thou art northward, and

southward, and eastward, and westward: For all the land which thou seest, to thee will I give it, and to thy seed forever. Then Abram removed his tent, and came and dwelt in the plain of Mamre… (vss. 14–15, 18).

What happened to Abraham when he separated himself from the spirit of the city and the spirit of unbelief? God blessed him. Right? God did not bless him until he made that quality choice and acted on the choice. Lot went with the spirit of the city and Abraham chose something else.

Where was Abraham heading? We get a clue from Hebrews 11:8:

By faith Abraham [not by the spirit of the city, or by trusting men's way of doing things, or by looking for the beauty of Egypt, but by faith—taking God at His Word], when he was called to go out into a place which he should after receive for an inheritance obeyed; and he went out, not knowing whither he went.

You see, the spirit of Egypt always seems to guarantee a result. Unfortunately, the result seldom materializes. But mankind, from the beginning of time, has always been suckered by the promise, by the illusory promise of the spirit of Egypt—the spirit of the city—promising social security, national medicine, denominational protection, or whatever. But it is illusory. It never seems to work out right. It has an appearance of substance, but it never satisfies. In fact, it creates more problems. It breeds unrest. Independence from God produces dependence on Egypt. Rather than freedom, there is bondage.

Countercultural Faith

In contrast, we see the countercultural faith of Abraham. "By faith he sojourned in the land of promise, as in a strange country…" (Heb. 11:9). He just seemed weird—socially strange. His ways did not jibe with what everybody else was doing. He was a stranger, just like Joshua and Caleb. An alien in the world, "dwelling in tabernacles [tents] with Isaac and Jacob, the heirs with him of the same promise." What was Abraham looking for? "…he looked for a city which hath foundations, whose builder and maker is God" (Heb. 11:10).

He was looking for a city, but it was a different city. It was the new Jerusalem. He sought the spirit of the new Jerusalem. But the new Jerusalem would not come down until the end time, and so he had to live as a sojourner—just a traveler in this world. He looked for that city with foundations whose builder and maker is God.

Abraham was the first of faith to come out of Egypt. From the beginning of the Book to the end of the Book, Abraham embodies the spirit of true faith. The Pharisees claimed him as "father," but they walked in a different spirit. Jesus excoriated their unbelieving "Egyptian" religious systems.

If ye were Abraham's children, ye would do the works of Abraham. But now ye seek to kill me…ye seek to kill me, because my word hath no place in you (John 8:36–40).

Unbelief is deadly. It is deadly to those who walk in unbelief, but it breeds within those who refuse to take God at His Word, a deadly attitude toward those who do. For this reason, the most serious persecution comes not from those "in the world" but from those within the "Egyptian" religious system, masquerading in the machinations of religious activity. Jesus faced the most serious opposition, not from the liberals, but from the conservatives—the "religious right" of His day. They conspired against Him, just as the leaders, priests, and prophets decreed death to Jeremiah "in the house of the Lord" (Jer. 26:8–9). Abraham had a different spirit.

By faith Abraham was justified, believing God for a son of promise. He staggered not at the promise of God (see Rom. 4:13–22). By faith Abraham offered Isaac, his son, upon the altar, believing that God was able to raise him from the dead to fulfill His promise. When asked by his son, "Where is the sacrifice, my father?" Abraham declared, "God will provide Himself a lamb" (Gen. 22:8).

Before taking Isaac up the sacrificial mount, he advised the young man that had borne the wood with him up to that place, "I and the lad will come again to you." Knowing that God had ordered him to sacrifice his son, he nevertheless declared, "I and the lad will come again to you" (Gen. 22:5). How could Abraham have such confidence? God had made a promise. God is God. He keeps His Word.

God had made a covenant with Abraham. And Abraham was strong in faith. Paul noted:

And being not weak in faith, he considered not his own body now dead, when he was about an hundred years old, neither yet the deadness of Sarah's womb: He staggered not at the promise of God through unbelief; but was strong in faith, giving glory to God; And being fully persuaded [in his heart, not his head] that, what he had promised, he was able also to perform (Rom. 4:19–21).

So Abraham represents, from the very beginning, the spirit of the new Jerusalem, the spirit of the city of the living God. He was the first one to come out of Egypt in spirit.

I Must Come Out to Lead Out

Generations after Abraham came out of Egypt, God called Moses, a man raised in the pomp and power of Pharaoh's own house, out of Egypt. God heard the cries of the "children of Israel," the children of Abraham's grandson.

God was still bound to His promise to Abraham. But God could not lead His people out of Egypt by the hand of one who had not first come out of the "house of bondage." It took forty years in the wilderness to get Egypt out of Moses. But in the fullness of time, God sent forth a deliverer with a divine mandate. The drama begins in Exodus 4:

> And thou shalt say unto Pharaoh, Thus saith the Lord, Israel is my son, even my firstborn. And I say unto thee, **let my son go**, that he may serve me… (vs. 22–23)

The children of God—God's kids—cannot serve God in Egypt. They cannot! You cannot! Why? Because the spirit of Egypt is the spirit of Antichrist. It is the spirit of doing things under my own power, my way. Any way other than trusting God. It is the spirit of modern America incarnated (on the secular side) in the life of Frank Sinatra and (on the religious side) in conservatism's bent on salvation by the power of conservative government. The problem is not with the conservative philosophy. The problem is our trust. **The believing minority are not defined by the "Moral Majority."**

Now I can **say** I trust God. The children of Israel did that over and over and over again. But when it came down to acting on what they said they believed, it never happened. They always went to Egypt. So a jealous God roared,

> And thou shalt say unto Pharaoh, Thus saith the Lord, Israel is my son, even my firstborn. And I say unto thee, **let my son go**, that he may serve me… (vs. 22–23).

"Let my son go that he may serve me" has been God's clarion call since Moses stretched forth the scepter of God over Egypt's pomp and power. But you and I have to make a choice. Christ took the keys of hell and the grave from Satan. That was just another way of saying, "Let my son go." But the question is, will I come out? I have to make the choice. **Christ may have given us the keys to His Kingdom, but we must walk out of the house of bondage.**

God declared to Moses, "Israel is my son, even my firstborn." But what does He say in the New Testament? Where does Jesus fit? Did not Paul refer to Christ as "the firstborn of **many** brethren"? In the same way, Israel, or Jacob (which was his name until it was changed) was also the firstborn of many brethren. The children of Israel symbolized all of God's people, from that time forward, who would leave Egypt by faith. God said, "I am calling my son out."

The prophet Hosea continued the theme:

> When Israel was a child, then I loved him, and called my son out of Egypt (Hos. 11:1).

96

Who was his son? His son was Israel—the firstborn of many brethren. Similarly His son by prophecy was Jesus, also the firstborn of many brethren. We would expect, then, that Jesus, Messiah, the Lord of the church, had to come out of Egypt in order to become the Captain of our salvation, leading many sons out of the house of bondage into the household of faith.

The Book of Matthew tells us very simply,

> And when they were departed, behold, the angel of the Lord appeareth to Joseph in a dream, saying, Arise, and take the young child and his mother, and flee into Egypt... (Matt. 2:13).

Did you know that Jesus had to go into Egypt before He came out? All of God's kids have gone into Egypt before they ever came out, starting with Abraham, the "father of faith." Moses came next, followed by Israel, then Jesus and you and I. Before we can come out of Egypt, it is obvious that we must have been in Egypt.

Matthew continued his narrative:

> When he arose, he took the young child and his mother by night, and departed into Egypt: And was there until the death of Herod: that it might be fulfilled which was spoken of the Lord by the prophet, saying, **Out of Egypt have I called my son** (Matt. 2:14–15).

Where was the prophecy spoken? In Hosea 11:1. Jesus, the only begotten Son of God, the Lord of the church, had to **come out of Egypt** that He might lead those who would follow Him out of the "house of bondage."

Have You Come Out of the Camp?

Now we must leap forward about thirty years to the completion of Christ's ministry. Consider these words from Hebrews 13:

> Wherefore Jesus also, that He might sanctify the people with His own blood, suffered **without the gate** (vs. 12).

What does "suffered without the gate" mean? Does that affect you and me? Listen to the writer to the Hebrew church:

> Let **us** go forth therefore [see that identification with Jesus?] unto Him **without the camp...** (vs. 13).

What is "the camp"? It is the spirit of the city. It is the spirit of Egypt. It is the spirit of humanism. It is the spirit of Antichrist.

> **For here we have no continuing city...** (vs. 14).

Have you ever wondered why God called Abraham out of his father's house? When Abraham was called out of Ur of the Chaldees, where he had been living, was he told to just go out and wander in the wilderness? We are told he went out "not knowing whithersoever he went" (Heb. 11:8). But was he to wander aimlessly? No! Abraham understood something more about what God expected. And unless you read the entire Bible and tie it all back together, you will never figure out why Abraham was called out of Ur of the Chaldees.

God never intended for Abraham to wander in the wilderness. God intended for him to look for a city with foundations whose builder and maker was God. Abraham never found the fulfillment of that city, but he refused to settle for an Egyptian substitute. He sought God Himself. That is why we are all called out.

Is it any wonder that the Scriptures confirm this pattern?

For here we have **no continuing city**, but we seek one to come (Heb. 13:14).

Moses took the tabernacle [which is the place where God resided in those days], and pitched it **without the camp** [outside the camp, not inside the city], afar off from the camp [far enough away so that it was obvious that there was a clear separation], and called it the Tabernacle of the congregation. And it came to pass, that every one which sought the Lord [obviously not everyone sought the Lord] went out unto the tabernacle of the congregation, which was without the camp (Exod. 33:7).

Isn't that interesting? So from beginning to end, God has always followed the pattern. He knew what man's propensity would be. He knew the propensity of men would be to adopt the spirit of religion. It would be to collectively create all kinds of religious structures and systems, structures of government, structures of tradition, institutions. God yearns for a spiritual organism; we yearn for an organization. But God, from the very beginning, so that there would be no confusion, called those who would truly follow Him **outside the camp**. Have you come **outside the camp**? Or are you still in bondage to the **spirit of the city**?

Crucified in Egypt?

What we are about to see may be a real revelation you. It certainly was to me when I first read it. The Holy Spirit used the particular scripture we are now ready to unfold as the "hook" to open to me the entire theme, "Out of Egypt."

First we must understand the context of this verse. There will be two great witnesses in the last days that God has appointed to do mighty miracles in the world. They will be God's final prophetic voice. Their power and purity will be known throughout the world, evidenced by mighty miracles. They will stand apart as men of God, in contrast to the Antichrist and his false prophet. These two prophets will be hated, despicable in the eyes of most of the earth's population, who will be operating in the spirit of deceit, the spirit of religion, the spirit of Egypt, and the spirit of Babylon. These prophets will be calling men to final accountability and obedience to God and His Word, calling them to come out of Egypt. This will inspire furious anger throughout the earth, because these prophets seem a threat to men's religious ways, false unity, and counterfeit peace. Men will conspire to get a hold of these two guys and kill them.

After three-and-one-half years, God's protective hand will be withdrawn, and they will be killed. Revelation 11:8 then gives us this seemingly contradictory statement:

> And their dead bodies [of the two witnesses] shall lie in the street of that great city, which spiritually is called Sodom and Egypt, where also our Lord was crucified.

How could Jesus have been crucified **outside the gate** of Jerusalem yet also in Sodom and Egypt? Remember, Lot set his eyes to Sodom and the cities. Abraham searched for a city with foundations whose builder and maker is God. Egypt and Sodom represent the same spirit, in the eyes of God. But here The Revelation says that Jesus was crucified in Sodom and in Egypt.

What does Jerusalem symbolize in the Word of God? THE city. Religion. The spirit of religion. Man's effort to comingle God's way with man's effort and pride. It embodies a system that looks spiritual but sounds in pride. It is a pragmatic system—one that we think "works." That is what Jerusalem was all about.

And so we find that the very people purporting to lead God's kids were the very ones who crucified Jesus. And we are told the reason they crucified Him. Pilate, a pagan Roman governor, saw through the system. He knew why they crucified Him. He understood it was "for envy" that they brought Him (Matt. 27:18; Mark 15:10). What was that envy? They had a form of godliness, but denied the power. Jesus had not only the form, but also the power. He refused to embrace the system.

When Jesus walked the face of the earth, the Bible says people observed that He did not talk as the other religious people did. Rather, He spoke with authority (see Matt. 7:29). He spoke outside the system. He had come out of Egypt—out of the house of bondage. He acknowledged who He was in God's eyes. Although the Son of God, His authority in the earth came not because He was the "Son of God," but because He was the "Son of Man"

(John 5:27; Psa. 8:4–6; Heb. 2; Phil. 2:5–11). And the religious system and its powerbrokers called Jesus a heretic, a "blasphemer."

Who are you? Do you know who you truly are in Christ? Who are you in the Kingdom of God? Are you in the Kingdom of God? You have the religious rhetoric down, but do you truly submit to the King? Do you speak with authority, and not as the scribes? Do you even speak? Do you crucify Jesus again by the spirit of your religion, because you do not accept what God says about you? Do you understand that you are the righteousness of God in Christ Jesus? Do you accept what He tells you in His Word about your body, about your spirit, about your mind, about your financial provision?

Do you accept Him? Do you not only accept Him, but also absolutely trust Him? Do you truly trust Him not only for salvation in "the sweet by and by," but also for your needs in the rough-and-tumble now? If not, maybe you are operating in unbelief or the spirit of pride, which is the spirit of Jerusalem, which is the spirit of religion. It is the spirit of false humility that says, "I cannot acknowledge that because that would be arrogance and pride." Therefore you do not claim or admit what God says to be true. What you are, in effect, saying is, "There are giants in the land. We are not able to overcome them." And God calls that an evil report. It is unbelief. It is the spirit of Egypt. And God, in these last days, is calling His people to absolute submission to His authority and absolute faith in His Word. To do otherwise is to crucify Jesus again in Egypt.

God's Final Call Out of Egypt

The prophet Zechariah advised, "Ask ye of the Lord rain in the time of the latter rain" (Zech. 10:1). Are these words for us today? What is the time of the latter rain? The prophet Joel told us that a time would come when "your sons and your daughters shall prophesy, your old men shall dream dreams and your young men shall see visions" (Joel 2:28). And the apostle Peter said that the time of the latter rain commenced when the Holy Spirit came down and empowered God's people to go out.

> But this is that which was spoken by the prophet Joel;…your young men shall see visions and your old men shall dream dreams (Acts 2:16–17).

Consider. If this "latter rain" is "that which was spoken by the prophet" then it must have started in Acts, chapter 2, with the outpouring of the Holy Spirit on the church—on you and me. Therefore, we must be living in the time of the latter rain. Of that time of the latter rain, Zechariah went on to prophesy:

> **I will bring them [God's children] again also out of the land of Egypt…"**
> (10:10).

How is God going to bring His children today out of the land of Egypt if they are not in the land of Egypt? Obviously, the bulk of God's children, in God's eyes, are still in the land of Egypt. That is why they must **come out** in the time of the latter rain. What does that mean for you and for me?

The questions in my mind are, "Am I still living in Egypt?" "Do I still need to come out of Egypt?" "Are you still living in the land of Egypt?" "Do you need to come out of Egypt?"

Zechariah recorded a wonderful promise for us: "...the scepter of Egypt shall depart away. And I will strengthen them in the Lord; and they shall walk up and down in His name" (10:11*b*–12). His name. Not in the name of Egypt. Who is he talking about? He is referring to us, to you and me. We will walk up and down in His name. But we will do that only **if** "the sceptre of Egypt departs away" from our lives.

God tells us that His children have not known His ways from the very beginning. Speaking of Israel, the writer of Hebrews stated, "They do always err in their heart; they have not known my ways." God is not concerned here with facts of the faith or religious rituals. Rather, He speaks of erring "in the heart." And then we receive a warning to "Take heed...lest there be in any of you an evil heart of unbelief, in departing from the living God" (Heb. 3:10–12).

How can we discern the spirit of Egypt lurking in our lives? Look at Israel. They were not satisfied with God or His ways. They were not satisfied with God's provision or God's rule over them. They wanted to be like everybody else. They refused to trust His protection and His promise. They did not want that dividing line outside the camp. They wanted to be inside the camp. They wanted a king to reign over them "just like them." Just like them! But God is crying out today: "I will be your king." Yet we, like ancient Israel, respond both in word and deed, "We want to be like them." "Give us a ticket to heaven, but let us live **like them** on earth." It is the choice of a city.

Every significant indicator reveals that there is no discernable difference between the lives of professing Evangelical Christians in America today and their secular counterparts. Attitudes and behavior reveal the same values, the same moral standards, the same thinking. The only observable difference is in religious forms, practices, and rituals. Folks, we are feeding on "Egyptian" leeks and onions and are destined for an Egyptian grave unless we turn and come "outside the camp." Mummies may have an extended temporal longevity, but they do not have eternal life. They look good on the outside, but they are dead on the inside. We have a choice to make.

Consider Your Ways

Haggai took the rational approach in pleading with God's people. Listen to him. Do these words ring true in your life as they did in the life of a young, churchgoing, attorney friend who confessed, "I do not know how to live by faith." Let the words of Haggai probe the recesses of your heart:

> Now therefore thus saith the Lord of hosts; Consider your ways. Ye have sown much, and bring in little; ye eat, but ye have not enough; ye drink, but ye are not filled with drink; ye clothe you, but there is none warm; and he that earneth wages earneth wages to put it into a bag with holes. Thus saith the Lord of hosts; Consider your ways (Hag. 1:6–7).

Isaiah took the more direct approach, thundering,

Woe to them that go down into Egypt (31:1).

Over and over again, in chapters 30 and 31 he pronounced, "Woe to them that go down into Egypt." Then, in Jeremiah 9:23–26, the prophet spoke of us being uncircumcised in the heart. And we found in Romans 2:29 that those are Israel which are circumcised in the heart and not in the flesh. And again in Romans 9: "...they are not all Israel which be Israel, but they are Israel which are Israel in heart," not in the flesh.

Who is the Israel that God is calling out of Egypt? There is only one honest answer. We are the Israel that He is calling out of Egypt. Say it verbally! "God is calling **ME** out of Egypt."

As we close this chapter, let me share with you a letter I received from one of America's prominent "Egyptian" companies: Prudential Insurance. I say "Egyptian" because the spirit of this letter is the spirit of Egypt. Consider the overarching mind and the underlying heart of this message:

> A house is not a home if it can be taken from your family. Fortunately, a "Piece of the Rock"—Prudential Life Insurance—can help make sure that your house remains a home.

As soon as I read this letter, I winced, "If that isn't preying upon the spirit of Egypt, I don't know what is." That is exactly what it is. It is a not-so-subtle effort to transfer our trust. It may appear innocent, but it is spiritually deadly. It says that "a piece of the rock"—Prudential Life Insurance Company—will do it for you. No need to trust God. He is "out there somewhere." Trust Prudential! Prudential will be your rock, your fortress, your protector. And then the words of a familiar chorus surged through my heart:

> Praise the name of Jesus...
> He's my rock,
> He's my fortress,

He's my deliverer,
In Him will I trust. [if I will]
Praise the name of Jesus!

In what "rock" or "rocks" do you trust? Why go for a piece of the rock when you can get THE Rock?

Moses lead Israel out of Egypt in powerful demonstration of the mighty, delivering hand of God. The providing and protecting hand of God was revealed continually as they wandered forty years in a physical wilderness, due to a continual hankering for Egypt in a spiritual wilderness.

Wrapping up a lifetime of struggle with the spirit of Egypt, Moses expressed God's own lament over Israel:

> I will publish the name of the Lord: He is **the Rock**...But [Israel] waxed fat and kicked: he forsook God which made him, and lightly esteemed **the Rock** of his salvation. Of **the Rock** that begot thee thou art **un**mindful, and hast forgotten the God that formed thee. And when the Lord saw it, He abhorred them...And He said, I will hide my face from them...for they are a froward generation, children in whom is no faith. For the Lord shall judge His people, and repent Himself or His servants, when He saith that their power is gone...And he shall say, **Where are their gods, their rock in whom they trusted...?** (Deut. 32:3–37)

Lest we should become smug, wondering how Israel could be so faithless and fleshly while we are so faithful, the apostle Paul warned us:

> Now all these things happened unto them for our ensamples [example]; and, they are written for our admonition; **upon whom the ends of the world are come**. Wherefore let him that thinketh he standeth take heed lest he fall (1 Cor. 10:11–12).

Do you realize that "the ends of the world are come" upon us, upon you and me? We are living in history's final hour. The great tributaries of history are converging in rapid, prophetic fulfillment, surging toward the Second Coming of Christ. It is time to leave Egypt once and for all time.

Remember, God lead Israel out of Egypt, but only two of the adult men who left Egypt entered the Promised Land, having left Egypt in spirit and truth. If these things were "written for our admonition; upon whom the ends of the world are come," the same division of spirit will prevail when it comes time to determine entry into the eternal promised land. Many churchgoing, Bible-toting people will say in that day, "Lord, Lord." Yet the Lord will say, "I never knew you: depart from me" (Matt. 7:21–27). Where will the lines be drawn?

Pray with Me

Father, thank You so much that You sent Jesus to be my Rock. He is my fortress and my deliverer. He is my strength. He is my salvation. He is my healing. He is my provision. And I will trust Him.

Reveal to me how I think like Egypt, believe like Egypt, and act like Egypt. Lord, I want to leave Egypt. I refuse to live in the house of bondage any longer.

I reject the spirit of the city. I will come back to You outside the camp. Forgive me for my lust to "be like them." I need Your help to escape the bondage of my own unbelief. By Your grace, I will walk by faith. I will take You at Your Word.

Forgive me for substituting my own thinking for Your wisdom and ways. Forgive me for shifting my trust to the government, to technology, to science, to corporate America, to religious traditions, to my denomination, and to anything that would subtly replace or displace my trust in You.

From this day forward, by Your power, I leave Egypt. I will no longer walk like an Egyptian. I am moving into the spirit of the city of the Living God. By faith, I will enter Your Promised Land. In the name of my deliverer, Jesus Christ. Amen!

What Lies Ahead?

In the chapters that follow, we will trace the theme "Out of Egypt" through many areas of our lives. We will test your trust quotient. We will measure whether you truly believe the message of the Master. Do you? Are you sure?

We will look at many of the major themes of the Bible as they relate to coming out of Egypt. For many it will be an eye-opening experience. You will have a fresh perspective of that Bible you own. And you will be challenged to a new life of faith—one you may never have known possible. The purpose: to prepare you as an overcomer for the Second Coming of Christ. It is right at our doorstep!

How You Can Come Out of Egypt

WHY WERE ONLY TWO MEN out of an entire nation of account-able adults—purportedly God's chosen people—allowed to enter the Promised Land? What implication does this have as professing Christians contemplate the rapidly approaching Second Coming of Christ?

Section three will continue to provoke your mind and challenge your heart. It may well cause some to rethink their traditional beliefs and doctrinal predilections. It may reveal some of the hidden motivations of the heart that have both established and perpetuated adamantly held positions and attitudes throughout much of the church, producing a chilling effect on the power of God in our time. Could it be Jesus "can do no mighty works" in our time (just as in ancient Nazareth) "because of our unbelief"?

We have become extraordinarily adept at casting religious cloak about us to camouflage the nakedness of our faith. Much of that which passes our pulpits and is entrenched in our pews is not faith but flesh wrapped in a myriad of religious excuses, justifications, and rationalizations. Such thinking kept an entire nation of accountable adults from the Promised Land. Yet God Himself had delivered Israel from the house of bondage in Egypt. Only two men entered the Land of Promise: Joshua and Caleb. The Scriptures note it was because they had "another spirit." Do you have that other spirit?

The writer to the Hebrew church observed "...they could not enter in because of unbelief." And he warns, "Take heed, brethren, lest there be in any of you an evil heart of unbelief..." How does your heart compare to those—the vast majority—who, having come out of Egypt, still died there in spirit? Do not answer too quickly. Your eternal destiny may be at stake.

For one last time, God is calling His people OUT OF EGYPT before the return of Christ for a pure and unspotted bride. Are you ready? The chapters that follow unfold how you can be better prepared by coming out of Egypt. Allow the searchlight of the Holy Spirit to probe deeply into your heart. Let us begin.

Chapter Ten

Spirit of Adoption

*Are you living in fear? If so, you are in bondage to
the spirit of Egypt. What will it take to walk
in the Spirit of Adoption?*

GOD HAS BEEN CALLING His children out of Egypt from
the Book of Genesis through the Book of Revelation. We have seen this
as one of the major themes, if not the overarching theme, of the Scriptures.
We have discovered that this is not a message to the world or to the sinner.
Rather, it is a message primarily to the person who calls himself by the name
of the Lord. It is addressed to the person who seeks to identify himself as a
child of God.

We must come out of Egypt. We must cease to live in the spirit of the
city. We must abandon the kind of thinking that locks us into the prison of
Satan's household. We must recognize that way as bondage.

Now we are going to see how God has called us out of that bondage,
out of the prison of a mindset that locks Christians into looking at life from
Satan's point of view.

We have thoroughly traced this pattern—this call of God, from Genesis to
Revelation, to come out of Egypt. We have observed the essence of the spirit
of Egypt expressed in the spirit of the city. Men gather together corporately to
exalt themselves above God, declaring in essence, "I am: my city is my own;
my river is my own; and I'll do it my way." It is the ultimate expression of
the carnal mind. It is enmity against God.

Children of Egypt

As we launch into our discussion of the "Spirit of Adoption," let us just put
one more hit on the nail to ensure we have this understanding locked well

into our mind and spirit. God wants us to come out of Egypt! We can find no stronger warning than in Isaiah, chapters 30 and 31:

> Woe to the rebellious children saith the Lord, that take counsel, but not of me; and that cover with a covering, but not of my spirit, that they may add sin to sin: That walk to go down into Egypt... (Isa. 30:1–2*a*).

Who is God speaking to here? The passage will have no impact on me whatsoever if I think God is talking here to the world and to the sinner. He is not. If He were, He would not address them as children. Throughout the Word of God, the children are those who claim to be God's family. That is why He addresses them as children. In God's eyes, the rest are (and pardon the clarity of this expression, but it is a biblical term) bastards. Why? Because they are not linked with the Father, God Almighty. They are living illegitimately. They are born of fornication with Egypt. They are of a different family. And we are going to see this very clearly.

When God speaks either *to* His children or *of* His children, He is addressing the children of Israel. In particular, He speaks to the children of promise—to those who are of faith with faithful Abraham. In that sense, we are the "Israel of God." All those who will walk according to the Spirit, who will link themselves to God through Jesus Christ, are the "Israel of God" and have standing for the spiritual promises of God. The Bible is a love letter that our Father provided to us as His children. Therefore, we can see that these words of Isaiah in chapters 30 and 31 are directed toward us, just as they were to ancient Israel:

> Woe to the rebellious children...That walk to go down into Egypt, and have not asked at my mouth; to strengthen themselves in the strength of Pharaoh, and to trust in the shadow of Egypt! Therefore shall the strength of Pharaoh be your shame, and the trust in the shadow of Egypt, your confusion. That this is a rebellious people, lying children, children that will not hear the law of the Lord (Isa. 30:1–3, 9).

God's concern is not that His children **cannot** hear, but they **will not** hear. Compare Jesus' words from Matthew 13:

> Therefore speak I to them in parables: because they seeing see not; and hearing they hear not, neither do they understand...lest at any time they should see with their eyes, and hear with their ears, and should understand with their heart, and should be converted, and I should heal them (Matt. 13:13, 15).

God laments His people who **will not hear** the Word of the Lord. Isaiah continued this heart-rending lament:

Wherefore thus saith the Holy One of Israel, Because ye despise this word, and trust in oppression and perverseness, and stay thereon: Therefore this iniquity shall be to you as a breach...For thus saith the Lord God, the Holy One of Israel; In returning and rest shall ye be saved; in quietness and in confidence shall be your strength: and ye would not. But ye said, No; for we will flee upon horses...and, We will ride upon the swift... (Isa. 30:12–13, 15–16).

What is God saying here? Is He talking about horses? No. He is not talking about horses. The horses are a symbol of the power of man. They did not have tanks in those days, but they used horses. They did not have nuclear warfare, but they used horses. The horse and the rider were the symbol of the strength of man. And they said, "We will not trust you, God. We will flee upon the horses. We will ride upon the swift."

Woe to them that go down to Egypt for help; and stay on horses, and trust in chariots, because they are many; and in horsemen, because they are very strong; but they look not unto the Holy One of Israel, neither seek the Lord! (Isa. 31:1)

You cannot get any clearer than that. "Woe to them that go down to Egypt." David translated it this way: "Some trust in chariots, and some trust in horses, but we will trust in the name of the Lord our God" (Ps. 20:7).

Translate that into the nitty-gritty. Look at the things you are concerned about in your life. What are the needs in your life? Where do you turn first for the resolution of those needs? What is the very first thought that passes through your mind when you see sickness attempt to strike your family? What is the very first thought that passes through your mind when you see financial needs begin to knock at your door?

Is it your banker? Is it your doctor? Your psychiatrist? Is that where you first turn? Is that the first thought that comes into your mind? Or is it, "But my God shall supply all my need according to His riches in glory by Christ Jesus" (Phil. 4:19)? See, "Some trust in chariots, and some trust in horses," but who will we trust in? That is what God is asking.

Let us be clear. God is not saying that doctors are evil and bankers are evil and lawyers are evil and psychiatrists are evil. So please do not draw that conclusion. God is probing deeply. Where do you truly put your trust? Whom do you trust? What do you trust?

For a moment, return with me to our Prudential Insurance illustration. I believe it reveals the spirit of the city—the spirit of Egypt—that concerns God so profoundly. I received this advertisement from Prudential Insurance Company. (If you are a Prudential agent, pardon me; this is not directed at you. It is directed to an idea.) Here is what it said: "A house is not a home if it can be taken away from your family. Fortunately, a piece of the rock, Prudential Life Insurance, can help ensure that your house remains a home." What is the spirit of this promotional piece? What is its message? You can trust a corporation. You can trust man-made devices. Anything that man can come up with, trust it.

But as I read this piece, the Holy Spirit spoke to me instantly: "Can you really trust Prudential? Is it true that Prudential Life Insurance can ensure that your house remains a home? Why should you trust a piece of the rock, when you can have THE Rock?" We sing the song "He's my rock. He's my fortress. He's my deliverer." Do we know what we are singing? Do we ever think about it? Do we truly believe it? Or do we just sing, and it sounds good? Does it rest in your spirit?

Look what Moses wrote in Deuteronomy 32:

> I will publish the name of the Lord; ascribe ye greatness unto our God. He is the Rock…" (vss. 3–4).

Not a piece of the rock. Not some rock. He *is* the Rock. What does that mean? The rock is the symbol of complete solidity, of dependability. Unshakable. Unmovable.

In a Howling Wilderness

We had a savings and loan in our community called Gibraltar Savings. Why do you think they used that name? Because it is the name of a rock. The Rock of Gibraltar. They wanted you to believe in your heart that you could trust that rock. Do you understand? You may think that this is nitpicking. But that is why God has had to call so loudly to His people. There have been a lot of "rocks" in the course of civilization that have cried out. People trust in those rocks. But they— including God's children—have not trusted in THE Rock, Jesus Christ.

> **He is the Rock,** His work is perfect: for all His ways are judgment: a God of truth and without iniquity, just and right is He. For the Lord's portion is His people; Jacob is the lot of His inheritance (Deut. 32:4, 9).

Notice, God is talking about His people. Not about some other people. Not about the world. About His people. Verse 10 says, "He found him…." Who did He find? His people. Who was the progenitor of His people? Jacob. What was Jacob's name changed to? Israel. Deuteronomy 32 tells us:

> He found him [Israel] in desert land, and in the waste howling wilderness; He led him about, He instructed him, He kept him as the apple of His eye…. He made him ride on the high places of the earth…then he forsook God…and lightly esteemed the Rock of his salvation (Deut. 32:10–15).

110

Theoretically they knew He was the Rock. They knew that God was the Rock of their salvation, but they lightly esteemed the Rock of their salvation. In their heart, God was not the rock.

Do you recall when God instructed Moses to speak to the rock because there was no water? God instructed Moses to speak to the rock, but instead, he hit the rock. Right now we do not need to go into the reason of why speaking and not hitting or hitting and not speaking. We are talking about the rock. What happened when Moses spoke to and struck the rock? The water came out, didn't it? And the apostle Paul told us, "...they drank of that spiritual Rock that followed them; and that Rock was Christ" (1 Cor. 10:4).

We do not really understand that, do we? It was a rock that they saw here. The water flowed out of a literal rock. Yet God was trying to give a graphic illustration. He was attempting to demonstrate vividly that He was going to be their rock. He was going to be the water of life that would flow for them freely and provide all their needs, because He was a father who loved His kids.

God expresses His heart over His children when He confesses, "...they are a very froward generation, children in whom is no faith" (Deut. 32:20).

He found His child wandering in a wilderness, in a desert land. He led him by the hand out of the wilderness. And He tried to lead him into prosperity of living, abundance of life. But the son pulled away and would not follow his Daddy.

Let My Son Go!

God gave instructions to Moses while the children were still in Israel. "And thou shalt say unto Pharaoh, Thus saith the Lord, Israel is my son, even my firstborn; And I say unto thee, Let my son go that he may serve me..." (Exod. 4:21–22).

Who is this son? It is Israel. Israel is the second name for Jacob, Abraham's grandson. Scripture refers to Jacob's seed as the "children of Israel." Scripture seldom speaks of Isaac. But it does talk a lot about Jacob, because Jacob was the last in the series of Abraham, Isaac, and Jacob.

Throughout the Bible, when God wanted to instruct His people that He intended to be their father and that He had made promises and covenants to be a father to them, what would He say? Instead of going through all that explanation, He would merely repeat, "I am the God of Abraham, the God of Isaac, and the God of Jacob." They knew exactly what He meant. That is all He had to say.

So here we have Israel, the firstborn son, called out of Egypt. John 3:16 says that "God so loved the world, that He gave His only begotten son." There is an only begotten son. And if there is an only "begotten" son, there must be other sons.

The Scripture tells us that Jesus was the firstborn of many brethren (see Rom. 8:29). If Jesus was the firstborn of many brethren, that means there would have to be some other brethren. And if Jesus was the "only begotten" son, the other brethren are going to have to get into the family another way. That is the thrust of this chapter: "Out of Egypt: The Spirit of Adoption." Consider Paul's statement to the Galatian church:

> But when the fullness of the time was come; God sent forth His Son, made of a woman, made under the law, To redeem them that were under the law, that we [you and I] might receive the adoption of sons (Gal. 4:4–5).

Jesus, the only begotten son, was sent that we might become adopted sons. The Book of Hosea tells us, "When Israel was a child, then I loved him, and called my son out of Egypt" (11:1). Then Mary and Joseph were instructed to take Jesus down into Egypt "that it might be fulfilled which was spoken by the prophet, saying, Out of Egypt have I called my son" (Matt. 2:15).

Jesus had to come out of Egypt as the only begotten son. Israel had to come out as the symbol of all adopted sons:

> And Moses said unto the people, remember this day, in which ye came **out from Egypt, out of the house of bondage**; for by strength of hand the Lord brought you out from this place…This day came ye out in the month of Abib (Exod. 13:3–4).

The month Abib was the first month of the year. It was the same month that Jesus was crucified, except they called it by a different name at that time. It was the time of the giving of the Passover when Jesus was brought to Jerusalem to be the Lamb that took away the sin of the world. That is why we celebrate Communion (which we will unfold when we discuss "Out of Egypt: Redemption and Atonement"). We are going to see what Communion really is. We will see why the apostle Paul warned, "…for this cause many are weak and sickly among you and many sleep." Often we do not truly understand the significance of Communion.

Rescued from the House of Bondage

In Exodus 13:3 we see that Egypt is called the "house of bondage." It is Satan's household. And many, if not most, professing Christians (at least in America) straddle households in unbelief. We are double-minded and duplicitous in our hearts. We claim blessing but live in bondage. This grieves our Father, God. This must change if we are to be readied as a bride for the Second Coming.

By the time you have completed this book, we will have looked at most of the major themes in the Word of God under the banner "Out of Egypt."

The goal is that you have a clearly painted vision of yourself as a child of your Father, God. You must begin to actually see yourself as a son or daughter of your Heavenly Daddy. It is not religious facts but righteous living that counts in the Kingdom of God. It is not the FACT that you are a son or daughter of God but that you live out that reality in your life that counts. And once you get that vision—when you see yourself as a son or daughter of your Heavenly Father—your whole world will change.

> For as many as are led by the Spirit of God, they are the sons of God (Rom. 8:14).

Not just anybody who calls themselves by the name of the Lord is a son of God (Matt. 7:21).

> For ye have not received the spirit of bondage again to fear; but ye have received the Spirit of adoption, whereby we cry, Abba, Father (Rom. 8:15).

Exodus reveals that Egypt was the house of bondage. Egypt is the symbol of bondage. The spirit of the city is the house of bondage.

Why did the apostle Paul use the words *again to fear*? Because that is what Egypt stood for. It stood for a life of fear. Bondage generates fear. Fear is the absence of faith. What does it take to please God? FAITH! Without faith you cannot please God (see Heb. 11:6). Therefore, you and I cannot please God in Egypt. Egypt is the house of fear and bondage. If you live in fear, you are living in the spirit of Egypt.

Scripture warns that men's hearts will be "failing them for fear," seeing that which is coming on the earth (Luke 21:26). Only those truly walking in the spirit of adoption will be able to walk in faith. Most, including professing Christians, will be paralyzed by fear. This is end-time preparation.

Consider the "spirit" of adoption. You can be adopted, in fact, and never live in the blessings of your adopted family. There are many who do that. That is a significant problem with adoption. The child, by choice, often refuses to live in the blessings of the adopted family. The child refuses to take on the ways of the adopted father and mother. Therefore, even though such a child appears, in name, to be a child of the family, in essence, he or she is not. Like-wise, we as Christians may call ourselves by the name of the Lord, but until we have taken on, by choice, the ways of our adopted Father's household, we will never experience the full blessings of what it means to live in that family. Nor will we have our Father's favor.

> The Spirit beareth witness with our spirit, that we are the children of God; And if children, then heirs; heirs of God, and joint-heirs with Christ... (Rom. 8:15–17*a*).

Abandoned

Let us explore this matter of adoption further. There are two basic ways in which a child can be adopted under the law while the natural parents are living: (1) by parental consent; or (2) by abandonment. There must be "grounds" for adoption.

A child can be adopted when the natural parents consent, in writing, with full knowledge of what they are doing, to release control of their child—to give up the child for adoption. Or, the state can take the child away from the parents because the parents have refused to fulfill their parental responsibility, usually by abandonment. To consider adoption based upon abandonment, we must know the basic needs of children.

What are the basic needs of children? We can answer that easily by evaluating our own basic needs, because we are children. You are somebody's child. God says we are His children. What are the basic needs of children? Love, health, protection, and food. Those are the things we need to live.

If that is true, we as spiritual children need to find out whether Satan was meeting those needs. Remember, the parent is obliged under the law to meet the basic needs of the child. And under the law, if the parent does not fulfill those needs, the court can properly step in and take the child away from the parent. Turn to John 8. We must find out who our father was. This may come as a shock to some people. And it came as a shock to some religious leaders in the biblical account. Fortunately, neither you nor I said what you are about to read.

In this passage we find some Jews present who believed a lot about what Jesus was saying. It is important that we understand that Jesus is addressing Jews that **seemed** to believe.

> Then said Jesus to those Jews which believed on Him, If ye continue in My word, then are ye My disciples indeed; And ye shall know the truth, and the truth shall make you free.
> They answered Him, We be Abraham's seed, and were never in bondage to any man; how sayest thou, Ye shall be made free? (John 8:31–33)

You cannot be made free if you were never in bondage, right? Obviously there was something in their thinking and understanding that was incomplete. Look at Jesus' response:

> Jesus answered them, Verily, verily, I say unto you, Whosoever committeth sin is the servant of sin (John 8:34).

Now Jesus is not talking about eating, drinking, chewing, and going with women who do. He is not talking about murder, adultery, fornication, and lying. He is talking about an attitude of the heart. Remember, these were the

Chapter Ten: Spirit of Adoption

religious leaders. They were not going out and killing people. So there was another kind of sin that rendered them guilty.

> And the servant abideth not in the house for ever: but the Son abideth ever (vs. 35).

Two Fathers, Two Households

In John 15:15, Jesus said, "I call you not servants; for the servant knoweth not what his lord doeth: but I have called you friends." The Son knows everything. And we have to come into the spirit of sonship—the spirit of adoption—to where we know what our Father doeth. And when I know what my Father doeth, I will know what His son must do too.

> If the Son therefore shall make you free, ye shall be free indeed. I know that ye are Abraham's seed; but ye seek to kill me, because my word hath no place in you (John 8:36–37).

This passage seems somewhat cryptic. It may appear as one of the more cryptic chapters in Scripture, as you read through it initially. Jesus admitted, "I know that you are Abraham's seed." They said, "We be Abraham's seed," and they spoke the truth insofar as they understood it. They thought that because Abraham was their father by fleshly heritage, that made them the heirs, as Abraham's seed, to the promises of Abraham. But Jesus' words dispute this belief. Today He might say, "You missed the whole boat, folks. Just because you were born into this does not mean you have any rights. That is not what it means to be the seed of Abraham." In the biblical encounter, Jesus then identified two fathers:

> I speak that which I have seen with my Father: and ye do that which ye have seen with your father (John 8:38).

If Jesus talked about His Father and then He turned around and talked about their father, that must indicate that there are two different fathers. And who is He talking to? He is addressing the religious leaders. In fact, He is addressing the "religious right" of His day—fundamentalists, evangelicals.

> They answered and said unto him, Abraham is our father. Jesus saith unto them, If ye were Abraham's children, ye would do the works of Abraham. But now ye seek to kill me, a man that hath told you the truth, which I have heard of God: this did not Abraham. Ye do the deeds of your father. Then said they to him, We be not born of fornication; we have one Father, even God (John 8:39–41).

115

And that is what people in religious circles believe in large measure. They think that God is the Father of all men. Some think God is the Father of churchgoers. It is not true! God is the Father only of the faithful. He is the Father only of those who decide by their choice to live within the confines of the family ways—God's family ways.

> Jesus said unto them, If God were your Father, ye would love me: for I proceeded forth and came from God; neither came I of myself, but He sent me. Why do ye not understand my speech? Even because ye cannot hear my word (John 8:42–43).

Obviously they could hear His word, in the sense that we think of hearing, because they were standing right in front of Him. They heard everything He said. But James warned, "Be ye doers of the Word, and not hearers only" so you will not deceive your own self (James 1:22).

The word *hearing* in Scripture almost invariably implies action—not passive reception, but action. And without the corresponding action, there is no hearing. Therefore Jesus told the religious leaders that they could not understand His speech because they could not hear His word. Then He made a daring, awful statement: "Ye are of your father the devil…" (John 8:44). Who was He addressing? He was talking to the religious leaders of His day. They were the Jews—the children of Israel. They were Jews who "believed on Him" (John 8:31). And He said, "You are of your father the devil." Do you know **this** Jesus? Apparently these "believers" only believed so far—to a certain extent. The Scripture does not go on to say exactly how far they did believe. Apparently it was an intellectualized belief of religious information without a corresponding transformation of heart—like many professing "Christians."

Jesus continued, "And because I tell you the truth, ye believe me not" (John 8:45). "He that is of God heareth God's words" (John 8:47). Why did Jesus say that? If you have children born or adopted into your household and you have certain ways, rules, and guidelines in your household, your children will understand and act on them when you speak. But if you have neighborhood children who come and flock into your home, unless they have been there a long time and have purposed in their heart to respond according to the ways of your household, you will say something to them that you would say to your children, and the neighbors will not even hear your words. They may hear the words with their ears, but they will not know what to do with them. The words will not be translated into the "warp and woof" of their living pattern and practice. That is what Jesus was saying here: "He that is of God heareth God's words."

If I am of God, I will hear what my Father is saying. My ear will be attuned, like a son to his father. It will "click" in my spirit, and I will be able to walk in that way. But these "believing" Jews were not attuned. There was something missing in their spirit. It was the spirit of adoption that was missing. They were of their father, the devil. They were pretending to walk in one household when, in fact, their modus operandi for living was in the household of their father, the devil. Yet they were "believers."

Jesus said there are two households. One is of the father the devil, and the other is of the Father of faith. Satan's household is getting more crowded by the day, crowded with "believers."

Why Jesus Came

"…For this purpose the son of God was manifested, that He might destroy the works of the devil" (1 John 3:8).

For this cause—one cause only. For this cause Jesus was sent into the world: that He "might destroy the works of the devil." Why did Jesus come to destroy the works of the devil? Because the Father God looked down. He saw that His children were being tormented by the works of the devil, that they were living in the wrong family, that their father was not providing all of their needs. They were sick. They were in poverty. They were walking in poverty of spirit. They were walking in financial poverty. They were walking in fear. Their ways were the ways of death. Everything that God wanted to do for them was missing in their life. They lived a religious sham.

And they were struggling. They were trying to make it on their own, but it was not working. Satan was not providing their needs. So the Father God sent Jesus—the only begotten son of God—to enter planet earth to legally prepare a way for the sons of men to become the sons of God. They could be adopted into a new family with a new Father. They could be taken, by the rule of the law, and ripped away from their father, Satan, who was not providing their needs. Just as the courts today will take a child away from the natural parents who are not providing the needs, so God is legally bound to strip from Satan parental authority for not providing the needs of the kids.

Legal Implications

Change of Name

The final words of the adoption decrees I've drafted over years of law practice read, "The name of this child shall henceforth be…" Adoption brings a change of name. When God imputed righteousness to Abram for leaving Ur and pursuing the city of God, He changed his name to Abraham, inserting identity from God's own name. When Abraham's grandson wrestled with God for His blessing, God changed his name from Jacob to Israel, declaring, "…as a prince hast thou power with God and with men" (Gen. 32:28).

When you and I truly leave Egypt—Satan's household and dominion— God calls us by His own name. "I have surnamed thee," says the Lord (Isa. 45:4). The whole family of true believers is called by the name of the Father of our Lord Jesus Christ (Eph. 3:14–15). Because of this adoption, "we have boldness and access with confidence by the faith of Him" (Eph. 3:12).

But change of name does not produce change of ways. Some of us either need to change our ways, or change our name.

CHANGE OF INHERITANCE

The decree of adoption provides that the adopted child "shall henceforth be treated in ALL respects as the natural child" of the adopting parents. For this reason the apostle Paul reported, "IF any man be in Christ…OLD things are passed away; behold ALL things are become new" (2 Cor. 5:17). Paul declared all true believers who are not walking in the spirit of bondage of Egypt "heirs of God, and joint-heirs with Christ" (Rom. 8:15–17). Think of the practical implications of such a decree. We become one with the "only begotten" Son.

That is why we must "get it together" on planet earth. Denominational and racial division between congregations is untenable in the same family. How can we "sit in heavenly places in Christ Jesus" while divided? We are living both a legal and relational fiction. It is a spiritual charade we endorse to protect and preserve our Egyptian value system of pride, position, and power.

Adoption is not a call to ecumenism but a call to embrace the Truth. Biblical unity is not birthed in compromise but is forged on the anvil of truth. We declare that "the truth shall make you free" (John 8:32), but we have not agreed with God in His Word that we might become His "disciples indeed" (John 8:31).

CHANGE OF AUTHORITY

With the decree of adoption comes a change of authority. The adopted child, by law, is no longer subject to the rule or values of the former parent. The legal relationship is severed. Yet as a practical matter, many adopted children continue to live as if they are still in submission to and dominated by their previous household. This is a serious problem for both the child and new parents. The child, while having every LEGAL right to the perks and provisions of the new household, refuses to partake, becomes rebellious, and breaches the spirit of the adoption. What might have been beautiful becomes an abomination.

This is precisely the position of professing Christians in America. God led us out of Egypt with a mighty hand. He adopted us into His family. But we refuse to walk in the ways of His household. We still love the ways of Egypt. We do not walk in agreement with our Father. We agree only with what we choose to agree with. We line up at His divine buffet table at His "bless-me club" and pick and choose what we will believe.

The family is fractured; the Father is frustrated; and the children are famished. The beautiful vision of our pilgrim and Puritan forefathers has become an abomination. The Father is pleading with us one last time before the "only begotten" Son's return, "Join My family. Agree with Me. Do things My way so we can fellowship together. Will you leave Egypt and come under My authority?"

Benefits of Adoption

"The Court finds that the interests and welfare of the child will be promoted by this adoption," reads the adoption decree. God has given you and me His own decree of adoption. Listen to His words:

> Wherefore come out from among them, and be ye separate, saith the Lord, and touch not the unclean thing; and I will receive you. And I will be a Father unto you, and you shall be My sons and daughters, saith the Lord Almighty (2 Cor. 6:17–18).

Father God has ordained practical benefits to flow to you from your adoption. If this were not so, God would have failed to provide for the kids just as Satan did. David, the man "after God's own heart," clearly understood those benefits. We love his words, but in reality do not trust enough to truly believe them.

> Bless the Lord, O my soul, and **forget not ALL His benefits**: Who forgiveth ALL thine iniquities; Who healeth ALL thy diseases; Who redeemeth thy life from destruction; Who crowneth thee with lovingkindness…Who satisfieth thy mouth with good things… (Ps. 103:1–3).

We must review the benefits again. Remember, we can reject them or receive them. The choice is ours. To reject them in whole or in part is to reject God as Father—to reject His ways, to reject His love, to reject His provision, and even to reject His authority. Rejection—in whole or in part—of God's declared benefits of adoption, is a declaration of unbelief.

Remember, **every** adult who experienced God's deliverance from Egypt refused the benefits—whining and bellyaching against God and Moses—and so was denied entrance to the Promised Land. Only two men, Joshua and Caleb, were permitted entrance because they had "another spirit" (Num. 14:26). What are those benefits that Father offers?

A NEW INHERITANCE

We have been declared "heirs of God" and "joint-heirs with Christ" (Rom. 8:15–17). Father lacks nothing. The earth is the Lord's (Ps. 24:1). He owns the cattle on a thousand hills (Ps. 50:10). And "no good thing will He withhold **from them that walk uprightly**" (Ps. 84:11).

INIQUITIES FORGIVEN

He "forgiveth ALL thine iniquities," declared David. Jesus, the Messiah, was "wounded for our transgressions, He was bruised for our iniquities" (Isa. 53:5). "The Lord hath laid on Him the iniquities of us all" (Isa. 53:6).

SONS OF GOD

"AS many as received Him, to them gave He power [authority] to become the sons of God, even to them that believe on His name" (John 1:12). But what if I do not believe all that Jesus provides under His name? Have I received Him? Can I receive Him in part and reject Him in part? That may be "receiving" American style, but not heavenly style. That is "soft" rebellion. But if we believe and receive, "Beloved, now are we the sons of God" (1 John 3:1).

HEALING AND HEALTH

God's adoption provides a health-maintenance plan, not Egypt's disease-maintenance plan. Father provided specific eating guidelines for His family to keep them healthy. We can choose to reject them. If they were given for our good by a loving God, how can that be "legalism"? Are we not reaping the devastating consequences of accumulated fallout from rebellious practices that God warned against for our own good?

All modern rationalizations aside, when did God repudiate or abrogate His guidelines for our good? You cannot find it in His Word! When the apostle Paul writes concerning the eating of meat, he speaks of meat offered to idols. It is this he addresses when he warns against the rules of "touch not, taste not." Loving guidelines become "legalism" only when we rise up against Father's authority.

Can we bless what God calls abomination and cleanse it for our healthy use? Are not the "diseases of Egypt" plaguing American Christians today, causing us to die like flies in the wilderness of our own rebellion? Our ways and traditions are powerful, aren't they? WE can justify almost anything, can't we? Please do not reject the substance of this book over your difficulty with this small section. Pray about it with the Word open before you. Does Father know best, or do His testy children know best?

He "healeth ALL thy diseases," declared David (Ps. 103:3). Then why do we have so many of them? Why are they multiplying? Why is *cancer* the most feared word in America? There may be a variety of contributing causes, but doctors increasingly admit the primary source is diet. Does this matter to those who cavalierly profess their bodies to be the "temple of the Holy Spirit"?

I will take sickness away from the midst of thee, says the Lord (Exod. 23:25).

If thou wilt diligently hearken to the voice of the Lord thy God...and wilt do that which is right, and wilt give ear to His commandments, and keep all His statutes…I will put none of these diseases upon thee, which I have brought upon the Egyptians: **for I am the Lord that healeth thee** (Exod. 15:26).

The Savior, Messiah, Christ, and Lord of the church, fulfilled, completed, and confirmed this promise: "That it might be fulfilled which was spoken by Isaiah the prophet, saying, Himself took our infirmities, and bare our sicknesses" (Matt. 8:17).

The bottom line again is a true trust. Do we trust God's wisdom enough to conform to His ways? Do we trust His healing promise enough to receive it, without Western rationalization, American equivocation, or twisted spiritualization that disembowels its clear meaning? Or will we continue walking with Egyptian minds in "Israelite" bodies, concocting triple-tier theologies to camouflage, in religious lingo, our profound refusal to believe. It could be a matter of life and death. Will we trust our traditional thinking, or will we trust God?

A FULL SUPPLY

"He brought them forth [out of Egypt] also with silver and gold" (Ps. 105:37). Why did God do that? Why was this important to be recorded? God declared Israel "abandoned." They had been under Satan's governance and family rule for four hundred years. He failed to meet their needs. So God "adopted" Israel, remembering His covenant with faithful Abraham. Abraham's seed would now inherit after him. They had no inheritance in Egypt. But when they came out, God made sure they had a full supply.

God the Father will make sure you have a full supply too, if you truly trust Him. But we must conform to the ways of His household. The apostle Paul confirmed the promise of provision to those who will believe God is Jehovah Jireh.

But my God shall supply ALL your need according to His riches in glory by Christ Jesus (Phil. 4:19).

A FOOD SUPPLY

The adopting Father provided manna to the many as they left Satan's household in Egypt. God takes great pain to inform us that He met their needs. "He that gathered much had nothing over, and he that gathered little had no lack" (Exod. 16:18).

Jesus confirmed God's commitment as adopting Father:

Take no thought, saying, What shall we eat? Or what shall we drink? Or Wherewithal shall we be clothed? For your heavenly father knoweth that ye have need of all these things. But seek ye first the kingdom of God, and His righteous; and ALL THESE THINGS shall be added unto you (Matt. 6:31–33).

FREEDOM FROM FEAR

"Ye have not received the spirit of bondage again to fear; but ye have received the spirit of adoption; whereby we cry, Abba, Father" (Rom. 8:15). The Psalmist put it this way: "I will say of the Lord, He is my refuge and my fortress: my God, in Him will I trust" (Ps. 91:2). The spirit of adoption is evidenced by the spirit of the household.

Household of Faith

There are only two households. Jesus chastised the religious leaders of His day for being of their father, the devil. Paul enjoined us to do good, especially to those of "the household of faith" (Gal. 6:10).

All those adopted into the household of faith are the seed of Abraham through the "son of promise," Isaac. The ways of the household are "faith that worketh by love" (Gal. 5:6).

Father's words are law in the household of faith (see Deut. 6:6–9). If God's Word on ALL of the issues of life is not law in your life, you must question whether you are truly in the household of faith.

> Not every one that saith unto me, Lord, Lord, shall enter the Kingdom of Heaven; but he that doeth the will of my Father which is in Heaven (Matt. 7:21).

Our Father God, in the spirit of adoption, pleads with you and with me to heed and honor His Word. He said, "This is not a vain thing for you. It is your life" (Deut. 32:47).

> My son, attend to my words; incline thine ear unto my sayings. Let them not depart from thine eyes; keep them in the midst of thine heart. For they are life unto those that find them, and health to all their flesh (Prov. 4:20–22).

You, as an adopted son or daughter, in the spirit of adoption, having left the spirit of Egypt, are entitled to walk in the words delivered to faithful Joshua as we move forward into the difficult days ahead, pressing toward the Promised Land on the near edge of the Second Coming.

> Be strong and of good courage, fear not nor be afraid…for the Lord thy God, he it is that doth go before thee; he will not fail thee, nor forsake thee…. Fear not, neither be dismayed (Deut. 31:6, 8*b*).

Chapter Eleven

Covenant Man: Part One

What did God promise that you are not receiving?

THEY ARE NOT ALL ISRAEL which are of Israel, but they are Israel which are circumcised in the heart and not in the flesh (see Rom. 9:6; 2:28–29).

The church does not fully replace Israel as contended by some, in what is known as "replacement theology." There are specific promises made to Israel, such as God's declaration that the Jews would be restored to their homeland and that Israel would again become a nation in one day, which was fulfilled May 14, 1948. God has not abrogated nor forgotten His promises to Israel, with whom He made covenant through Abraham. But there are two Israels. There is the Israel of national origin and geographical location, an Israel by birth. And there is an Israel by new birth. True "Christians"—whether of Gentile or Jewish descent—are the Israel by new birth, or adoption. Abraham is the link.

Yet it has always been God's intention that His spiritual promises and blessings go to Israel, not by birth alone, but by faith, or "new birth." Whether by walking in faith according to the law, or walking by faith in obedience to the law of the spirit written on the tablets of our hearts through Jesus Christ, God's intention was always the same. As it is written, "Jesus Christ, the same yesterday, today and forever" (Heb. 13:8). Jesus neither changed nor abrogated the law. Rather, He fulfilled it, giving the law full application.

With that brief introduction and overview, let us begin our trek through the Abrahamic Covenant in Exodus 2.

What Does God Remember?

> And it came to pass in process of time, that the king of Egypt died: and the children of Israel sighed by reason of the bondage, and they cried, and their cry came up unto God by reason of their bondage. And God heard their groaning, and **God remembered His covenant with Abraham**, with Isaac, and with Jacob (Exod. 2:23–24).

Now you may be surprised! The reason why God brought His people out of Egypt was not because of their plaintiff cry alone. The main reason God brought His people out of Egypt was because He had made a promise. It was an unbreakable promise. As a Father He had made a promise to a man called Abraham. God swore by Himself because it was impossible for God to lie. He swore by His own name, because there was none greater. By His own word, God, under the eternal integrity and authority of His name, entered into a covenant with Abraham. And because of the covenant, God hearkened to the cry of Israel, delivering them from Egypt and the spirit of bondage.

God's deliverance of Israel from Egypt cannot be severed from God's covenant with Abraham. It is foundational. Abraham had been a man of faith. His faith was imputed to him as righteousness. Therefore God entered into covenant with him. The God of covenant heard the cry of Abraham's seed, who were physical heirs according to the promise, and He delivered them from Egypt.

He sent them a deliverer. That deliverer was Moses. Moses, the temporal deliverer, was a type of Christ who is the eternal deliverer. Moses delivered that men would follow the letter of the law. Jesus delivers that men might follow the spirit of the law, a higher standard. Each is an expression of God's grace, mercy, and covenantal commitment to Abraham.

The law was never abrogated. In Matthew 5 Jesus declared, "I am not come to destroy the law...but to fulfill" the law (vs. 17). Anyone who thinks we are living in a new dispensation—that the law is abrogated, and that we are subject only to mercy and grace in the Spirit—has not properly understood the Word of God. The Word of God does not say that the law was rejected, abolished, or changed. It merely tells us that Jesus, as the "Word made flesh," revealed the full purpose, intent, and application of the law. Those who are "in Christ" are able to fulfill all of the law in Christ Jesus, since Christ is the fulfillment of the law. Failure to understand and receive this has lead to massive disobedience within the professing church, and has given rise to a brand of glib grace that borders on disgrace. Only the ceremonial law of sacrifices was replaced by its fullness or completeness in Christ. God's laws for living remained to be lived out, both in spirit and in truth.

What Is the Abrahamic Covenant?

Understanding the Abrahamic Covenant is essential to understanding the Scriptures. Therefore, we must look at it carefully. So what exactly is the Abrahamic Covenant? Your appreciation of your Bible may well expand dramatically.

> Now the Lord had said unto Abram, Get thee out of thy country, and from thy kindred, and from thy father's house, unto a land that I will shew thee: And I will make of thee a great nation, and I will bless thee, and make thy name great; and thou shalt be a blessing; And I will bless them that bless thee, and curse him that curseth thee: and in thee shall all families of the earth be blessed. So Abram departed, as the Lord had spoken unto him… (Gen. 12:1–4*a*).

The Book of Hebrews tells us that Abraham went out, not knowing where he went, but "he looked for a city with foundations whose builder and maker was God" (Heb. 11:10). He was not going out to wander aimlessly in the wilderness. He was going out to look for a particular thing. He was looking for a different city. Remember our lengthy study into the spirit of the city in our journey out of Egypt? God's Word reveals the spirit of the city to be the spirit of humanism. It is the spirit of man attempting to do for himself—including being his own provider, being his own healer, being his own salvation—everything that God wants to do for him. So Abraham went out looking for something different. And God made a promise to him.

> And the Lord appeared unto Abram, and said, Unto thy seed will I give this land… (Gen. 12:7).

> …and Abraham went down into Egypt… (Gen. 12:10).

Coming Out Requires Going In

All of God's people go into Egypt before they ever come out. You cannot come out of a place you have never been. Right? All of God's people must come out of Egypt, because all have been in Egypt, spiritually speaking. Jesus came out of Egypt that it might be fulfilled "Out of Egypt have I called my son" (Hos. 11:1, Matt. 2:14–15).

Abraham was no different. He was the father of the faithful. Let us follow him out of Egypt.

> And Abram went up out of Egypt, he, and his wife, and all that he had, and Lot with him, into the south. And Abram was very rich in cattle, in silver and in gold (Gen. 13:1–2).

Notice! When Abram came out of Egypt, he came out with great substance. That is very important to understanding the totality of what it means to live in the Abrahamic Covenant. We will pick that up in more detail later.

Continuing in Genesis 15, God came to Abram again:

> After these things the word of the Lord came unto Abram in a vision, saying, Fear not, Abram: I am thy shield, and thy exceeding great reward (Gen. 15:1).

God was saying to Abram, "I AM." "I am everything you need. I am everything you desire. I am everything you want. Everything that life requires of you, I am."

> And he [Abram] believed in the Lord; and he counted it to him for righteousness (Gen. 15:6).

Was Jesus Abraham's Son?

Abram, as a matter of history, became THE original faith man—the model, the image. He was the prototype of faith that God requires in order to please Him. Abram believed God.

God told Abram that He was going to extend His promise. The covenant to Abraham was first declared in Genesis 12. But God encouraged him—or improved, or increased upon that covenant—expanding it for his understanding over a period of years. It was twenty-five years from age seventy-five, when the covenant was first made in chapter 12, until Abram saw any indication of the fulfillment of that promise at nearly 100. So God reminded him along the way, just like He reminds you and me. The question is, do we heed the reminders and remain faithful, or do we get discouraged and fall away, looking at our circumstances and not at the promise? That is our perpetual problem, isn't it? We look at the circumstances around us rather than to the promise of God?

Look at this man Abraham as described by the apostle Paul:

> And being not weak in faith, he considered not his own body now dead, when he was about an hundred years old, neither yet the deadness of Sarah's womb: He staggered not at the promise of God through unbelief; but was strong in faith, giving glory to God; And being fully persuaded that, what He had promised, He was able also to perform. And therefore it was imputed to him for righteousness (Rom. 4:19–22).

His perseverance, his endurance against doubt, is what was imputed to him for righteousness.

In Genesis 15:14, we see God extending His covenant:

> And also that nation, whom they shall serve, will I judge: and afterward shall they come out with great substance.

What nation was it that Abraham's seed would serve? Egypt! First, Abraham came out of Egypt. Then God told Abram that his seed, Israel, the children of Abram's grandson, were going to go back into Egypt. Israel was Abraham's seed and heir according to the promise. Yet God said they were going back into Egypt. Why? Because you cannot come out unless you go in. And all who truly believe must come out of Egypt.

Abraham went into Egypt and then came out. His seed was going to have to go in and come out. And in Matthew 1, we are told that Jesus was the son of Abraham. He was the son of David by lineage and the son of Abraham by faith. Therefore Jesus needed to come out too.

Genesis 15:14 makes it clear. Not only was Abraham's seed going into Egypt, but afterward they would come out with great substance. What happened when Abraham came out of Egypt? He came out with great substance. What was happening now as God spoke again to Abraham? God was prophesying, telling Abram what He was going to do for His children, Israel, when they came out of Egypt. They were going to come out with great substance. And what does God have for all of His kids when they decide to come out of Egypt? Answer the question yourself. That is what God is trying to show here. God follows both patterns and promises.

There Is Something in a Name

Genesis 17 presents God's final declaration of the promise. God was again reminding Abram when Abram was ninety-nine years old—one year before the fulfillment of the initial stage of the promise.

> And when Abram was ninety years old and nine, the Lord appeared to Abram , and said unto him, I am the Almighty God; walk before me, and be thou perfect (Gen. 17:1).

God has always wanted His children to be perfect. The author of the Book of Hebrews exhorted in the New Testament to "move on to perfection" (6:1). And yes, even in the Old Testament, God's kids were to walk in perfection. Abraham believed God, but God also believed in Abraham. He reiterated His covenant in Genesis 17, refreshing the memory of the man-of-faith.

> And I will make my covenant between Me and thee, and will multiply thee exceedingly. And Abram fell on his face: and God talked with him,

saying, As for me, behold, my covenant is with thee, and thou shall be a
father of many nations (vss. 2–4).

That was a personal covenant. God made a personal promise to Abram.
And then, in order to encourage him along, He changed his name. As the
fulfillment of this promise was coming near, when the temptation would be
great to wander away and doubt, when hope deferred threatened to make
old Abram's heart sick, God changed his name from Abram to Abraham.
He inserted part of His own name into that of His faithful son. Every time
Abraham now spoke to Sarah and every time Sarah spoke to Abraham, they
declared the promise: "Father of many nations, go tie up the goats." "Mother
of many nations, come wash the dishes." They reminded themselves by their
own name of the promise of God. And you are no exception. God has called
you by your name (see Isa. 43:1). And He has surnamed you with His own
name (see Isa. 45:4).

Isn't God a good God? A good Father? To help His kids along? To even
change their names to help them remember the promise so they will not falter?
That is what God did.

> I will establish my covenant between me and thee and thy seed after thee
> in their generations for an everlasting covenant, to be a God unto thee, and
> to thy seed after thee (Gen. 17:19).

"Everlasting covenant...." That means a covenant that has no end. It
means it must still be going on. That is what is so exciting about it. It is still
going on. So we need to find out a little bit more about it, don't we?

God says He will be "a God unto thee, and to thy seed after thee." I have
written in the margin of my Bible, "FATHER." He will be a God, but He
will be a father. He will be all that true fatherhood means. The fatherhood
of God means He will provide for the children. That is what God is trying
to say to Abraham: "I am going to be your personal God. I am going to be
everything you need. Everything! And I will be everything to your seed after
you." Who are the seed? We will explore that later on.

Sealed in Blood, Rolling Away Flesh

God wants to seal the deal. He has done everything He can, swearing
by His own name, even inserting part of His name into Abraham's. But
Abraham needs to do something:

> And ye shall circumcise the flesh of your foreskin: and it shall be a token
> of the covenant betwixt me and you (Gen. 17:11).

Circumcision was going to be the sign that would confirm this covenant.
Abraham and his seed must continue the practice of circumcision the rest of

their days. The requirement is not made because of the inherent virtues of circumcision but as a reminder so you will never forget, similar to changing the name from Abram to Abraham. Circumcision required the shedding of blood and the rolling back of the flesh to confirm the covenant.

What kind of a covenant was this?

> Fear not, Abram: I am thy shield, and thy exceeding great reward…. And behold the word of the Lord came unto him, saying, This shall not be thine heir… (Gen. 15:1, 4).

Abraham was trying to figure out in the natural how he could make the promise of God come true—just like you and I frequently try to do. We read a promise in the Word of God, and we go around trying to conjure up ways we can make the promise of God come true. That is essentially trying to live in the kingdom of God and in Egypt at the same time. We have all done it.

Abraham was not any different than you and me. Abraham was supposed to be walking toward perfection, but he was not perfect. He needed help and encouragement in his faith. Abraham was trying to figure out how in the world this ridiculous promise God had made was ever going to happen, seeing that he was already well near ninety years of age. And he knew that he could not have a child. He said, "…seeing that I go childless…" and began talking about the stewards in his house.

Eventually, Abraham's patience weakened. He still believed God but he figured he needed to help God out. He even actually went out and tried to fulfill the promise of God in collusion with his own wife. They put their minds together and figured out that the only possible way this "promised son" could happen would be through Hagar. Consider the devastating world-struggle that has echoed through history to this very hour because two people tried to do God's part of the work for Him. Despite our best intentions, there are consequences to our unbelief and impatience.

Look at the volatility in the Middle East. Is that not why we have those problems? All the Arab community are descendants from Ishmael, who was the son of the Egyptian Hagar's relationship with Abraham (with the approval of Sarah). All was in attempt to do God's work in the flesh, outside of the Spirit. Think about it! Hagar was Egyptian; **Abraham, the father of the faith, had intercourse with Egypt in his attempt to do God's will.**

But God did not hold that against Abraham, because He knew Abraham's heart was right. The record says Abraham believed God. He tried to do some of God's work for Him, but He did not falter in his belief in God. He was fully persuaded that what God had promised He was able to perform.

So Abraham asked, "How am I going to know that your promise is going to come true?" God responded:

> And He said unto him, Take me an heifer of three years old, and a she goat of three years old, and a ram of three years old, and a turtledove, and a young pigeon (Gen. 15:9).

Then God told Abraham to divide the animals in half, fold over the parts and lay them out. Now that sounds like a gruesome thing to do, but that is what God told Abraham to do. And so he did it. He laid out the parts. And we are told the vultures came down and tried to eat up the carcasses and Abraham was shooing them away, violently. Can you just imagine old Abraham trying to keep those vultures away?

Then a deep sleep fell on Abraham, and in the midst of the horror of a dream, the Spirit of God came down and walked through those bloody pieces, to establish His own covenant of blood. A blood covenant. That was the kind of covenant that God entered into with Abraham.

> In the same day the Lord made a covenant with Abram, saying, Unto thy seed have I given this land… (Gen. 15:18).

Abraham's seed repeated the sacrifices of this covenant until the promised "only begotten Son"—the Lamb of God, Jesus the Christ—died once and for all to confirm this covenant of blood through the body of God Himself. And so we are told that Jesus became the mediator of a "better" covenant. Why was it better?

> But now hath he [Jesus] obtained a more excellent ministry, by how much also He is the mediator of a better covenant, which was established upon better promises (Heb. 8:6).

> But Christ being come an high priest of good things to come, by a greater and more perfect tabernacle, not made with hands, that is to say, not of this building [the tabernacle God had instructed the Israelites to build, with all the details]; Neither by the blood of goats and calves, but by His own blood He entered in once into the holy place, having obtained eternal redemption for us. For if the blood of bulls and of goats, and the ashes of an heifer sprinkling the unclean, sanctifieth to the purifying of the flesh: How much more shall the blood of Christ, who through the eternal Spirit offered Himself without spot to God, purge your conscience from dead works to serve the living God? And for this cause He [Jesus] is the mediator of the new testament [covenant] that by means of death, for the redemption of the transgressions that were under the

first testament, they which are called might receive the promise of eternal inheritance (Heb. 9:11–15).

So it is a continuing promise. It was an everlasting covenant. Jesus is the fulfillment of God's blood covenant with Abraham. And without shedding of blood there is no remission of sin.

Beyond Sin

Yet the covenant goes beyond sin. It is a total covenant, which we will eventually see. But here it is a blood covenant. It is similar to blood brothers who mix their blood, confirming a solemn promise between each other. It is a promise that cannot be broken. It means that everything that I have is yours and everything that you have is mine. David and Jonathan had such a profound covenant. We do not know that it was a blood covenant, but it was a solemn commitment that they had to each other. "What I have is yours, and what you have is mine." That is the kind of covenant God entered into with Abraham and the kind of covenant that God enters into with you and me. Marriage is such a covenant, and therefore is permanent.

Moses understood this covenantal significance of the blood. It confirmed God's Word that could not be broken.

And Moses took the blood, sprinkled it on the people, and said, **Behold the blood of the covenant**, which the Lord hath made with you concerning all these words (Exod. 24:8).

It is important to read every word. Note the phrase "concerning all these words." That means there is more than one word. If it is "these" words, it is referring to specific words that belong as part of this covenant. It is not what I construe it to be or what you or your denomination construe it to be. "Behold the blood of the covenant, which the Lord hath made with you **concerning all these words**." Let us find out what those words are. "These" refers back to something specific that has been received.

Just previous to this, Moses had been giving the Ten Commandments, perhaps talking about the year of Jubilee and talking about taking care of strangers and the way God's people are supposed to treat their land. Then verse 15 declares, "Thou shalt keep the feast of unleavened bread." What was the feast of unleavened bread? Remember, it had to do with the Passover blood on the doorpost. It was a blood covenant. God's covenant has always been a blood covenant from the very beginning.

Thou shalt keep the feast of unleavened bread: (thou shalt eat unleavened bread seven days, as I commanded thee, in the time appointed of the month of Abib; for in it thou camest out from Egypt…) (Exod. 23:15).

In the context of the blood covenant, in the fulfillment of the blood covenant, they came out of Egypt. Note God's requirement: "none shall appear before me empty." In other words, God is saying, "I am not doing this for nothing. It is not a lame or empty gesture, and I want you to appear before Me with expectation." God is saddened—yet more probably incensed—by our vain and empty religious forms and rituals that are not accompanied by a high level of covenantal expectation.

> Your words have been stout against me, saith the Lord, Yet ye say, What have we spoken so much against thee? Ye have said, It is vain to serve God; and what profit is it that we have kept His ordinance… (Mal. 3:13–14).

God is saying, "Come before Me with expectation in heart and hand. It is not a vain thing or empty religious gesture. It is going to be for a purpose, and I am going to fulfill that purpose because I am making a solemn promise with you. I am continuing the promise that I made to Abraham. You now stand in my friend Abraham's shoes."

By the way, when you read the Word of God with respect to the promises of God, do not forget the "ifs." It is so easy to read the promises without obeying the "ifs." The promises are all conditional. And we are going to look at some of the conditions later.

> But **if thou shalt** indeed **obey** his voice, **and do** all that I speak; **then I** will be an enemy unto thine enemies and an adversary unto thine adversaries (Exod. 23:22).

God continued His promise, stating He was going to kick out all the heathen in the Promised Land so that Abraham's children could enter.

> And ye shall serve the Lord God; and He shall bless thy bread, and thy water [provide all that I need to keep me going] (Exod. 23:25).

What did He do when the Israelites were in the wilderness? He provided manna. He provided quail. And He provided water. Their shoes did not even wear out. Talk about "I AM"! He was everything they needed. Now consider what Jesus tells us:

> Therefore take no thought, saying, What shall we eat? Or, What shall we drink? Or, Wherewithal shall we be clothed? (For after all these things do the Gentiles seek:)…But [you] seek ye first the kingdom of God, and His righteousness; and all these things shall be added unto you (Matt. 6:32–33).

What Did God Say?

What did God say was included in His covenant? He said, "I will take sickness away from the midst of thee." Did He say I will take spiritual want away from the midst of thee?" No. He says, "I will take **sickness** away from the midst of thee." There is no way to mistake what that word is or what it means. And it is important. This point is made for a reason, because the Body of Christ has, for a long time, tried to rationalize, spiritualize, and therefore trivialize the word *sickness*. God said *sickness* because He meant sickness. We see sickness around and figure that God must not have meant what He said. He must mean spiritual misery or sin. If God meant that, God would have said so. We will look at this matter again later, but these are the words. God said these are the words of the covenant. These words are part of the words of the blood covenant. These words are:

> I will take sickness away from the midst of thee. There shall nothing cast their young, nor be barren, in thy land: the number of thy days I will fulfill (Exod. 23:25*b*–26).

Can you believe what God has said? Will you believe? Remember, unbelief of God's Word cost Israel dearly. Only two men entered the Promised Land out of the multitude who walked out of Egypt.

Go back to Exodus 22. The engines of your mind are whirring fast and furiously and you are wondering. "How come, then, do I see sickness in the Body of Christ? How come I see people casting their young (miscarrying), as well as barrenness in the Body of Christ?" Verse 22 explains, "If…, then…" "If thou shall indeed obey his voice,…" The Body of Christ has not been obeying the voice of God. Not even close. We have not been walking in His ways. We do not agree with His clear words. We have not even believed what He says in His Word, let alone walked in His ways. We give the left foot of fellowship to brave souls among us who dare to believe. We, like ancient Pharisees, certainly do not want Jesus upsetting out religious applecart.

We pick and choose what we will believe, which includes only whatever suits our fancy or seems to jibe with our experience or party line. How can we receive the benefit of a contract when we do not even know what the benefits are? or never read the contract? or reject the clear words and choose to allegorize or spiritualize words that are unequivocally clear on their face? How would you feel if someone tried to do that to the clear words of a contract you had made? How do you think God feels?

You can have a contract that is twenty-five pages long, and if all you know is one provision of the contract, you will never assert your rights with respect to the rest of the contract. You are ignorant and hold that contract in vain. And the Body of Christ does not know the contract. We do not truly know what God has said. Therefore we cannot walk in the ways of the contract.

Therefore God cannot perform it. He has bound Himself to perform. He said He would. I will either believe Him or I will not. We will see some situations in which the children of Israel did not receive the benefits of the promise. God has said over and over, "If you will…, then I will…"

You may be thinking, *Well, that is just one passage of Scripture.* The Word of God says, "In the mouth of two or three witnesses shall every word be established" (2 Cor. 13:1). Note that for that very reason I try never to use one passage of Scripture to support a principle. There may not be more than one scriptural citation for every sentence, but if you follow the themes, you will find abundant references to support the emphases within each chapter. There should be more than one authority to support a given principle. If there is not, according to my Bible, it is not true. "In the mouth of two or three witnesses shall **every** word be established."

Leviticus 26:3 repeats God's conditional terms: "If ye walk in my statutes, and keep my commandments, and do them…" What does the Book of James tell us in the New Testament? "Be ye doers of the Word, and not hearers only, deceiving your own selves" (James 1:22). Why do you think God said that? Because He knew people have always been the same. I am the same as you are. You are the same as I am. And we are the same as Abraham was and the same as the apostle Paul was and the same as James was. We are all the same. We are flesh and blood.

God knows human nature. He knows that people tend to listen, that they even tend to give mental assent to the credibility or truth of what has been said, but they also tend not to act on what they've heard. That is human nature. And human nature is the carnal or fleshly nature. Human nature or the fleshly mind of Egyptian thinking cannot receive the things of the Spirit of God, for they seem foolish" (1 Cor. 2:14). But God says, "Be ye doers of the word and not hearers only" because we deceive our own selves, disqualifying ourselves from God's benefits.

And then we get discouraged. Can you relate? We listen. We hear all the good stuff. We hear someone's testimony about walking in the promises and doing the Word of God. Then we step out on a spiritual binge to make things happen, and if we do not see immediate results, we cannot understand it. We give up, whining, "The Word does not work for me. Therefore, it must mean something other than what it says." Then we define deviancy down by substituting our experience over the clear words of Scripture, in effect rewriting God's Word to conform to our traditions, ways, and experiences. Believing what God has said—actively agreeing with Him even in the face of seeming insurmountable odds or conditions—is an essential part of what God means when, repeatedly, we are advised to "endure to the end." It is not passive putting up with the situation. It is actively, even almost violently against unbelief, choosing to embrace what God has said.

Consider Your Ways

God reminds us that His ways must become a way of life. It is a walk.

> **If ye walk** in my statutes, **and keep** my commandments, **and do** them; **Then I will give** you rain in due season, and the land shall yield her increase... (Lev. 26:4).

God is not a counterfeiter. People look for God's provision and expect God to punch His heavenly slot machine when they call. God will not be manipulated by technocratic American button-punchers who demand a "Mac Answer." God works through a completely different set of mechanisms than those by which we operate here "in Egypt." That is why God calls His people out of Egypt so that He can get us operating in a different system—His system.

That is part of what tithing is all about. It is a symbol of our commitment to operate in a different system. And that is all it is. It is a MINIMUM commitment of our finances. And when we demonstrate our faithfulness in that commitment, then God follows through with His commitment described in Malachi 3:10, when He dared, "Prove me now saith the Lord...."

> And I will walk among you, and will be your God, and ye shall be my people. I am the Lord your God, which brought you forth out of the land of Egypt, that ye should not be their bondmen; and I have broken the bands of your yoke, and made you go upright (Lev. 26:12–13).

God does not want you walking around with a crooked back all the time, struggling all the time. He wants you to walk upright, because you are a King's kid, God's adopted son or daughter. He has broken that yoke of bondage from off your back. That was the spirit of Egypt. Remember? Israel always tried to lean on the staff of Egypt. Ezekiel pointed out that the Egyptian reed was piercing their hand; it was so sharp. It was breaking and crumbling under them. And if you lean on it in your life, it will give you a crooked back. But when you don't have to lean on the rod of Egypt anymore, you can walk with the staff of God, like Moses did. You can straighten up.

Moses went on to warn Israel in the verses that follow. If God's children do not do what God tells them to do, if they walk a different way, then they are going to reap different rewards.

> I will even appoint over you terror, consumption, and the burning ague, that shall consume the eyes, and cause sorrow of heart: and ye shall sow your seed in vain, for your enemies shall eat it. And I will break the pride

of your power; and I will make your heaven as iron, and your earth as brass: And strength shall be spent in vain... (Lev. 26:16, 19–20).

Haggai expresses a similar warning:

Now therefore thus saith the Lord of hosts; Consider your ways. Ye have sown much, and bring in little; ye eat, but ye have not enough; ye drink, but ye are not filled with drink; ye clothe you, but there is none warm; and he that earneth wages earneth wages to put it into a bag with holes. Thus saith the Lord of hosts; Consider your ways (Hag. 1:5–7).

You see, it is a way. A walk. It is learning to follow the ways of your adopted Father, God, and His household of faith. It does not happen in one day. It may not happen tomorrow. Not in a week. Not in a month. Maybe not even in a year. For Abraham it was twenty-four years before he saw the first inkling of the fulfillment of the promise. Twenty-four years! That is why Abraham is the "father of the faithful." That is why Jesus was the son of Abraham, by faith. And that is why you and I are heirs according to the promise of Abraham, by faith (Gal. 3:29). But even Abraham had to leave Egypt.

This chapter should not be seen as an effort to belittle your faith. Jesus talked about great faith, but He also addressed His own disciples with "O ye of little faith." Our goal is great faith. And great faith begins simply by choosing to believe God, to take Him at His every Word. What kind of faith do you have? What kind of faith do you think will be required to be an "overcomer" when times truly get tough? This is the time to address the problem of weak, waning, and sometimes almost nonexistent faith among God's people. Will you believe God?

In the next chapter, we will unfold the legal nature of a covenant as it relates to what God has for us. We will further explore the relationship between the Old Covenant and the New Covenant. And then we will talk about some of the benefits of the New Covenant, the bond of the covenant, the importance of knowing your contract, and how to appropriate the incredible benefits God provides under His expansive covenant. This is survival food for end-time Christians.

Pray with Me before We Continue

Lord, again I want You to know how grateful I am to be Your child. I thank You that You are everything that I need. Help me, as Your son/daughter, to see with the eyes of the Spirit. Help me to see and faithfully follow the walk that You have for me. When my vision becomes clouded or distorted, when the clouds of Egypt blow in and drift upon me, threatening to obscure my path, whisper direction to me, saying, "This is the way, walk ye in it."

Then give me the courage to be a doer of Your Word. I do not want to be self-deceived. Reveal Your Word, Your plan, and Your purposes to me. I embrace Your covenant now in its fullness. Help me Lord, with my unbelief. In Jesus name and by Your grace, I rest on Your promises and commit to walk in loving obedience to fulfill Your covenantal conditions that Your Kingdom will be manifested through my life and example. In Jesus' name. Amen.

Chapter Twelve

Covenant Man: Part Two

God wants you to be a Kingdom conduit, not a worldly reservoir. But are you pursuing MANNA rather than the MASTER? Have we prostituted ourselves with the sons of Egypt?

GOD'S BOTTOM LINE IS FAITH! A faith revealed in loving obedience. And when we talk about His covenant, essentially we are talking also about faith. There is nothing you can talk about in the Word of God that does not find its bottom line in faith that is revealed by loving obedience. Nothing. You may not use the word *faith*, but ultimately, the bottom line is faith.

As a matter of fact, if you enter into a contract with any person here on earth, the bottom line of that contract is faith, is it not? When someone makes a promise to you, and you make a promise to him, you are trusting that each of you is going to perform according to the promise. And that is precisely what the nature of God's covenant with us is about. It is a promise that was made by God who is expecting an act on our part. He said, "If you..., then I..." "If you will..., then I will..." He did not expect a promise from us. He expects obedience. An act.

A Promise for an Act

There are two kinds of contracts in the law. There are unilateral contracts and bilateral contracts. A bilateral contract is a promise for a promise. A unilateral contract is a promise for an act. God made a unilateral covenant. He said, "If you will **do**..., then I will **perform** what I promise." The solemnity of this covenant is so profound that "when God made promise to Abraham, because He could swear by no greater, He swear by Himself" (Heb. 6:13). It was a covenant that could not be broken. It is God's own Word. His name is on the line.

We have found God's covenant to be a blood covenant. That further adds to its solemnity and importance. It was a covenant in God's own blood. Ultimately, the New Covenant was a restatement of the Old Covenant. Jesus said, "I came not to destroy the law, but to fulfill it." So Jesus was the fulfillment or incarnation of the law, not the destruction of the law. It was a covenant in His own blood (see Heb. 10:1–22).

Then, we discovered, in Exodus 24, that "these are the words of the covenant." God specifically said, "…behold the blood of the covenant." Look and see the blood of the covenant. He gave us these words in Exodus 23:

> Thou shalt keep the feast of unleavened bread: (thou shalt eat unleavened bread seven days, as I commanded thee, in the time appointed of the month of Abib; for in it thou camest out from Egypt and none of you shall appear before Me empty:) (vs. 15).

> And ye shall serve the Lord God; and He shall bless thy bread, and thy water; and I will take sickness from the midst of thee. There shall nothing cast their young, nor be barren, in thy land: the number of thy days I will fulfill (vss. 25–26).

Those were the specific words of the covenant, at least as restated in Exodus 23.

Now, we must look specifically at how the Israelites, God's children at that time, understood the Abrahamic covenant. What did they understand that covenant to mean?

The covenant means substantially more than what the majority of Christians think it means when we read blithely over the words. But we are not going to brush lightly over the words. We are going to look at them in great detail. David's son Solomon declared, "**Every Word** of God is pure:…Add thou not unto His Words [or subtract from them], lest He reprove thee and thou be found a liar" (Prov. 30:5–6). Since Jesus was to "sit on the throne of David," if the covenant was important at all, David should have something to say about it. If the covenant was so important to God's heart—and David was a man after God's own heart—then David would have something to say about that covenant. Consider Psalm 25:10, 14:

> All the paths of the Lord *are* mercy and truth unto such as keep the covenant and His testimonies.... The secret of the Lord *is* with them that fear Him; and He will show them His covenant.

139

Covenant of Fathers, Confidence for Future

Now if you want to build faith, the way to build faith is not to look into the future and commiserate about all the potential problems. The way to build faith is to look into the past and begin to recount what God has done. When you see what God has done, you might have a little stronger hope for the future. And that is precisely what the Psalmist did in Psalm 105:

> O give thanks unto the Lord; call upon His name: make known His deeds among the people. Sing unto Him, sing psalms unto Him; talk ye of all His wondrous works. Glory ye in His holy name: let the heart of them rejoice that seek the Lord. **O ye seed of Abraham** His servant, ye children of Jacob His chosen. He is the Lord our God, His judgments are in all the earth. **He hath remembered His covenant** for ever, **the Word which He commanded to a thousand generations** (vss. 3, 6–8).

Have you ever considered that God had to remember anything? God made a promise, and He swore by his own name so He would not forget it. He wanted to make sure we would not forget that He would not forget it. That is very important. We are going to see a very exciting and shocking passage of Scripture at the end of this chapter. It has to do with just this: God remembering His covenant.

> Which covenant He made with Abraham, and His oath unto Isaac; And confirmed the same unto Jacob for a law, and to Israel for an everlasting covenant (Ps. 105:9–10).

And who is the Israel of God? To whom does the Abrahamic covenant pertain? It is to those who believe with faithful Abraham (Rom. 9:4–8; 2:28–29; Gal. 3:13–14).

Think with me for a minute about three names: Abraham, Isaac, and Jacob. As you have read through the Old Testament, how many times do you remember hearing the phrase "the God of Abraham, Isaac, and Jacob"? Sometimes we read "the God of Abraham and Jacob" or "the God of Jacob." But it all means the same. Over and over again we have seen it. It almost seems boring, doesn't it? Why did God continue to use that form of expression?

Those three names, whenever mentioned, brought forth out of the heart of Israel (of those who believe) a whole raft of understanding. Embodied in those three names is everything that we are going to unfold in this chapter. It is an entire covenant. It covers the whole of life. To the Israelites, it was a big deal! Every time they mentioned "the God of Abraham, Isaac, and Jacob," everything that was included in the covenant of Abraham was implicated. We must discover what Israel understood. Israel's difficulty in embracing that covenant as they left Egypt conscripted them to forty years in the wilderness, longing for Egypt. Our failure to do so has cut us short and, in a significant sense, left us wallowing in the mud of Egypt.

Does God Mean What He Says?

Let us begin in Psalm 105. The Psalmist reminded the Israelites of how God brought them out of Egypt. He then recalled, "He brought them forth also with silver and gold" (vs. 37). Do you remember? We saw that when Abraham came out of Egypt, he came forth with silver and gold (Gen. 13:1–2). That was long before the children of Israel ever went into Egypt. Abraham went into Egypt. When he came out, he came out a rich man, with silver and gold. When the children of Israel went in and came out, they came out with great substance.

Similarly, God told Abraham that his offspring, his seed, would go into a strange land, would be there for four hundred years, and would come out with great substance (Gen. 15:13–14). God told that to Abraham hundreds of years before they ever went into the land of Egypt. He told Abraham what was going to happen. There is a reason why God said that. He chooses His words carefully. He means them! God's statement has been consistent from Genesis to Revelation. When God's kids truly come out of Egypt, they will, as a whole, come out with great substance. He is not talking here about some sort of ethereal, spiritual substance. He is talking about material substance. God is concerned about you—body, soul, and spirit. His promises apply to your entire being.

> Beloved, I wish above all things that thou mayest prosper and be in health, even as thy soul prospereth (3 John 2).

God is concerned first about our soul and spirit. But He is also concerned about our health and material provision. This is why Jesus could so simply say in His Sermon on the Mount, "But Seek ye **first** the Kingdom of God, and His righteousness" (Matt. 6:33). The spiritual covenantal relationship is the fountain from which all other blessings flow. Note carefully: Jesus completed His statement, "...and all these **things** shall be added unto you." What things? "ALL THESE THINGS." He wants us to "take no thought" worrying about finances, houses, food, transportation, health, etc. Why could He say this so simply and confidently? Because all "these things" had already been provided for in God's covenant with Abraham and his seed who would walk by faith. Look closely at the psalmist's report in Psalm 105:

> **Egypt was glad when they departed**: for the fear of them fell upon them. He spread a cloud for a covering; and fire to give light in the night. The people asked, and He brought quails, and satisfied them with the bread of heaven. He opened the rock, and the waters gushed out; they ran in the dry places like a river (vss. 38–41).

What does this mean? The Psalmist was declaring that, as part of the Abrahamic covenant, God provided even the minuscule survival needs of the people. When nothing was available, He brought it from seemingly nowhere. Do you remember when the people cried out for flesh? God replied, "I'm going to provide you so much flesh it will stink in your nostrils." And Moses said, "Come on, God. How in the world are you going to do that? There is no flesh around here except these meager cattle we have wandering around. Do you want us to kill them all?" God said, "I AM." And the next day there were so many quail that blew in off the sea that the people got deathly sick because of their refusal to trust.

God provided the meat. He provided the bread, the manna. Their shoes did not wear out. And He provided the water: "They drank of that spiritual Rock that followed them: and that Rock was Christ" (1 Cor. 10:4). That Rock was Christ—back then, before He even came to earth.

For He remembered His holy promise, and Abraham, His servant (Ps. 105:42).

That was the covenant. God remembered what He promised and performed according to the promise. God means what He says. He kept the contract. Now look at these words carefully:

He brought them forth also with silver and gold; and there was not one feeble person among their tribes (Ps. 105:37).

What is He saying here? He is reminding that there was no sickness among the entire nation of Israel. Now that is an astounding statement. Israel had been in slavery for four hundred years. They had been beaten, had worked in the mud and the slime. And yet, when they came out, there was not one feeble one among them. They came out, not only with all their material needs met and an abundance of material goods, but also they came out without sickness. This is very important to understand, admit, and receive. This is not some spiritual transliteration of the words. This is talking about sickness in body. There was not one feeble one among them. This baffles our human understanding. But if we believe God's Word regarding our spiritual salvation, we must also believe the rest of His Word that we have difficulty receiving. To fail to do so is to place us back in Egypt by unbelief. We cannot pick and choose what we will believe. To do so is to undermine the very integrity of God's Word. It is sheer arrogance.

Did Israel Understand the Covenant?

The Psalmist, many hundreds of years after the children of Israel came out of Egypt, believed in the full implication of the words "Abraham, Isaac, and Jacob." And he recorded that God had performed according to His covenant.

God had remembered the covenant, and that is why Israel was delivered from Egypt. Let us go back to that period of time and find out what Moses understood and what the people understood that covenant to mean in very explicit terms.

> Beware that thou forget not the Lord thy God, in not keeping His commandments, and His judgments, and His statutes, which I command thee this day... (Deut. 8:11).

That is the performance part of the contract on our behalf. If we perform, then God will keep His promise. For salvation from sin, the only required "performance" is our faith-filled belief, followed by the fruit of a holy and obedient life, revealing that belief. We then have "standing" or a place of legal "eligibility" to receive the other covenantal benefits, also by faith-filled belief through Abraham, confirmed in Christ, the "son of Abraham" (Matt. 1:1). Listen to Moses:

> Lest, when thou has eaten and art full, and hast built goodly houses, and dwelt therein; And when thy herds and thy flocks multiply, and thy silver and thy gold is multiplied, and all that thou hast is multiplied... (Deut. 8:12–13).

God is presuming that things will be multiplied. And He is warning the people: "I am going to keep my covenant with you, but I am going to warn you, there is going to be great temptation to you. When all those things come according to the covenant, you will be tempted to say that your might and your power got you this wealth."

America's Prostitution with Egypt

The root of all sin is pride. The breeding ground of pride is often ungratefulness. It is a subtle shifting of recognition of the source of position and prosperity. The problem is not the prosperity. Wealth comes from God. It is a significant part of His covenant. To deny that is to arrogantly and selectively edit the Scriptures. Read these words from Deuteronomy 8 very carefully:

> Then thine heart be lifted up, and thou forget the Lord thy God, which brought thee forth out of the land of Egypt, from the house of bondage...And thou say in thine heart, My power and the might of mine hand hath gotten me this wealth. But thou shalt remember the Lord thy God: **for it is He that giveth thee power to get wealth, that He may establish His covenant which He sware unto thy fathers...** (vss. 14:17–18).

What is God saying here? "I give you power to get wealth in this earth, because I made a contract with your father Abraham, your father in faith, the father of Jesus in faith." Jesus was the son of Abraham and the son of David (see Matt. 1:1). He was of the house and lineage of David, but He was of the house of faith through Abraham.

And God said, "Because I have made that covenant with Abraham, that covenant will extend to you, and I give you—specifically John Jones or Mary Smith, or whoever else believes and receives my covenant—power to get wealth, that I might establish [make perfect, fulfill] the terms of my contract with Abraham and with his seed thereafter."

Consider seriously! God has not just committed to provide basic needs but to provide an abundance for every good work. Is that not precisely what the apostle Paul explained? God intends to supply not only your basic needs, but also you will have an abundance for every good work that He desires you to perform (2 Cor. 9:8). That is what God expects us to do with the wealth that He puts in our hands.

This is not the "Prosperity Gospel" as applied by worldly Christians or by preachers pandering to the lusts of the people while refusing to preach the tremendous responsibility attendant to God's blessings. This is trustee-ship. It is stewardship! God endows His children with the tender (or goods) of the world to accomplish His Kingdom business. The problem is not with the message but with carnal messengers and Christians who still live by the fleshpots of Egypt.

How are we going to get the gospel out? Prosperity is not about building personal wealth and bigger barns to display it to the world in self aggrandize-ment. It is not about being in castles and isolating ourselves from the world. No! It is about "being a blessing." It is about becoming a Kingdom conduit, not a worldly reservoir.

This has become America's problem. We revel in unprecedented prosper-ity issuing from the fulfillment of our forefather's seeding a nation in humble covenant with the God of Abraham. Now our prosperity has turned our minds. We have become conformed to this world in pride and self-sufficiency while professing to have hearts toward God. We pursue MANNA rather than the MASTER. We have interbred Egyptian minds with spiritual hearts and have produced bastard sons who now live off of the spiritual capital of our forefathers. No longer trustees for God's Kingdom, we have become lords of our own kingdoms. We are no longer conduits of blessing but consumers. The church has prostituted herself with the sons of Egypt.

Rebellion Frustrates God's Covenant
God wants a love affair with His people. He says, "Ye have not chosen me, but I have chosen you..." (John 15:16). He loves us, but He wants us to love Him. His covenant extends only to those who love Him. But there is a test of that love. It is called obedience.

For thou art an holy people unto the Lord thy God: the Lord thy God hath chosen thee to be a special people unto Himself, above all people that are upon the face of the earth (Deut. 7:6).

But because the Lord loved you, and because He would keep the oath which He had sworn unto your fathers, hath the Lord brought you out with a mighty hand, and redeemed you out of the houses of the bondmen, from the hand of Pharaoh, king of Egypt. Know therefore that the Lord thy God, He is God, **the faithful God**, which **keepeth covenant** and mercy **with them that love Him and obey His commandments** to a thousand generations (Deut. 7:8–9).

God's covenant extends ONLY to those who "keep His commandments." You say, "I disagree! That is Old Testament talk. We are 'under grace.'" My dear friend, we have not been given an entirely true picture of the TRUTH, of the Word of God in our generation. It did not fit our freewheeling American spirit that grasps for God's blessing without the biblical burden. Jesus said that His "burden is light." It is obedience. It is light (not heavy) because we love Him. We obey, not because we ought to but because we want to. If you do not want to obey Him, you do not love Him. You have become a legalist. The law must compel you to obey. Were you aware that John, the apostle of love, defined love as obedience? Listen to his words:

By this we know that we love the children of God, when we love God, and **keep His commandments**. For this **is** the love of God, that we **keep His commandments**: and His commandments are not grievous (1 John 5:2–3).

And whatsoever we ask, we receive of Him, *because* we **keep His commandments**, and do those things that are pleasing in His sight (1 John 3:22).

Jesus—the Lord of the church, the completer and fulfiller of the law—reinforced this point. It may not agree with your personal or church doctrine (born of modern-American "churchianity" and "gospel-lite") or with the teachings of some church father you have chosen to follow, but here are the words of the "only begotten son" of God:

If ye love me, **keep my commandments** (John 14:15).

He that hath my commandments, and keepeth them, he it is that loveth me (John 14:21).

Judas (not Iscariot) asked of Jesus,

Lord, how is it that thou wilt manifest thyself unto us, and not unto the world? Jesus answered him: **If a man love me, he will keep my words:** and my Father will love him, and we will come unto him, and make our abode with him. **He that loveth me not keepeth not my sayings** (John 14:22–24).

The covenant is to those who love God, but **love is defined or confirmed by obedience. Obedience is the true revealer of faith.** You cannot obey God's Word unless you step out on what God says, whether you understand it or not, whether your experience tells you that it is valid or not. Americans define truth by their experience. True believers define their experience by God's Word. One way is "Egyptian." The other is the way of the "sons of promise." **Refusal to obey is rebellion.** Rebellion frustrates the covenant. That is why Samuel told King Saul (whose actions revealed a kind of now-Americanized, half-baked obedience): "To obey is better than sacrifice, and to hearken than the fat of rams" (1 Sam. 15:22).

Moses made the record undisputedly clear! Read these words carefully, American Christian. Your ability to claim the covenental promises of God in the difficult days of trial and persecution ahead will depend upon your heart and mind embracing these conditions:

Thou shalt therefore keep the commandments, and the statutes, and the judgments, which I command thee this day, to do them. Wherefore it shall come to pass, *if* ye hearken to these judgments, and keep, and do them, that the Lord thy God shall keep unto thee the covenant and the mercy which He swore unto thy fathers: And He will love thee, and bless thee, and multiply thee: He will also bless the fruit of thy womb, and the fruit of thy land, thy corn, and thy wine, and thine oil, the increase of thy kine, and the flocks of thy sheep, in the land which He swore unto thy fathers to give thee. Thou shalt be blessed above all people; there shall not be male or female barren among you, or among your cattle. And the Lord will take away from thee all sickness, and will put none of the evil diseases of Egypt, which thou knowest, upon thee… (Deut. 7:13–15).

That is almost a restatement of Exodus 23:25–26, isn't it? "There shall be nothing barren or cast their young in their land…. I will take sickness away from the midst of thee…. The number of thy days I will fulfill." Out of the mouth of two or three witnesses let every word be established. And there are many more witnesses than just these. We are just highlighting some of the more direct ones here.

Can We Live without Fear?
The times that are coming upon us will be the most perplexing and frightening times ever experienced in human history. We are warned "men's

hearts will fail them for fear." Must Christians experience this terror? What if the popular "pretribulation rapture" doctrine should be in error. After all, it is a doctrine rooted primarily in Americanized Christianity in this last century, lacking even one direct, unequivocal scriptural support, built entirely upon inference. Would your present faith-walk sustain you and your family to "endure to the end" before God's wrath is poured out on the children of disobedience? Do not answer this question with the glib, American rhetoric, "We'll be out of here." Do you have the faith that endures when times of prosperity fail? Will your faith endure if radical social change prevents public worship and the fickle feelings of Americans become openly hateful or violent to true Christians?

God desires that we live, walk in, and breathe the oxygen of faith when the fires of end-time reality begin to burn. His covenant promises are sure to those who obey Him. They are as dependable in the end-times as in Bible times. Thoughtfully consider these words of encouragement:

> …and ye shall eat your bread to the full, and dwell in your land safely. And I will give you peace in the land, and ye shall lie down, and none shall make you afraid…. And ye shall chase your enemies, and they shall fall before you by the sword. And five of you shall chase an hundred, and an hundred of you shall put ten thousand to flight… (Lev. 26:5–8).

What is God saying here? He is telling us the same thing that Paul told us in 2 Timothy 1:7: "For God hath not given us the spirit of fear; but of power, and of love, and of a sound mind."

He is saying, "When you are redeemed out of Egypt and you come out of Egypt and you are trusting Me and you are walking in My covenant, one of the benefits of the covenant is that you will walk without fear." Why can we walk without fear? Because we have absolute trust in our God! Do you?

Let's Be Honest!

We have found that God's covenant, which is extended to those who come out of Egypt, includes freedom from material want, freedom from physical sickness, and freedom from fear. Let us talk about this in real, practical terms.

God tells us we will come out without sickness. We are told, "If thou wilt diligently hearken to the voice of the Lord…and give ear to His commandments" that none of the diseases of Egypt will come upon us…that He is "the Lord that healeth thee" (Exod. 15:26). In other words, as you walk in this way of life, as you walk in faith, under the covenant, you will find that sickness in your family and sickness in your body will begin to diminish. Now, it is not going to diminish overnight, because that process did not get started overnight. Our ways are producing after their kind. But we have found, in our family, that as we have diligently sought to open our eyes and hearts to the whole of God's Word and conform our ways to it, as we have been operating in this covenant and believed it and taken God at His Word and entered into the bond of the covenant, that our health improved and our medical bills diminished.

That does not mean we do not have any sickness. Even as I write, I have endured an unprecedented attack on my body that has taken me to the hospital, has defied medical explanation, and has threatened to intimidate me from declaring to you these covenental promises God commanded "to a thousand generations" (Ps. 105:8). But we are walking in a way of life. And as you begin to walk in the covenantal way of life, your pattern of life will begin to change—your thinking, your values, perhaps even your eating.

We have found in our family that the pattern of life economically began to change. It changed our business. It changed our way of looking at things. It changed our perception of responsibility to open our hearts and hands far beyond our own family. It opened a heart of hospitality, enabling our family to become a "Kingdom conduit" of blessing. Yet even as I completed final editing of this book, our family has been assaulted financially in unprecedented ways, again daring me to declare God's timeless truth. My wife and I will not be intimidated, even if it costs us all. For the consequesces of stifling these end-time truths could be devastating to many weakened believers.

But God also began to deliver me from the spirit of fear. Before embracing His full covenant, I could not speak before groups without freezing. My throat would swell, and tears would fill my eyes. But God has loosened my tongue to be able to speak—with boldness and gladness and joy—the Word of God. It was a process of embracing, by faith, His promise. I must continually rebuke Satan's temptation to fear, as I would any other temptation.

I say that precisely because there is always a question. Well how come Sister Jones had cancer? How come Brother Smith has this or that? The question for us personally is not Sister Jones or Brother Smith, because we went through that whole issue with Joshua and Caleb and ten other spies. We found a whole nation failed to get the blessing of God. Only two men out of the entire nation got the blessing of God, because they chose to say what God said. Can we truly walk with God unless we agree with Him? (see Amos 3:3). Let God be concerned with Sister Jones. In the words of Jesus, "What is that to thee? Follow thou me" (John 20:22).

Changing Thinking, Changing Ways
Isaiah says that the inhabitants shall not say, "I am sick" (Is. 33:26). The prophet Joel says, "Let the weak say, I am strong" (Joel 3:10). So who are you going to believe? Are you going to believe the testimony of your senses? Or are you going to begin to put the covenant of your God in your mouth, on your lips, and begin to speak what God says?

This is not name-it-and-claim-it theology based in self-centered pursuit of ungodly, fleshly purposes to consume God's blessing upon our own lust, as we've been warned against in James (see 4:3). This is merely a coming into agreement with God's Kingdom Covenant. All heresy is merely perverted truth. Shall we throw out the truth because some, or even many, choose to pervert the faith with fleshly desires or with fleshly demonstrations? To discard truth because of its abuse is as heretical as the abuse or misuse of truth.

American medicine is not a health-care system but a disease-care system. As Americans, our focus has not been on health but on remedy. Our mind-set has created a drug culture, which has seriously shifted the trust of American Christians. Like the Egyptians of old, we think first of physicians rather than of the Great Physician. We prefer doctors' prescriptions for remedy rather than God's prescriptions for health.

Joshua, one of the two men who entered the Promised Land, gave us a succinct picture of God's expectation in Joshua 1:8. Let's dissect it together:

> This book of the law [covenant] shall not depart **out of thy mouth**, but thou shalt **meditate** therein day and night, that thou mayest observe **to do** according to all that is written therein:… (Josh. 1:8*a*).

- "Out of thy mouth…" Not out of thy head, not off thy coffee table, not out from under thy arm, but out of thy mouth, the scripture says.
- "But thou shalt meditate therein…." Here *meditate* means "to mutter softly to yourself, to ruminate like a cow chewing its cud."
- "That thou mayest observe to do…" Note the words *to do*. James 1:22 says, "But be ye doers of the word, and not hearers only, deceiving your own selves." Why deceiving? Because you read what it says, yet it never happens, because you never do it. God pleads with us: "Just do it!" He wants His children to participate in His full covenant.

Joshua learned the secret:

> …that you may observe **to do** according to all that is written therein: for then thou shalt make thy way prosperous and then thou shalt have good success (Josh. 1:8*b*).

Notice the pattern again: If…, then…. "If you…, then I…." If you observe to do, then the covenant will become operative so that "thou shalt make thy way prosperous and then thou shalt have good success."

Moses repeated the theme in Leviticus 22, hinging obedience to holiness:

> Therefore shall ye **keep my commandments, and do them**: I am the Lord. Neither shall ye profane my holy name; but I will be hallowed among the children of Israel: **I am the Lord which hallow you**, That brought you out of the land of Egypt, to be your God: I am the Lord (vss. 31–33).

When "I brought you out of Egypt, I hallowed you," God says. In Hebrew, that word *hallow* really means "to sanctify, to purify, to set you apart." A further benefit of the covenant, then, is that God sanctifies, or sets apart. He makes separate from the rest of the world His people who will, by their own will, be established in the bond of the covenant. The covenant benefits extend only to those who will agree with the covenant, who will accept it, who will make it theirs.

Can We Stand on the Promises if We Do Not Know What They Are?

What is the New Covenant? Did it eliminate the entirety of the Old Covenant? If it is a better covenant, how is it better? Hebrews 8 gives us the answers:

> But now hath He obtained a more excellent ministry, by how much also He is the mediator of a better covenant, which was established upon better promises. For if that first covenant had been faultless, then should no place have been sought for the second. For finding fault with the first, He saith, Behold, the days come, saith the Lord, when I will make a new covenant with the house of Israel and with the house of Judah. Not according to the covenant that I made with their fathers in the day when I took them by the hand to lead them out of the land of Egypt; because they continued not in my covenant, and I regarded them not, saith the Lord. For this is the covenant that I will make with the house of Israel after those days, saith the Lord; **I will put my laws into their mind, and write them in their hearts**; and I will be to them a God, and they shall be to me a people (vss. 6–10).

Jesus, the "Living Word," provided a new and better covenant established on better promises. Now what is that new and better covenant? Hebrews 9 and 10 make it clear that the thing that is new and better about the New Covenant is that we no longer have to sacrifice hundreds or thousands of animals every day and have the Levites walk up to their knees in blood as they slit the throats of those animals, day after day after day, hour after hour. We will not have to wince as the blood gushes from animals' severed arteries, reminding us of the sin and the awfulness of the penalty that has come upon us through Adam. And we will no longer have to endure, as with the Old Covenant, the haunting pallor of sin weighing our memory with guilt.

No! We do not have to do that anymore, since Christ died once and for all. He was the sacrificial Lamb. And from that moment on, we have been entitled to the covenant blessing through Jesus. We no longer have to go through those forms, which were but a shadow of the things to come. That is a summary of the whole of Hebrews 9 and 10, because we do not have sufficient space to recite it specifically.

But turn to Romans 15:8. "Now I say that Jesus Christ was a minister of the circumcision...." Circumcision was the evidence, or manifestation, of the covenant required of Abraham and his seed. In the Old Testament we are told that all the boy babies would have to be circumcised on the eighth day to establish the covenant that God had made with Abraham.

> Now I say that Jesus Christ was a minister of the circumcision for the truth of God, **to confirm the promises made unto the fathers** (Rom. 15:8).

Jesus was the minister of that circumcision to confirm all those promises that were made to the fathers. So we see in 2 Corinthians 1:20, that "all the promises of God in Him [in Jesus] are yea, and in Him Amen, unto the glory of God." **All the promises of God from Genesis to Revelation are "yes" and "so be it" to those who will believe them,** because Jesus was the minister of the circumcision to confirm the promises made unto the fathers. But what are those promises? Can you articulate the principle promises made to and through Abraham, Isaac, and Israel? What promises were extended to Israel—God's son—as he came out of Egypt? When Moses took the blood from the burnt offering and peace offering, sprinkled it on the people to remind them of the Abrahamic blood covenant, and declared, "Behold the blood of the covenant" (Exod. 24:8), what was included?

THE PROMISE OF CLEANSING FROM SIN

First and foremost, God desires and demands a holy people. Although we will look at this most important part of the covenant in particular detail in the chapter "Redemption and Atonement," we should at least give meaningful emphasis here, lest someone think other provisions are elevated unbiblically above this overarching aspect of the covenant.

Abraham believed God when the Word of the Lord came to him, despite all scientific and natural evidence to the contrary. His faith was imputed to him as righteousness (Gen. 15:4–6). The Lord made a covenant of blood with Abraham to confirm the covenant, including right-standing with God, giving the right to inherit the Promised Land (Gen. 15:7–18).

When Moses led Abraham's seed out of Egypt, God then provided atonement for the sin of an entire people: the congregation. The elders were to lay their hand on a bullock and kill it before the Lord. The priest was to dip his finger in the blood and sprinkle it seven times, putting some on the horns of the altar. When the priest completed the sin offering for the people, Moses wrote, "...it shall be forgiven them" (Lev. 4:20). The bullock was then to be burned outside the camp. Again Moses repeated, "...it is a sin offering for the congregation" (Lev. 4:21).

But this practice was only a shadow of the once-and-final sacrifice to come. A high priest named Caiaphus counseled the Jews as they enviously plotted to rid the world of "the WORD of God" (who threatened their tidy religious traditions and positions of prominence). Caiaphus stated, "…it was expedient that one man should die for the people" (John 18:14). And so the apostle Paul wrote of Jesus:

> For He hath made Him to be sin for us, who knew no sin; that we might be made the righteousness of God in Him (2 Cor. 5:21).

Jesus (who knew no sin) was made to be sin for us, that I, [put in your name], might be made the righteousness of God in Christ Jesus. That I might be sanctified, hallowed, set apart as a son of God, a son of Abraham. I am adopted into His very family and given His surname, that I might love His Word as I walk and live in the household of faith. I will make His words my words because He is my Father. Jesus became sin that I would not have to live under the curse and unending plague of conscience of sin (Heb. 10:10–22). That was the new and better promise. The rest of the Old Covenant remains the same because God remains the same—fulfilled, fleshed out, and revealed in Christ.

The Promise of Physical Healing

The prophet Isaiah foretold the continuance of physical healing in Christ, as contained in the Abrahamic covenant:

> Surely He [Jesus] hath borne our griefs, and carried our sorrows: yet we did esteem Him stricken, smitten of God, and afflicted. But He was wounded for our transgressions, He was bruised for our iniquities: the chastisement of our peace was upon Him; and **with His stripes we are healed** (Isa. 53:4–5).

Now if you think Isaiah was talking about some sort of spiritual healing, you need to turn with me to Matthew 8 where it is clearly written,

> When the even was come, they brought unto Him [Jesus] many that were possessed with devils; and He cast out the spirits with His word, and **healed all that were sick: That it might be fulfilled which was spoken by Esaias the prophet, saying, Himself took our infirmities, and bare our sicknesses** (vss. 16–17).

Jesus was the fulfillment of the covenant, which says, "I will take sickness away from the midst of thee" (Exod. 23:25). Why is this so difficult to accept or believe? Why is it we can accept the promise of forgiveness of sin as literal, but we insist upon converting the clear and obvious words of Scripture regarding healing—in both Old and New Testaments—into some spiritualized application? Could it be because of tradition? Could it be that some of our spiritual fathers and teachers have really not believed, just as the religious leaders of Jesus' day did not? Could it also be that we are paralyzed by the spirit of science, as we were the ancient Egyptians? Has our Egyptian thinking mummified our spirits?

Could it be that, down deep, our pride is at stake because we fear that our faith will be empirically tested and we might be thought to have "little faith?" Are we more afraid of the opinions of man than the opinion of God? Do we not partially trample His promise and sacrifice when we choose to disregard or disbelieve? Could this be part of what Paul referred to when discussing the Lord's Supper: "For he that eateth and drinketh unworthily, eateth and drinketh damnation to himself, not discerning the Lord's body. For this cause many are weak and sickly among you, and many sleep" (1 Cor. 11:29–30)? We trifle with, trivialize, or tamper with any portion of the Word of God at our peril.

THE PROMISE OF A FULL PROVISION

One need only read the incredible blessings catalogued by Moses in Deuteronomy 28:14, to be convinced of God's commitment to bless an obedient people. As is always the case, God's promises are conditional. Failure to obey would produce the most horrendous curses (Deut. 28:15–68). American Christians need to be reminded that God's blessings are conditional, both to individuals and to nations. We can see ourselves progressively reaping the gut-wrenching destruction promised to a people who refuse to obey God. Read Deuteronomy 28:45–68 prayerfully. Do not shrink from it. It is part of the inspired Word. Read it! Read it again!

We have already seen Abraham come out of Egypt with silver and gold. Israel came out of Egypt "with great substance" as promised to Abraham. And every biblical theme is consistent. The New Covenant does not provide less in any way.

Jesus said He came to fulfill or give full meaning to the Old Covenant. He did not destroy, undermine, or replace it. He fleshed it out. His death was a substituting sacrifice for sin. His stripes extended and confirmed the covenant of physical healing. And His voluntary poverty took our place that we might have everything we need for every good work. Read the following words of scripture slowly and ask yourself these questions: What do they say on their face? Do they appear clear? Remember, "Every word of God is pure." Let us look at them carefully:

> For ye know the grace of our Lord Jesus Christ, that though He was rich, yet for your sakes He became poor, that ye through His poverty might be rich (2 Cor. 8:9).

If you look up the word *rich* in Webster's dictionary, you will find that one of the primary definitions is "to have a full supply." That is precisely what God has promised. Jesus was the fulfillment of the Abrahamic covenant. When you come out of Egypt, you will have an abundance. You will come out with great substance. Jesus said, "I became poor that you might be rich and have a full supply." He did not promise you a mansion on earth, but He did promise a full supply. He did promise prosperity, but not necessarily American-style. Prosperity is having sufficient provision to fulfill every purpose God has for you on planet earth. Do not sell Him short by your unbelief. Neither allow the lust of the flesh, the lust of the eyes, nor the pride of life to corrupt His provision. Some may have mansions here; others may not. But we are all promised one in the "promised land" (John 14:1–3).

A PROMISE OF FAITH FOR FEAR

Paul's letter to Timothy reminds us, "For God hath not given us the spirit of fear; but of power, and of love and of a sound mind" (2 Tim. 1:7). You will find the same theme repeated in Romans: "For ye have not received the spirit of bondage again to fear; but ye have received the spirit of adoption…" (8:15). This same theme was repeated to Israel in various ways, the essential message being, "Faith and confidence if you obey, fear and terror if you disobey or refuse to believe" (see Deut. 28).

So what are we saying? We are saying that the entire covenant, if summarized, consisted of:

- Being hallowed (set apart to God; justified; saved from sin; set in right relationship with God; restored; cleansed from sin);
- Experiencing deliverance from sickness (diseases of Egypt);
- Receiving financial and material provision (an abundance for every good work);
- Having fear removed from the midst of us.

This is, in essence, a distillation of God's covenant to His people, from Genesis to Revelation. This has not been intended to be an exhaustive discourse on the subject. Rather, it is an honest, biblically balanced overview, sufficient to restore faith and build necessary trust in the God who declares, "I AM." Is it not interesting that the provisions of the covenant are would-be answers to the most common prayer requests heard in the Body? Does this not reflect God's incredible, fatherly foreknowledge of our needs? Does it not also reflect our unbelief in and failure to faithfully embrace that which He has already promised?

Know Your Covenant; It May Be a Matter of Life or Death

God has spoken through the prophet Ezekiel, wooing and warning us:

> Like as I pleaded with your fathers in the wilderness of the land of Egypt,
> so will I plead with you, saith the Lord God.

And God is continuing to plead with His people. He is continuing to plead with me. He is pleading with you—with all His people who claim to be called to His name. Come into the bond of my covenant.

> And I will cause you to pass under the rod, and **I will bring you into the bond of the covenant** (Exod. 20:37).

Why "pass under the rod"? Because we are His children. Hebrews warns that if we do not receive chastisement, we are not a son or daughter. A loving father and mother chastise those who are of their own seed. Children who are not chastised, God calls "bastards" (Heb. 12:8). So God says if you err from His ways, you are going to suffer some consequences. The love and the mercy of God are rounded out by the justice of God. God is not just a God of mercy and peace and love—ooshy, gushy, mushy, lovey-dovey. He is "a consuming fire," as well (Heb. 12:29).

Then God decreed, "I will bring you into the bond of the covenant" (Exod. 30:37*b*). What is "the bond of the covenant"? God told Abraham that because of the covenant He was making with Abraham, He wanted him to do something tangible—to never forget. "I want you to circumcise every one of the boy babies from this day on," God said. It was a permanent covenant. Circumcision was the bond of the covenant at that time (Gen. 17:11).

In Romans 15:8 we see that Christ is (and was) the minister of the circumcision to all that will believe. Paul made it clear in Galatians 5:6: "neither circumcision availeth any thing, nor uncircumcision; but faith which worketh by love." So today faith is the bond of the covenant. Faith, not circumcision, is the bond of the covenant, because circumcision was a temporal sign. And God has said, "I am calling my people into the bond of the covenant" (Ezek. 20:37). There is no faith without trust. Trust requires rolling away the flesh from my heart.

You can have the greatest contract in the universe. You can have a million-page contract with page after page of provisions and benefits. But if you do not know what is in it, you are not going to reap the benefit of it. My experience in the course of twenty years of law practice was that people tend not to perform based upon of the terms of their covenant. Sometimes they have to be reminded. And sometimes, when they are reminded, they still do not perform. But God always performs when we fulfill His preconditions. He also asks us to put Him in remembrance, just as Moses did (see Isa. 43:26 and Exod. 32:11–14).

First of all, we must establish the beneficiaries under the covenant. Paul established the beneficiaries:

> And if ye be Christ's, then are ye Abraham's seed, and heirs according to the promise (Gal. 3:29).

Do you have any idea who the heirs according to the Abrahamic covenant, or promise are? You and me—if we have established relationship with Jesus Christ. Have you confessed Him as Savior, and do you obey Him as Lord? If you have not confessed Him as Savior, there is no salvation, for you have not employed God's designed instrument of faith. The apostle Paul again has made it abundantly clear: "…with the heart man believeth unto righteousness; and with the mouth confession is made unto salvation" (Rom. 10:10). So there is no such thing as a "closet Christian." Jesus said that if you will not acknowledge Him before men, neither will He acknowledge you before His Father in heaven (see Matt. 10:32–33). You cannot be a closet Christian. Your mouth is tied in directly to faith. And we will discuss that more fully in the chapter "Taming the Tongue."

You Must See Yourself in the Covenant

So we see that we are beneficiaries of the covenant. You must see yourself in this covenant. I must see myself in this covenant. Jesus did not begin to walk in the authority of His ministry until He found the place where it was written in the Book of Isaiah:

> The Spirit of the Lord is upon me, because He hath anointed me to preach the gospel to the poor; He hath sent me to heal the brokenhearted, to preach deliverance to the captives, and recovering of sight to the blind, to set at liberty them that are bruised, To preach the acceptable year of the Lord. And He closed the book, and He gave it again to the minister, and sat down. And the eyes of all them that were in the synagogue were fastened on Him. And all bare Him witness, and wondered at the gracious words which proceeded out of His mouth (Luke 4:18–19, 22).

That was the commencement of His ministry. But it made the people angry. Why? Because He admitted that He was in God's Word. He saw Himself in the Word and had the audacity to admit it. Have you ever admitted that you are in God's Word? Are you a son of God? Are you a daughter of God? The scripture says, "Beloved, now are we the sons of God" (1 John 3:2). Is it true of you? Is it? Listen again to these words:

> Who are the Israelites; to whom pertaineth the adoption, and the glory, and the covenants…for they are not all Israel, which are of Israel (Rom. 9:4, 7).

> But he is a Jew [or an Israelite], which is one inwardly; and circumcision is that of the heart, in the spirit… (Rom. 2:29).

How do you claim under the covenant? God was very angry with the children of Israel because they were not walking as children. Rather, they were walking as those who were not the seed of Abraham.

And the Lord said unto Moses, I have seen this people, and behold, it is a stiffnecked people: Now therefore let me alone, that my wrath may wax hot against them, and that I may consume them: and I will make of thee a great nation. And Moses besought the Lord his God, and said, Lord, why doth thy wrath wax hot against thy people, which thou hast brought forth out of the land of Egypt with great power, and with a mighty hand? Wherefore should the Egyptians speak, and say, For mischief did He bring them out, to slay them in the mountains, and to consume them from the face of the earth? Turn from thy fierce wrath, and repent of this evil against thy people. Remember Abraham, Isaac, and Israel [Jacob], thy servant, to whom thou swearest by thine own self.... And the Lord repented of the evil which He thought to do unto His people (Exod. 32:9–14).

How do I, as God's child, claim my position under the covenant. First, I must own up to that position. I must be willing to verbalize it, to declare it as an act of faith with my own tongue. Second, I must remind God, just as a son reminds his father of promises made. "Daddy, remember you promised...." Our heavenly Father longs to hear those words spoken in loving respect. You and I have been grafted in with Israel. In Christ, "all the promises of God in Him are yea, and in Him Amen, unto the glory of God by us" (2 Cor. 1:20). Here is a sample prayer of how you can talk with God about your position in His covenant:

Father, I thank You that You have made me the seed of Abraham, an heir according to Your promise. Father, it is written in [give reference] of Your covenant with Abraham and Israel, which You have also extended to me because You said that I am an "Israelite" as I walk by faith and not by sight. I am accepting Your Word. I believe it was not just for yesterday but for today. Father, I call You to remembrance of Your Word, as Your son. You have promised that by the stripes of Jesus, I am healed. You have promised to provide all my needs and an abundance for every good work You want me to do. I thank You that You will honor Your WORD. You are not a man that You would lie. You are God, my God. You are my healer and my provider.

Father, I thank You that it is written in Your Word that I do not have the spirit of fear but of power and of love and of a sound mind. I thank You that, notwithstanding the thoughts in my mind right now and notwithstanding the trepidation I feel, that You have promised in Your Word—2 Timothy 1:7—that I do not have the spirit of fear. Satan, in the name of Jesus, get thee behind me. It is written, "By the stripes of Jesus I am healed." God has not given me the spirit of fear. I have a sound mind. And I declare these things and thank You, Father, for hearing me, In Jesus name. Amen.

That is how to claim your covenant benefits under the Word of God. It does not happen overnight. It is a way of life. It must become your way of life. Start today. Do not delay. For the battle is about to intensify.

A Final Word

The walk of faith is a life of patience and sometimes dogged endurance. That is why we are repeatedly told, "He that endures to the end shall be saved" (Matt. 24:13). Be an overcomer. Become a covenant man or woman of faith. Here is some instruction and encouragement to set you on course:

Be not slothful, but followers of them who through faith and patience inherit the promises (Heb. 6:12).

Cast not away therefore your confidence, which hath great recompense of reward. For ye have need of patience, that, after ye have done the will of God, ye might receive the promise (Heb. 10:35–36).

Let Us Commit Together in Prayer

Father, I thank You that I have heard this word. I have received it with a heart of faith, and I am going to walk as an heir according to the promise. I am going to understand my covenant privileges, because You want me to, because You gave them to me as Your child. Open Your Word to me. I purpose to walk by faith and not by sight. I am going to put Your words in my mouth and claim Your promises. And I am going to walk in holiness, purity, and obedience. Lord, I believe. But help me in my unbelief. In Jesus name. Amen.

Chapter Thirteen

Redemption and Atonement

Most Christians live on the edge of Egypt, taking frequent excursions across the border. Do you? Are you chasing Egypt, or is Pharaoh pursuing you?

I WILL REDEEM YOU!" "I will redeem you with a stretched out arm," declared the Lord, as He prepared to deliver Israel from Egypt. It was God's first explicit promise of a redemptive plan. And it all issued out of God's covenant with Abraham.

We are beginning to see how most, if not every, significant theme in the Word of God finds its root in the idea of "coming out of Egypt." God has been calling His children out of Egypt ever since Abraham. Abraham came out of Egypt, and God made unbreakable promises to him. He told Abraham that his seed—the children of Israel—would go into a strange land for four hundred years and that when they came out, they would come out with great substance. The children of Abraham, Isaac, and Israel did, in fact, go into that strange land, the land of Egypt. And when they came out 430 years later, they came out with great substance, just as God said they would.

We have seen that Jesus went down into Egypt that it might be fulfilled which was spoken by the prophet Hosea, "…out of Egypt have I called my son." We are told that Jesus was the firstborn of many brethren and that we are Israel—the Israel of God, not by circumcision but by faith. And God now calls us out of Egypt, calls us to follow after His only begotten son. Because those who truly embrace Christ are now beloved sons of God.

Redemption—Both IN Egypt and FROM Egypt

We begin our journey toward redemption with the "father of the faithful," Abraham. And we find him mentioned, not in Genesis now, but in Exodus.

> And God spake unto Moses, and said unto him, I am the Lord. And I appeared
> unto Abraham, unto Isaac, and unto Jacob, by the name of God Almighty,
> but **by my name Jehovah was I not known to them** (Exod. 6:2–3).

Here is an interesting tidbit—a special insight. Here we see even more of
the greatness of Abraham's faith. He did not even understand God as "Jehovah,"
the eternal God. He did not understand God that way, yet he had the kind of
faith that led him to go out, not knowing where he went. He would look for
that city with foundations whose builder and maker is God. He would believe
that the promise of God—that he and Sarah would have a son beyond the age
of childbirth—would come true. And then, after having received that son, he
would be willing to offer him up, even believing that God was able to raise
Isaac from the dead in order to fulfill His promise. That is some kind of faith
when you do not even fully understand that God is the eternal one. Yet the
eternal God made an eternal covenant with this man, a covenant that affects
you and me.

> And I have also established my covenant with them [the children of Israel],
> to give them the land of Canaan, the land of their pilgrimage, wherein
> they were strangers. And I have also heard the groaning of the children of
> Israel, whom the Egyptians keep in bondage; and **I have remembered my
> covenant** (Exod. 6:4–5).

> Wherefore [because God has remembered His covenant] say unto the children
> of Israel, I am the Lord, and will bring you out from under the burdens of
> the Egyptians, and I will rid you out of their bondage, and **I will redeem you**
> with a stretched out arm, and with great judgments (Exod. 6:6).

Here is the promise of redemption to God's children.. The promise comes
out of Egypt. The promise comes **in** Egypt. It is when God's children are in
Egypt that He makes the promise of redemption. That is when God made
the promise of redemption to you and me—when we were yet in Egypt.

The New Testament puts it differently. We are told that "while we were
yet sinners, Christ died for us" (Rom. 5:8). When we were yet in Egypt, Christ
died for us. Egypt is a type (or symbol) of sin and its bondage—of sinful
ways—and also of a lifestyle of unbelief, even after coming into the family of
faith in Christ.

Here we find in Exodus that God has made His first outright, explicit
promise of redemption. We have other symbolic or veiled promises of the
coming of Christ, such as in Genesis 3:15, which speaks of the seed of the
woman crushing Satan's head, and we have God making His promise to Abraham: "In thee shall all nations of the earth be blessed." But this, I believe, is
the first time in the Bible where God specifically says there is going to be a

redemption plan and that He is going to redeem (or "buy back") His children out of Egypt, the house of bondage.

Again, it is important to see it is the covenant that God made with Abraham that precipitated the redemption plan. That is why we first talked about the covenant. Redemption flows out of the covenant. We have studied the fullness of implication of that covenant.

As we talk about the fullness of redemption and atonement, in many respects you will find a repetition back to some of the things we discussed surrounding the covenant. Why? Because God has used many illustrations, or threads of emphasis, throughout His Word to try to get across the same message. Sometimes they are seen as different doctrines. But essentially they are just different windows through which we view the overarching message and receive its aggregate truth.

Obviously, then, the ultimate results are going to sound similar, because in fact, they are. According to Hebrews 13:8, Jesus Christ is the same yesterday, today, and forever, so we need to rethink this idea of all these special little doctrines. God is not much concerned about doctrines, in the abstract. What He is concerned about is faith. Do we believe or do we not? Do we take Him at His Word? That is God's bottom line. Not all, but much of our obsession with doctrinal nuances becomes a smoke screen of words to obfuscate the real issue: obedience. It is not the mere assertion of facts, however correct, that pleases God. It is our day-to-day conformity and obedience to God's Word—doing what it says—that is ultimately relevant. Correct assertion of biblical facts, without correct attitudinal and behavioral response, is pure deception in religious cloak (James 1:22).

> And I will take you to me for a people, and I will be to you a God: and ye shall know that I am the Lord your God, which bringeth you out from under the burdens of the Egyptians (Exod. 6:7).

What Was God's Intention?

What was God's intention in His redemptive plan? His intention from the very beginning was that we would come out and be His sons and daughters. And so we have been reminded by the apostle Paul:

> Be ye not unequally yoked together with unbelievers.... Wherefore come out from among them, and be ye separate, saith the Lord.... And [I] will be a Father unto you, and ye shall be my sons and daughters, saith the Lord Almighty (2 Cor. 6:14–18).

This is exactly what God was saying in Exodus: "I'm going to redeem you out of Egypt, and when I redeem you out, then you will have the inheritance of sons." He wanted to be Father. He wanted to "buy back." *To redeem* means to "buy back, to buy out of."

We discussed the fatherhood of Satan when we considered living in the spirit of adoption. We found that Satan **was** our father. God wanted to buy us back from the household of Satan into His household of faith. There, we could live as sons and daughters of Almighty God, our Father, who wanted to provide all of our needs. A father who does not provide the needs of his children can have his children taken away. Even under the law of men, the state has the right to take a child away from the natural parent if the natural parent does not provide the necessities of life for that child. Satan did not provide those necessities of life.

In that light, consider the oft-quoted words in John 10:10:

> The thief cometh not, but for to steal, and to kill, and to destroy: I am come
> that they might have life, and that they might have it more abundantly.

From this passage we can see that God's redemptive intention never changed. He always intended that we would become His sons and daughters, that He would take us from Satan's abusive clutches.

Moses disclosed the primary response of the people to God's offer of redemption. Response patterns have not changed from then until now.

> And Moses spake so unto the children of Israel: but they hearkened not unto
> Moses for anguish of spirit, and for cruel bondage (Exod. 6:9).

It is the old phrase, "You can't see the forest for the trees." We get so locked up in the bondage of living in the spirit of Egypt, that even as Christians—as ones who have received redemption—we still, because of anguish of spirit and the focus of our eyes and our senses, refuse to hearken to the spirit of redemption. We do not walk in the spirit of redemption, but rather in the spirit of Egypt. God's kids have always wanted to go back into Egypt. God calls His people out of Egypt. But His people continually want to go back. This is the continuing drama of the Bible. And it will continue to the end of the church age.

God First Speaks in Egypt

We see clearly the promise of redemption. Now let us look more closely at God's beginning of this plan. God's children had been in Egypt for four hundred years. They had been oppressed, repressed, and suppressed. We will begin in Exodus 12:

> And the Lord spake unto Moses and Aaron in the land of Egypt...
> (Exod. 12:1).

Notice! They were **in** Egypt. Not out of Egypt. God first speaks redemptively to us in Egypt. And He speaks to us one message. That message is "Come out." Make a decision to come out. That is the beginning of the redemption plan. God calls, but we must walk out in body, mind, and spirit.

God continued instructing Moses:

> Speak ye unto all the congregation of Israel, saying, In the tenth day of this month… (Exod. 12:3).

What month is that? Look at verse 2:

> This month shall be unto you the beginning of months: it shall be the first month of the year to you (Exod. 12:2).

Now, that is significant. We will soon see what significance these details have in tying the Old and the New Testaments together.

> Speak ye unto all the congregation of Israel, saying, In the tenth day of this month they shall take to them every man a lamb, according to the house of their fathers, a lamb for an house:…Your lamb shall be without blemish, a male of the first year…. And they shall take of the blood, and strike it on the two side posts and on the upper door post of the houses, wherein they shall eat it…. And thus shall ye eat it; with your loins girded, your shoes on your feet, and your staff in your hand; and ye shall eat it in haste: it is the Lord's Passover. For I will pass through the land of Egypt this night, and will smite all the firstborn in the land of Egypt, both man and beast; and against all the gods of Egypt I will execute judgment: I am the Lord. And the blood shall be to you for a token upon the houses where ye are: and when I see the blood, I will pass over you, and the plague shall not be upon you to destroy you, when I smite the land of Egypt (Exod. 12:3, 5, 7, 11–13).

The redemptive promise was made in Egypt. It was the first month of the year. Exodus 23:15 tells us it was in the time appointed of the month Abib. That was the Hebrew word for the first month of the year. It was in that month they were told to conduct this first Passover feast. It is continually referred to as "the Passover" from this chapter on. And so we find in Matthew 26:16–20:

> Now the first day of the feast of unleavened bread [another name for the extended Passover] the disciples came to Jesus, saying unto Him, Where wilt thou that we prepare for thee to eat the Passover? And He said, Go into the city to such a man, and say unto him, The Master saith, My time is at hand; I will keep the Passover at thy house with my disciples. And the disciples did as Jesus had appointed them; and they made ready the Passover. Now when the even was come, he sat down with the twelve.

A Lamb vs. *the* Lamb

The first Passover, which we call "the Lord's Supper" or "Communion," was held in Exodus 12. Verse 3 instructed, "...they shall take to them every man a lamb." In John, chapter 1, Jesus came to John the Baptist to be baptized, and John the Baptist cried out, "Behold **the** Lamb of God which taketh away the sin of the world." In Exodus they were to take every man "**a** lamb," one for every household. But John cried, "Behold **the** Lamb of God, which taketh away the sin of the world."

Then we find in Hebrews 10:10 that we are "sanctified by the body of Jesus, once for all." We then understand why John declared, "Behold THE Lamb of God." Jesus was that sacrifice. Once for all. He was **the** Passover Lamb, once for all. The apostle Paul repeated the words of Jesus when He introduced the Lord's Supper: "This is my body [the symbol of My body]...He then took the cup, saying, "...drink all of it in remembrance of me." Where is the remembrance? It extends back beyond Christ to the Passover in Egypt. And so we sing the wonderful words of the song that reminds us of what God said:

When I see the blood,
When I see the blood,
When I see the blood,
I will pass, I will pass over you.

The blood covers it all. Without the shedding of blood there is no remission of sin (Heb. 9:22; Lev. 17:11). "The life of the flesh is in the blood" (Lev. 17:11). We all died spiritually in Adam's bloodline. But Christ, as the second and last Adam through the virgin birth, gave us the opportunity to be "reborn" into the bloodline of Christ, uncontaminated by death-producing sin, that we might be "made alive" (1 Cor. 15:21–22).

Are You without Spot, without Blemish?

Moses instructed Israel, "your lamb shall be without blemish" (Exod. 12:5). We are told that Jesus was without spot (Heb. 9:14). **The** Lamb of God was without blemish, without spot. And we too must be without spot. Jesus, when He ascended back to the Father, left a visible church as His visible presence in the earth to be both salt and light (see John 20:21). When Christ returns He will not receive a blemished church. This is serious business! We can claim to be "washed in the blood," but if we are not walking in righteousness, we are blemished and unreceivable in His presence (see Eph. 5:27).

Peter also warned that we must be found "without spot, and blameless," requiring that we "be diligent" (2 Pet. 3:14). These scriptures fight with some folks' theology, but they cannot be ignored. We ignore or attempt to explain away inconvenient passages at our personal peril. God needs to get His bride shaped up and cleaned up, because His bride is all spotted and blemished. We cannot enter the presence of a Holy God with spot or with blemish. That means a lot of cleaning up for most of us. And the message of this book deals with these issues closest to God's heart, as the time of Christ's return approaches.

God required that the blood be on the doorposts and lintel (Exod. 12:7). That symbolized being over everything in the life of the inhabitant. It was on the sides and on the top. It was all over everything. Similarly we find other places in the Old Testament where the priests had to put blood on the tips of the ears and on the nose. It was a symbol of being over everything—covering all. And without the shedding of blood there could be no remission of sin.

In Exodus 12:46 we have been told, "...neither shall ye break a bone..." of the sacrifice, or of the lamb. Likewise, we find in John 19:33–36 that when Jesus was on the cross, with the thieves on both sides, the soldiers came and broke the legs of the thieves. But when they came to Jesus, they found that He was already dead. So they thrust the sword in His side, the blood flowed out, but they did not break His legs because He was already dead, "that the scripture should be fulfilled, A bone of him shall not be broken" (John 19:36). Unspotted and unblemished. A perfect sacrifice.

So there we have the basic picture of the Passover. The Word of the Lord regarding the Passover came when they were in the land of Egypt. In Egypt.

We must return now to Revelation 11. It is a very unusual passage, but it has great import for us as Christians. It speaks about the two great witnesses in the last days. In the time of the seven-year period often referred to as "the tribulation," there will be two great witnesses for the Lord who will be given power to do great miracles. They will be preaching the Word with great boldness and will be hated by the inhabitants of earth so much so that those on planet earth will seek to get rid of them. Finally they will be killed, and we are told:

> And their dead bodies shall lie in the street of the great city, which spiritually is called Sodom and Egypt, where also our Lord was crucified (Rev. 11:8).

Where was Jesus crucified? In the eyes of God, Jesus was crucified in Egypt. Now, you say, "He was crucified just outside of Jerusalem on a hill called Golgotha." That is true. But in God's eyes, He was crucified in Egypt, because Jerusalem—her people and leadership—were, spiritually speaking, living in Egypt.

They were going through religious forms. They were very religious. They even claimed to believe God's Word. They even believed that God was. They believed it all. Their doctrine and creed were correct. But they did not operate in them. They lived religiously but did not believe God. And faith is not something abstract. Faith is taking God at His Word. It is walking step by step on the Word of God.

The Jews of Jerusalem were not willing to truly take God at His word. They suffered from a case of severe head-knowledge. Like ours, theirs was a creedal faith but not a credible faith. And from God's viewpoint, they were walking in Egypt. God's Word declares that Jesus was crucified in Egypt. That is where the redemption took place. In Egypt. That is why we had to go back to Exodus 12:1 and see that the message of redemption came to Moses in Egypt. And so also it came to Jesus in Egypt. He was crucified in Egypt. That is where the redemption was fulfilled.

How Did Jerusalem Become Egypt?

Let us take another look at why God declared Jesus' crucifixion outside the gates of Jerusalem, a crucifixion "in Egypt." We will find the key in Exodus. We are going to see a pattern that is, and has always been, the same.

> And Moses and Aaron came in unto Pharaoh, and said unto him, Thus saith the Lord God of the Hebrews. How long wilt thou refuse to humble thyself before me? Let My people go, that they may serve Me (Exod. 10:3).

God has said and is saying, "How long, Pharaoh? How long, Egypt? How long, God's kids, who are living in Egypt, will you refuse to humble yourself before Me?" How long will you stay in Egypt? Pharaoh had a choice. You and I have the same choice. Will we humble ourselves? Will we choose to submit to God's authority when our personal notions, traditions, ideas, education, or beliefs disagree, in whole or in part?

The Egyptians knew about God. They knew a lot about God. Pharaoh knew about God, but he hardened his heart, and he refused to humble himself. He made a choice to stay in Egypt and to keep Israel there as well. We will find that God's kids were redeemed out, but they made a choice to go back. They made a choice to go right back in to the house of bondage. It seems foolish, but most of us do the same thing. We all have our reasons. But the problem is pride. Pharaoh refused to humble himself, and so do we.

A rough-and-tumble, crusty Gentile governor understood why Jesus was crucified. This understanding did not come out of the church or the synagogue. It came from a Roman governor who found himself personally trapped in a Judean web of political correctness. But he could see the problem very clearly: "For he [Pilate] knew that for envy they had delivered him [Jesus]" (Matt. 27:18). What is the source of envy? Pride! That is what it is. And we are about to see just how stinky such envy, born of pride, can get.

We must look at the story of Lazarus, whom Jesus loved. Lazarus had died. His body had been in the grave three days, and Jesus came to minister to him.

> Much people of the Jews therefore knew that He [Jesus] was there: and they came not for Jesus' sake only, but that they might see Lazarus also, whom He had raised from the dead. **But the chief priests consulted that they might put Lazarus also to death. Because that by reason of him many of the Jews went away, and believed on Jesus** (John 12:9–11).

The chief priests had a pride problem. They wanted to be in control. They loved the perks that followed from power and position. They believed that God existed, but they wanted to be in control of the religious system. And anything that got in the way, whether it was a doctrine or a person—anything that they perceived to threaten their ability to hang on to the reins of their religion—they were going to do away with. It was a severe pride problem.

People today in the church have the same problem, from pulpit to pew. That is one reason why people cannot or will not believe God's Word. They run up against a portion of the Word that contradicts their tradition or what somebody taught them, or that is different from what their experience tells them, or that threatens their position or power. And they would rather hold on to their experience or what somebody told them, or to grasp on to power than to yield to what God tells them. They want to be in control of the situation. And so their pride and stubbornness keeps them locked up in Egypt, just like it kept Pharaoh, and ultimately Israel, locked up in Egypt.

And yet we still go through the motions. We may attend church on the Sabbath, or twice on Sunday and again on Wednesday nights. We may sing in the choir. But we are still in Egypt because we cannot or will not receive. We do not want to let go of the reins and let God be our Father.

Some may find this a little hard to grasp or understand. To others it may seem harsh. Hopefully it is beginning to come across. John gives us a further window on this faith-quenching, spirit-killing problem. There were even some religious leaders who wanted to believe Jesus, and did.

> Nevertheless among the chief rulers also many believed on Him; but because of the Pharisees they did not confess Him, lest they should be put out of the synagogue: **For they loved the praise of men more than the praise of God** (John 12:42–43).

What did they love? They loved the system, the spirit of the city. They loved the religious organization of things that kept them in control. They loved power, perks, and position. And even when they could see the truth, they refused to accept it and confess it with their own mouth. They refused to publicly agree with God. Paul advised us of the unmistakable consequences of such spiritual gamesmanship.

> That if thou shalt confess with thy mouth the Lord Jesus, and shalt believe in thine heart that God hath raised Him from the dead, thou shalt be saved.

For with the heart man believeth unto righteousness; and with the mouth
confession is made unto salvation (Rom. 10:9–10).

If you do not confess it, you do not have it! Jesus said if you will not confess
Him before men, neither will He acknowledge you before His Father in heaven
(see Matt.10:32–33). This is a fundamental spiritual principle that pertains
to all of God's Word and promises. It has to do with humility. If you cannot
or will not confess it with your mouth—grab ahold of it, and appropriate it
for yourself, boldly and openly—you are still walking in Egypt. You are still
walking with Pharaoh, refusing to humble yourself. It is a tough place to be.
It is the point of decision. It is the fulcrum over which faith turns. And that is
true, whether we are speaking of redemption or embracing any of the principles
and promises of God. Jerusalem becomes Egypt in the mind of God through
religious pride, the lust for power, and refusal to agree with Him at each point
of His Word.

Egypt Is Pursuing You!

We are going to see what happened right after God's redemption in the
Passover. Remember, God had explained to Moses the significance of the
Passover:

Remember this day, in which ye came out from Egypt, out of the house
of bondage; for by strength of hand the Lord brought you out from this
place...in the month of Abib (Exod. 13:3–4).

God told Moses that the Passover would be a memorial forever. It would
be a permanent memorial from that time on for the children of Israel (see
Exod. 13:9). "But the Egyptians pursued after them..." (Exod. 14:9). Do
you know Egypt is pursuing after Christians today? It pursues after us more
than we know. We are not usually aware of it. But Egypt is always pursuing
us. It is pursuing you. And here Egypt pursued them: "...all the horses and
chariots...."

Why do you think David said, "Some trust in chariots and some trust in
horses, but we will trust in the name of the Lord our God" (Ps. 20:7)? What
do you think he is talking about? Egypt is symbolized by chariots and horses,
or any man-made device designed to take the reigns away from God. That is
true even of religious systems, especially if they purport to be Christian. God
said, "I'll be a father unto you. I'll be your healer. I'll be your provider. I'll be
your Savior, your Lord, your protector. I'll be everything. I AM."

But many of us say, "No, Lord. I'll receive only salvation from sin. I
don't believe in the rest of those things. My mother did not believe it. My
pastors said it was not for today. So I do not believe it." What do you call it
when a person elevates human wisdom, experience, or teachings over what

God clearly says in His Word? It is PRIDE wrapped tightly in religious cloak to camouflage its rebellion in religious trappings. And we end up shifting our trust to "chariots and horses." Our chariots and horses may be doctors, conservative politics, liberal politics, religious traditions or systems. Anything that becomes a substitute for God's power.

"And when Pharaoh drew nigh, the children of Israel lifted up their eyes" (Exod. 14:10*a*). That always gets God's people in trouble: when they lift up their eyes and their ears and they start looking around to the circumstances. That is the first step toward going back to Egypt. And every time God's kids did it, they went back to Egypt. That is what happened when they saw the giants, in Numbers 13–14; that is what happened when they saw no water; that is what happened when the water was bitter; that is what happened when there was no food. They whined and complained, preferring to trust their lot to the power of Egypt rather than the power of God. Each time, they cried to go back to Egypt: "Would God that we had died in Egypt!" "Were it not better for us to return into Egypt?" "Let us make us a captain; and let us return into Egypt" (Num. 14:2–4).

> And when Pharaoh drew nigh, the children of Israel lifted up their eyes, and behold, the Egyptians marched after them; and they were sore afraid; and the children of Israel cried out unto the Lord. And they said unto Moses, because there were no graves in Egypt, hast thou taken us away to die in the wilderness? Wherefore hast thou dealt thus with us, to carry us forth out of Egypt? (Exod. 14:10–11)

Have You Also Longed for Egypt?

They wanted to go back. When did they want to go back? Right after they came out. They were sitting in front of the Red Sea. That is when they wanted to go back. They had spent four hundred years in bondage, and they still wanted to go back. And God's kids are still wanting to go back, even though they have been in bondage. Can you honestly say that you have not struggled with going back to Egypt? I fear most Christians live at least on the border of Egypt and take frequent journeys across the border, driven largely by fear and by inability or refusal to truly trust God.

Remember with me. The children of Israel were told to go into the Promised Land. Ten spies came back with an evil report, but two spies—Joshua and Caleb—came back with a good report that agreed with God. And God observed that Joshua and Caleb had "another spirit" (Num. 14:24). It was a different spirit. It was a spirit that would inherit the promises of the kingdom of God. Note! Only two men received the promise of God. Only two men stood in the position of being true children of God, children who would inherit the promise of their Father. Only two stood as family members to receive a father's promise. Yet all of them professed to be children of God.

They were of the "chosen" people, the children of Israel, by name. But they did not receive the promise. They were living in the spirit of Egypt, yet God was looking for men that had another spirit: His spirit.

> Woe to the rebellious children, saith the Lord, that taketh counsel, but not of me; and that cover with a covering but not of My spirit, that they may add sin to sin: That walk to go down into Egypt, and have not asked at my mouth; to strengthen themselves in the strength of Pharaoh, and to trust in the shadow of Egypt! Therefore shall the strength of Pharaoh be your shame, and the trust in the shadow of Egypt your confusion (Isa. 30:1–3).

"Woe...to them that go down into Egypt." We can now understand why the writer to the Hebrew church gave dire warning:

> Today if ye will hear his voice, harden not your hearts...Take heed, brethren, lest their be in any of you an evil heart of unbelief, in departing from the living God (Heb. 3:7–8, 12).

> To whom sware he that they should not enter into his rest, but to them who believed not? So we see that they could not enter in because of unbelief. Let us therefore fear, lest a promise being left us of entering into his rest, any of you should seem to come short of it (Heb. 3:18–19, 4:1–2).

Communion: Cup of Blessing or Damnation?

You say, "What in the world does this all have to do with Communion, and the Lord's Supper and the Passover?" Well, God ties His whole Word together. It is all part and parcel of the same theme. Consider again the familiar words regarding the Lord's Supper:

> For I have received of the Lord that which also I delivered unto you, That the Lord Jesus the same night in which He was betrayed took bread: And when He had given thanks, He brake it, and said, Take, eat: this is My body, which is broken for you: this do in remembrance of Me. After the same manner also He took the cup, when He had supped, saying, This cup is the new testament in My blood: this do ye as oft as ye drink it, in remembrance of Me. For as often as ye eat this bread, and drink this cup, ye do shew the Lord's death till He come. Wherefore whosoever shall eat this bread, and drink this cup of the Lord, unworthily, shall be guilty of the body and blood of the Lord. But let a man examine himself, and so let him eat of that bread and drink of that cup. **For he that eateth and drinketh unworthily, eateth and drinketh damnation to himself, not discerning the Lord's body.** For this cause many are weak and

sickly among you, and many sleep. For if we would judge ourselves, we should not be judged (1 Cor. 11:23–31).

In Exodus 23, God has given us a summary expression of what He understands the meaning of Passover to be. In 1 Corinthians 11, the apostle Paul has warned us that we should not eat or drink of the cup unworthily, not discerning the Lord's body. Let us look again at Exodus 23:

> Thou shalt keep the feast of unleavened bread [Passover, communion, the Lord's supper]:…for in it thou camest out from Egypt: and none shall appear before me empty…. But if thou shalt indeed obey his voice [the voice of the Lord through the angel], and do all that I speak; then I will be an enemy unto thine enemies, and an adversary unto thine adversaries…. And ye shall serve the Lord your God, and He shall bless thy bread, and thy water; and I will take sickness away from the midst of thee. There shall nothing cast their young, nor be barren, in thy land: the number of thy days I will fulfill. I will send my fear before thee, and will destroy all the people to whom thou shalt come, and I will make all thine enemies turn their backs unto thee…. Thou shalt make no covenant with them [i.e., the people in the land], nor with their gods. They shall not dwell in thy land, lest they make thee sin against me: for if thou serve their gods, it will surely be a snare unto thee (vss. 15, 22, 25–27, 32–33).

Will you take a closer look with me? First of all, this is a celebration of coming out of Egypt. **Communion, for God's children, is always a celebration of coming out of Egypt**, as well as of our Lord's death and resurrection. If it is a celebration purely **in** Egypt, then it is not a memorial. It is a celebration of coming **out** of Egypt. If we do not understand or comprehend the implication and meaning of what it is to come out of Egypt, it probably means that we are still in Egypt, and therefore, Paul has written in 1 Corinthians 11: "For this cause many are weak and sickly among you, and many sleep [die]." Paul was calling his readers, and us, to a knowledge and understanding of what this means.

Exodus 23:33 says that God will be an enemy unto our enemies. In other words, He is going to be a protector. God wants to be your protector. Is that not what a father is supposed to do in the family? He is supposed to be the protector for the family.

Verse 25 declares, "And ye shall serve the Lord your God, and He shall bless thy bread, and thy water." What is God saying? He is going to be our provision: "I AM your provider. I AM Jehovah Jireh. In every situation, I AM. And I will be the provider of all of your needs."

Verse 25 also says, "I will take sickness away from the midst of thee." That is not spiritual sickness, it is physical sickness. That is part of God's concern. He is concerned about your physical and spiritual sickness, as well. It is all-encompassing.

Then in verse 27, God says, "I will send my fear before thee, and will destroy all the people...." In other words, because of His power and His concern, God is going to send His fear, so that we need not fear. Isaiah understood it this way when he wrote God's message: "Fear not: for I have redeemed thee, I have called thee by thy name; thou art mine." He will be with you when you "pass through the rivers" and when you "walk through the fire" (Isa. 43:2).

Finally, we read in verses 32 and 33: "Thou shalt make no covenant" with those other people or their gods; "they shall not dwell in thy land, lest they make thee sin against me." God is saying, "Be ye holy, for I am holy."

In simple language God says, "If you are going to take on the ways of my household, you must know that it is the household of faith. I am a holy God and you should be holy people. Come apart and be separate. Trust me completely. Leave Egypt."

Let us look even further at 1 Corinthians 11:29–30:

> For he that eateth and drinketh unworthily, eateth and drinketh damnation to himself, not discerning the Lord's body. For this cause many are weak and sickly among you, and many sleep.

"Not discerning the Lord's body." What does this mean? First of all, 2 Corinthians 5:21 tells us that Jesus became sin for us, because He knew no sin, that we might be made the righteousness of God in Him. He became sin. He became the sin man. Sin was put on Him just like it was put on that scapegoat back in Exodus. Once a year, the Israelites would lay their hands on that scapegoat and send him out into the wilderness to take away the sin of the people. That is what Jesus became: our scapegoat. All of the sin of the world—my sin and your sin—was laid on Him, and He became sin for me, because He knew no sin, that I might be literally made the righteousness of God in Him. He took the death penalty that God's justice required for my sin.

Yet it is not my own righteousness, because my righteousness is like filthy rags (Isa. 64:6). It is His righteousness that I have been given. I must confess it with my mouth. If all I confess is filthy rags, I am not owning up to and acknowledging the good thing that God has done in me through Christ Jesus. Therefore faith does not come. My faith will be made effectual, operational, and active only by acknowledging every good thing that is in me in Christ Jesus (Philem. 6).

Are you partaking of the Communion cup unworthily? Are you properly discerning the Lord's body? If I eat and drink unworthily—not properly discerning, accepting, and confessing all that Christ did for me—Paul says I eat and drink damnation to myself rather than blessing (1 Cor. 11:29–30). This must not be taken lightly.

Have You Received All His Benefits?

We discussed first the idea of redemption from sin, because that is the most important thing. It restores our relationship with God. David has given us further insight into the fullness of the redemptive plan. The psalmist was remembering God's promises to His people as they came out of Egypt:

> Bless the Lord, O my soul: and all that is within me, bless His holy name. Bless the Lord, O my soul, and forget not **all** His benefits: Who forgiveth all thine iniquities; who healeth all thy diseases (Ps. 103:1–3).

David began with benefit number one: "who forgiveth all thine iniquities." Then he told of benefit number two: "who healeth all thy diseases." When we pray, we have two primary prayer requests. Number one is for healing of the soul, of forgiveness of sin, and reception of the redemption of Christ. Number two is for healing of the body. David was no different. He saw healing of the body as part of the redemptive package. And the God of Abraham, Isaac, and Israel (who has established His Kingdom through Christ upon the throne of David) has not changed. God's reminder continues: "Remember **all** my benefits."

Our celebration of the Lord's Supper is a time of remembrance. It is a remembrance not only of His sacrifice but also of ALL the benefits flowing from Christ's substitutionary sacrifice. For this reason, the apostle Paul has warned that if we are not fully "discerning the Lord's body," then "many are weak and sickly among [us] and many sleep" (1 Cor. 11:29–30).

Isaiah foretold the completeness of the Messiah's mission and redemptive offering of Himself as the Lamb of God:

> Surely He [Jesus] hath borne our griefs, and carried our sorrows: yet we did esteem Him stricken, smitten of God, and afflicted. But He was wounded for our transgressions, He was bruised for our iniquities: the chastisement of our peace was upon Him; and with His stripes we are healed (Isa. 53:4–5).

The word *grief* in the Hebrew means "disease, malady, calamity, sickness, and anxiety." That is right from *Strong's Concordance*. Surely Christ has borne my disease, malady, calamity, sickness, and anxiety. Isaiah then declared, "...with His stripes we are healed." Yes we are "healed" spiritually by being forgiven and reconciled to God. But that is not to the exclusion of physical healing. The Gospel of Matthew makes this abundantly clear, compelling us to embrace the full implications of redemption or else risk intellectual dishonesty and spiritual unbelief. Matthew made direct reference to the specific passage in Isaiah 53:4–5, which we have just reviewed.

> When the even was come, they brought unto Him many that were possessed with devils: and He cast out the spirits with His Word, and healed

all that were sick: **That it might be fulfilled which was spoken by Esaias the prophet, saying, Himself took our infirmities, and bare our sicknesses** (Matt. 8:16–17).

I must admit that I do not understand all of that. And neither does the most learned theologian. We do not fully understand salvation from sin either, nor the resurrection. My job is not to understand how God divided the Red Sea when Moses stretched out his rod over it. My job is, as Moses' was, to put the rod over the sea and let God do the rest of it. It is ALL by faith! But notice, before he stretched the rod over the sea, Moses was crying and commiserating, acting anything but faith-filled. He gave the religious look of faith saying, "The Lord shall fight for you…" (Exod. 14:14). Yet inside, his unbelief shouted, "What am I going to do? All these people are screaming and hollering!" He could hear the horses of Pharaoh thundering down. He was terror stricken, but trying desperately to muster courage.

Then God spoke to him and said, "Moses, what do you cry out to me for? **You** stretch out the rod." Now Moses did not divide the Red Sea, but Moses had to stretch out the rod. In other words, Moses had to **do** an act of faith to demonstrate that he believed God. Then God performed on his behalf. The same is true of salvation from sin. I must come to God in total humility and in total faith. It is by faith, and faith alone. Yet I must repent, I must believe, and I must confess. My acts reveal my faith.

The Psalmist understood what happened when the children of Israel came out of Egypt. He reported there was not one feeble one among them—not one among the whole nation, which had been under physical, mental, and emotional oppression. There was not one feeble among them when they came **out** of Egypt. When they were **in** Egypt, they had all they could stand. But when they came out, Scripture records there was not one feeble among them. Amazing!

Returning to our "Lord's Supper" passage, we find a similar focus, yet a reverse report: "For this cause many are weak and sickly among you, and many sleep." When we fully and completely "discern the Lord's body," the Scriptures—from Old Covenant to New Covenant—reveal unequivocally that redemption from sin is accompanied also with health and restoration by God, who is also Jehovah Rapha, the Lord our healer. If we accept salvation from sin without the rest of the package, we have, in a sense, been delivered from Egypt but refuse to enter the Promised Land. It was precisely such unbelief that kept a nation of "chosen people" from receiving the full benefit of leaving Egypt.

Deliverance from material need is similarly promised. Again, the apostle Paul has made a striking statement, linking the substitutionary life and death of Christ to His meeting even the practical needs of the human condition.

> For ye know the grace of our Lord Jesus Christ, that though He was rich, yet for your sakes He became poor, that ye through His poverty might be rich [or have full supply].

That is the New Testament. We cannot escape it. We can rationalize it, editorialize it, or spiritualize it. But then we are confronted with the very obvious, practical, and material references in the Old Testament to the same redemptive program. God made the promise to his children when they came out of Egypt: "…ye shall not go out empty" (Exod. 3:21). Moses reported that when the Israelites left Egypt, they came out with "great substance" just as God had promised Abraham four hundred years earlier (see Exod. 12:35–36; 15:13–14). Remember, we are talking about properly "discerning the Lord's body" as part of the fullness of the redemptive plan.

Consider deliverance from fear. The apostle Paul again has reminded us in Romans 8:15:

> For ye have not received the spirit of bondage again to fear; but ye have received the Spirit of adoption, whereby we cry, Abba, Father.

This is language drawn from (and leading us again to consider) the fear endemic to the bondage of Egypt.

> For God hath not given us the spirit of fear; but of power, and of love, and of a sound mind (2 Tim. 1:7).

And finally, Paul has told us that "the last enemy that shall be destroyed is death" (1 Cor. 15:20). Death was conquered by Jesus, but we do not receive the benefit of that until the last resurrection. Until our resurrection. All of these other benefits we have discussed are present benefits. "Forget not all his benefits." Are you properly and fully discerning the Lord's body?

What Is Your Response?

So what should be our response? God, through Moses, brought ten devastating plagues upon the land of Egypt to display His power and to crush Pharaoh's pride.

> But against any of the children of Israel shall not a dog move his tongue, against man or beast: that ye may know how that the Lord doth put a difference between the Egyptians and Israel (Exod. 11:7).

When the plagues came on the Egyptians, none of the hail fell on the Israelites. None of the plagues fell on the Israelites. None of the flies. None of the lice. None of the darkness. None of it fell on the Israelites. And whoever, by faith, painted the redemptive blood of the sacrificial lamb on his door posts was saved from the deadly wages of sin as the death angel passed on to destroy the firstborn.

What do you think God was trying to tell his kids? He was and is still trying to say that He puts a difference between those who will live in the spirit of Egypt and those who will live as the Israel of God. By faith we must totally trust Him and take Him at His Word. And there will be a difference. Even in the church "of the redeemed" there will be many who will refuse to receive the promised benefits. We have turned unbelief into an art form that smells and looks religious. Remember, that is precisely why God declared Jesus to have been crucified in Sodom and Egypt (see Rev. 11:8).

There will be those who, by faith, will reach for the health and healing of Jehovah Rapha. As a pattern, they will grow in health and strength. Others will continue to deny it is for today.

There will be some who will always be in poverty and embrace it as a friend. Then there will be others who, increasingly, as they walk in God's ways, begin to walk out of poverty and into a full supply. That does not mean we are all going to have mansions covering every hilltop. We are not talking about a display of wealth. We are talking about walking in God's supply in order to fulfill our individual purpose on the earth.

There will be those who will walk in fear all their life, because they choose to walk in fear. But those who will begin to walk under the Fatherhood of God and walk out of Egypt will begin to walk out of fear, as well.

That is the promise of God. That is part and parcel of the fullness of the redemptive plan. "I put a difference between Egypt and Israel," declares the Lord. **We must fully discern the Lord's body before He returns for His Bride.**

> For this cause many are weak and sickly among you, and many sleep.

Pray with me: Father, I partake of the elements of Communion with You and with those of like faith whom You have placed in my life. I confess—even though my heart's desire is to walk in the fullness of Your promise and redemptive plan—that I have fallen far short in unbelief. I confess that I will walk as the "Israel of God." I will take You at Your Word. I will take step one, as You will reveal it to me. Then I will take steps two and three, that I may discern Jesus' body and not trample it under foot again, as the high priests did. Open my heart now, as I partake. Lord, I believe.

Why Are Some Not Healed?

Let us become brutally honest! Some are not healed. Some walk in poverty. Many walk in fear. And most walk in unbelief. We should cry out with doubting Thomas, "Lord, I believe. Help thou my unbelief." But is all sickness, all poverty, all fear due to unbelief. None of us truly knows for sure, but probably not. Yet that should not be an excuse for us to embrace denial or unbelief. Down deep, you know whether you truly accept God's Word as we have opened it in this chapter. God certainly knows. And Satan will play upon your weakness.

But we must also realize we live in a fallen world. All died in Adam. With sin came disease, selfishness, poverty, sickness, fear, and ultimately death. If, as Paul says, "The last enemy that shall be destroyed is death" (1 Cor. 15:26), apparently the other enemies, from God's viewpoint, are already destroyed, including poverty, sickness, fear, and the agent of fear himself: Satan. Is there a reason, then, why we do not see the full manifestation of these promises in "real time" in our lives? The answer is yes. But again it should not be shouldered as a holy cop-out for not taking God wholly at His Word on these points.

The answer has to do with the nature of the Kingdom of God. Simply stated, the Kingdom is both NOW and LATER. The promises are fully for NOW, but we will not experience them in their absolute totality until LATER. This is why the apostle Paul reminded us, "For now we see through a glass darkly" (1 Cor. 13:12). But because we do not fully comprehend does not excuse us from fully believing.

This should not be that difficult to understand if we consider the matter of sin. Have you received the redemption of Christ for sin? Have you received His forgiveness? Do you have assurance of eternal life? Do you sin? Of course you do. Then why has the apostle John so boldly said that "whosoever is born of God sinneth not" (1 John 5:18)? The answer, again, is that we live in a fallen world. Even the great apostle Paul struggled against the flesh and sin (see Rom. 6–7).

Our flesh battles against the Spirit constantly. That is the primary nature of Christian warfare. But if the battle was already won at the cross, why must we yet do battle with sin? Why has the apostle Paul warned us, "Take heed, brethren, lest there be in any of you an evil heart of unbelief, in departing from the living God" (Heb. 3:12)? It is because the Kingdom is both NOW and LATER.

We are reminded, "we have this treasure in earthen vessels" (2 Cor. 4:7). Why? Because while "the Kingdom of God is within you" and "All the promises of God in Him are yes, and in Him Amen," we still live this side of glory, or heaven (see Luke 17:21 and 2 Cor. 1:20). For this reason, Jesus dramatically declared, "From the days of John the Baptist until now the Kingdom of Heaven suffereth violence, and the violent take it by force (Matt. 11:12). This is not physical or political violence. It is a serious confrontation with the spirit of this world, the spirit of Antichrist, the spirit of Egypt. We must press on and continue to press into kingdom living and believing. You will be sorely tempted to unbelief. But unbelief is sin and can, if indulged long enough, relegate you to the "lake that burneth with fire" (Rev. 21:8).

Any denial or refusal to accept ALL God's benefits and His clear instructions in His Word is walking in unbelief. It is walking back to Egypt. Jesus came to give us "rest," but Paul warned the church that it must labor to enter into that rest. Why? Because the spirit of Egypt is pressing upon us.

Let us conclude this chapter with Paul's serious warning against all forms of unbelief. His words are an express reference to Numbers 13 and 14 in which we are informed that only two adult men—men of God's chosen people who walked out of Egypt—entered the Promised Land. Through stubborn unbelief, the rest died, not having received the promise.

> And to whom sware he that they should not enter into his rest, but to them that believed not. So we see that they could not enter in because of unbelief. Let us therefore fear, lest a promise being left us of entering into His rest, any of you should seem to come short of it. For unto us was the gospel preached, as well as unto them: but the word preached did not profit them, not being mixed with faith in them that heard it (Heb. 3:18–19; 4:1–2).

Take God at His Word in every area. Trust Him as to ALL His benefits. Then leave the results to Him, not allowing your faith to waver. Believe God! You will need such faith for the times that are coming.

Chapter Fourteen

Covenant and Curse

*How does the curse come? Can a "Christian" be under the
curse? Is America under the curse? Can we walk
free from the curse?*

GOD'S SALVATION IS COMPLETE SALVATION! It is salvation from the entire curse of the law. You may be thinking, *What curse? I didn't know I was under a curse!* But God's Word clearly indicates that everyone created in His image is under a curse. It is called "the curse of the Law." This should interest and concern every professing Christian. Yet many have never been taught concerning this serious matter. Therefore, you may need to ask the Lord to open your mind and heart concerning the truths we are about to discuss.

Did the Prophets Understand the Curse?

To get correct bearings regarding the curse of the Law, we must look at Israel and the curse. What understanding did Israel have throughout her history as to the meaning of the curse of the Law? We will begin with the prophet Daniel, who has given us such a bold example of faith and courage.

> In the first year of his [King Ahasuerus'] reign I Daniel understood by books the number of the years, whereof the word of the Lord came to Jeremiah the prophet, that he would accomplish seventy years in the desolations of Jerusalem. And I set my face unto the Lord God, to seek by prayer and supplications, with fasting, and sackcloth, and ashes: And I prayed unto the Lord my God, and made my confession, and said, O

Lord, the great and dreadful God, **keeping the covenant and mercy to them that keep His commandments** (Dan. 9:2–4).

God is a God of mercy, but He is a dreadful God, keeping covenant and mercy. Covenant is something that is legal—"If you…, then I…" Purely legal. No issue about it. It is the law. And God gave the Law. But He also gave Israel mercy. That is what the "mercy seat" was all about. God could look at Israel's performance of His Law through the mercy seat, extending His enabling grace, even though men and women were not perfect.

You may have thought that the New Testament is the place where God instituted the doctrine of grace. Not so. Jesus Christ is the same yesterday, today, and forever (Heb. 13:8). The grace of God was always manifested, and God revealed that when He gave instructions for Noah's ark, for the creation of the ark of the covenant, and for the mercy seat. He said that the mercy seat was going to be there so that when God looked down on the Law positioned under the mercy seat, He not only would see the perfection of the Law, but also would see men's imperfect performance through mercy.

It is important to know that the grace of God has always been there. God has not changed. God has always been a God of grace. But He also has always been a God of justice and a dreadful God. Noah "found grace" we are told in Genesis 6:8, but God still brought judgment and destroyed the earth with a flood.

Daniel, looking historically at the actions and the behavior of the children of Israel, and then taking a faith photograph of their present behavior, cried out to God in repentance, identifying himself with the sins of God's people.

> We have sinned, and have committed iniquity, and have done wickedly…. O Lord, to us belongeth confusion of face, to our kings, to our princes, and to our fathers, because we have sinned against thee. Neither have we obeyed the voice of the Lord our God…. Yea, all Israel have transgressed thy law, even by departing, that they might not obey thy voice; **therefore**… (Dan. 9:5–11).

The word *therefore* is a linking word. It indicates that something preceding it resulted in what followed. It is a causative linking word. Daniel continued:

> Yea, all Israel have transgressed thy law, even by departing, that they might not obey thy voice; therefore [because Israel transgressed] **the curse is poured upon us**, and the oath that is written in the law of Moses the servant of God, **because we have sinned** against Him (Dan. 9:11).

What is the curse? Daniel understood that many hundreds of years after Moses gave the Law, there was a curse of the Law. And Daniel said, "…**the** curse is poured upon us." He did not say it was **a** curse but called it "**the curse.**" Verse 13 of Daniel's account tells us where the pronouncement of the curse can be found:

> As it is written **in the law of Moses,** all this evil is coming upon us....

Daniel understood that there was a causative relationship between the behavior of God's children and the curse that came upon them. This principle is restated in the New Testament. God has warned through the apostle Paul:

> Be not deceived; God is not mocked: for whatsoever a man soweth, that shall he also reap (Gal. 6:7).

If we sow unbelief, we will reap the consequences of unbelief. If we sow anticovenant behavior, we will reap anticovenant behavior. God will not be mocked. He will not allow the spiritual laws and principles that He put into effect to be violated. They will work whether we understand them or not, whether we believe them or not, just as the law of gravity works. The law of gravity works, not because you can see it, but because God put it into place. No one on earth ever awoke comfortably resting on the ceiling of his house after sleeping all night! Whether or not you understand the law of gravity, it works. Whether or not you believe in gravity does not prevent its operation.

Whether or not you understand spiritual principles, they work. They are in operation. You may not recognize how they work today. You may not recognize how they work tomorrow or next week or next month or next year. But God said that we should not be deceived. He will not be mocked. What we sow, we will reap. And it will most likely be manifested some time in our life, as it was manifested in the time of Daniel.

Jeremiah also gave serious warning to God's people of the continuing application of the curse:

> The word that came to Jeremiah from the Lord, saying, Hear ye the words of this covenant, and speak unto the men of Judah, and to the inhabitants of Jerusalem; And say thou unto them, Thus saith the Lord God of Israel; **cursed be the man that obeyeth not the words of this covenant, Which I commanded your fathers in the day that I brought them forth out of the land of Egypt,** from the iron furnace, saying, Obey my voice, and do them, according to all which I command you: so shall ye be my people, and I will be your God: That I may perform the oath which I have sworn unto your fathers, to give them a land flowing with milk and honey, as it is this day. Then answered I, and said, So be it, O Lord. Then the Lord said unto me, Proclaim all these words in the cities of Judah, and in the streets of Jerusalem, saying, Hear ye the words of this covenant, and do them. For

> I earnestly protested unto your fathers in the day that I brought them up
> out of the land of Egypt, even unto this day, rising early and protesting,
> saying, Obey my voice. Yet they obeyed not, nor inclined their ear, but
> walked every one in the imagination of their evil heart: therefore I will bring
> upon them all the words of this covenant, which I commanded them to do;
> but they did them not. And the Lord said unto me. A conspiracy is found
> among the men of Judah, and among the inhabitants of Jerusalem. They
> are turned back to the iniquities of their forefathers, which refused to hear
> my words; and they went after other gods to serve them: the house of Israel
> and the house of Judah have broken my covenant which I made with their
> fathers. Therefore thus saith the Lord, Behold I will bring evil upon them,
> which they shall not be able to escape; and though they shall cry unto me, I
> will not hearken unto them. Then shall the cities of Judah and inhabitants
> of Jerusalem go, and cry unto the gods unto whom they offer incense: but
> they shall not save them at all in the time of their trouble. For according
> to the number of thy cities were thy gods, O Judah; and according to the
> number of the streets of Jerusalem have ye set up altars to that shameful
> thing, even altars to burn incense unto Baal (Jer. 11:1–13).

Please note again. It was the spirit of the city of men that caused the
children of Israel, God's children, to violate the covenant principles, thereby
bringing the curse upon them. That is why we spent three entire chapters
discerning the spirit of the city. And if you look back to Daniel 9, you will
find that he, too, mentions the city as being the key. The spirit of the city and
the curse merge.

If There Is a Curse, Is There a Blessing?

We see how the leaders and prophets of Israel understood, many hundreds
of years after the Exodus from Egypt, that there was a curse in active operation
and that it would come upon those who did not actively follow the covenant.
That theme echos into the New Testament. The apostle Paul stated:

> Christ hath redeemed us from the curse of the law, being made a curse
> for us: for it is written, Cursed is everyone that hangeth on a tree. That the
> blessing of Abraham might come on the Gentiles through Jesus Christ; that
> we might receive the promise of the Spirit through faith (Gal. 3:13–14).

Christ has redeemed us from the curse of the Law. He has redeemed us from a
curse related to His people coming out of Egypt, and it behooves us to find out
what the curse of the Law really is. Moses should be able to give us some help.

> For if ye shall keep all these commandments which I command you, to
> do them, to love the Lord your God, to walk in all his ways, and to cleave

unto him; Then will the Lord drive out all these nations from before you.... There shall no man be able to stand before you: for the Lord your God shall lay the fear of you and the dread of you upon all the land that ye shall tread upon, as he hath said unto you. **Behold, I set before you this day a blessing and a curse; A blessing, if ye obey** the commandments of the Lord your God, which I command you this day: **And a curse, if ye will not obey** the commandments of the Lord your God, but turn aside out of the way which I command you this day, to go after other gods, which ye have not known (Deut. 11:22–28).

God, through His servant Moses, warned the people of God. He was not speaking to the world here. He was not speaking to the Canaanites, the Amorites, the Amelekites, or any other "ites." He was speaking only to the Israelites, God's kids. It was a message to the children of God, not to the sinners. He said, "If you…, then I…" If you will obey this covenant, there will be a blessing. If you do not follow in it—if you wander away from turning your heart wholly to serve the Lord and to trust Him, to obey Him, to love Him, to walk by faith and not by sight—then there will be a cursing.

In Deuteronomy 28, we find a detailed account of the blessings and curses of the Law. It is the most full-blown recitation found in Scripture regarding these things. God is a God of justice, as well as of mercy. He says, "If you…, then I…" And He means business. Consider these wonderful words of blessing:

And it shall come to pass, **if thou shall hearken diligently** unto the voice of the Lord thy God, **to observe and to do all his commandments** which I command thee this day, that the Lord thy God will set thee on high above all nations of the earth. And **all these blessings shall come on thee, and overtake thee**, if thou shalt hearken unto the voice of the Lord thy God. **Blessed** shalt thou be in the city, and blessed shalt thou be in the field. **Blessed** shall be the fruit of thy body, and the fruit of thy ground, and the fruit of thy cattle, the increase of thy kine, and the flocks of thy sheep. **Blessed** shall be thy basket and thy store; **Blessed** shalt thou be when thou comest in, and blessed shalt thou be when thou goest out. The Lord shall cause thine enemies that rise up against thee to be smitten before thy face: they shall come out against thee one way, and flee before thee seven ways. **The Lord shall command the blessing upon thee** in thy storehouses, and in all that thou settest thine hand unto; and shall bless thee in the land which the Lord thy God giveth thee. **The Lord shall establish thee** an holy people unto Himself, as He hath sworn unto thee, **if thou shalt keep the commandments** of the Lord thy God, **and walk in His ways.** And all people of the earth shall see that thou art called by the name of the Lord; and they shall be afraid of thee. And the Lord shall grant you plenty of goods, in the fruit of your body, in the increase of your livestock, and in the produce of your ground, in the land of which the Lord swore to your fathers to give you. And the Lord shall open to you His good treasure, the heavens, to give the rain to your land in its season, and to bless all the work of your hand. You shall lend to many nations, but you shall not borrow. **And the Lord shall make you the head and not the tail**; you shall be above only, and not be beneath, **if you heed the commandments** of the Lord your God, which I command you today, **and are careful to observe them.** So you shall not turn aside from any of the words which I command you this day, to the right hand or to the left, to go after other gods to serve them (Deut. 28:1–14).

That is the blessing of the covenant! Can you receive that? Do you believe God said it? Have you noticed how readily Christians embrace the promises set out in the Old Testament? We love them! But have you also noticed how we cavalierly ignore or deny the conditions upon which those promises are based? We conveniently dismiss the conditions as so-called legalism.

Lest anyone should think, *Well, that is Old Testament; we are not in that dispensation any more. We are in the dispensation of Grace,* I would not hesitate to remind you of the words of James. The apostle warned New Testament Christians to "be…doers of the word and not hearers only, deceiving your own self." Christians of the early church were tempted to abandon obedience then, too. They were tempted to think that now they were operating under grace, and they no longer had to do what God said. And James took them to task.

As a matter of fact, there were apparently even some people at that time who thought it was enough just to believe that God exists. And James said, "Why do think you should pat yourself on the back and think that you are so great because God exists? Even the devil believes, and trembles" (see James 2:19). So it is not enough to believe that God is, "for He that cometh to God must [not only] believe that He is, but that He is the rewarder of them that diligently seek Him" (Heb. 11:6). The whole Word ties together. Jesus Christ is always the same, yesterday, today, and forever.

What Is the Curse?

We must now look at the curse of the Law, beginning with Deuteronomy 28:15:

Cursed shalt thou be in the city, and cursed shalt thou be in the field. **Cursed** shall be thy basket and thy store. **Cursed** shall be the fruit of thy body, and the fruit of thy land, the increase of thy kine, and the flocks of thy sheep. The Lord shall send upon thee cursing, vexation, and rebuke, in all that thou settest thine hand unto for to do…. The Lord shall smite thee with a consumption, and with a fever, and with an inflammation, and with an extreme burning, and with the sword, and with blasting, and with mildew…. The Lord shall smite thee with the botch of Egypt, and with the emerods, and with the scab, and with the itch, whereof thou canst not be healed. The Lord shall smite thee with madness, and blindness, and astonishment of heart; And thou shalt grope at noonday, as the blind gropeth in the darkness…" (vss. 15–29).

This is not pleasant to read. Yet it is just as important as the blessing. In fact, there are more than three times as many verses devoted to the curses of the law as are devoted to the blessings. They extend from verse 15 to verse 68 of this chapter. The blessings and curses were revealed to Israel just after they came out of Egypt. God wanted to keep them out of Egypt's ways and direct them to His ways.

Let us identify the curse with particularity. What constituted the curse of the Law?

CURSE OF MATERIAL AND FINANCIAL HARDSHIP

Verses 16–20 speak of being cursed in the city, and in the field, in the basket, and in the store. In other words, there is going to be financial hardship. It is going to be a real struggle, and you are not going to make it. It will be a struggle beyond merely working by "the sweat of the brow." God is going to cause the heaven to be brass. Even though you cry out for help, God is not going to hear, because He is not going to listen. Isaiah explained the reason.

> Behold, the Lord's hand is not shortened, that it cannot save; neither His ear heavy, that it cannot hear: But your iniquities have separated between you and your God, and your sins have hid His face from you, that **He will not hear** (Isa. 59:1–2).

God will not be mocked. He is a God of mercy, but He expects faithful obedience and trust. When Israel cried to God for deliverance, having left Egypt but still refusing to trust, believe, and obey God, Moses recorded God's response:

> Ye returned and wept before the Lord; but **the Lord would not hearken to your voice,** nor give ear to you (Deut. 1:45).

This is not pleasant, but we must take the "whole council of God" if we purport to believe the Bible as the Word of God.

CURSE OF SICKNESS AND DISEASE

God has warned that He will smite with consumption, fever, blasting, and mildew. The botch of Egypt, emerods, itch and things whereof Israel could not be healed could be expected. And then would come great plagues, even plagues of long continuance and sore sickness (Deut. 28:22–61). We are seeing an increasing manifestation of things matching these descriptions today. Just think about it. AIDS. Rampant sexually transmitted diseases. Ebola. Phisteria. Monstrous crop-crushing, fruit-destroying floods, droughts and freezes have baffled meteorologists for nearly a generation across America.

God completed this terrible warning, decreeing that "every sickness, and every plague, which is not written in the book of this law" will come upon you (Deut. 28:61). That is awful stuff!

CURSE OF FEAR

Then came the warning of consuming and paralyzing fear. Our loving God does not take kindly to those who breach His covenant, whether they call themselves "Israel" or the "chosen people" or "American Christians."

> The Lord shall cause thee to be smitten before thine enemies: thou shalt go out one way against them, and flee seven ways before them: and shall be removed into all the kingdoms of the earth (Deut. 28:25).

> Thy life shall hang in doubt before thee, and thou shalt fear day and night, and shalt have none assurance of thy life. In the morning thou shalt say, Would God it were even! For the fear of thine heart... (Deut. 28:66–67).

CURSE OF EGYPT

So we have financial difficulties and hardship and poverty. We have sickness and disease. We have fear—constant fear. Then God lowers the final boom. It is His final, ultimate warning to a "chosen people" who refuse to believe Him fully and to obey His covenant. Here it is:

And **the Lord shall bring thee into Egypt again**....

That is God's ultimate response to Israel. Except for the birth, death, and resurrection of Christ (whom Israel rejected as Messiah), the number-one event in Israel's history—from the day the people came out, even up to the present day—has been their escape from Egypt. To be remanded back to Egypt registered as a blow to their national solar plexus.

> And the Lord shall bring thee into Egypt again with ships...there ye shall be sold unto your enemies for bondmen and bondwomen, and no man shall buy you (Deut. 28:68).

What is God talking about here? He is speaking of spiritual death with very practical, earthy implications. He is talking about being sold back into the bondage of Egypt from which He had already redeemed them. Remember, Israel kept wanting to go back in. No sooner had they walked out, but they stood before the Red Sea and said, "Would to God we had stayed in Egypt. Why in the world did Moses have to bring us out to die here in this place." Over and over again, they cried, "Would to God we could go back into Egypt and die there where we had meat and onions and garlic."

They were always living in the spirit of the city. Always looking to anyone, anything, other than God to meet and provide for their needs. And so God warned them. The ultimate penalty for breach of His covenant is to go back into Egypt. It is death to freedom. It is death to national pride and power. And it is death to the relationship between a people and their God.

Does the Curse Apply to Me?

The question is, of course, whether you and I have gone back into Egypt. Or is it possible we never truly or fully came out? The Israelites came out in body, but they never came out in spirit. They **never** came out in spirit! Why do you think God had to continually call them out? "Woe to them that go down into Egypt," warned Isaiah (30:1–2; 31:1). And ultimately, God had to call His own son out of Egypt, that it might be fulfilled what was spoken by the prophet, "Out of Egypt have I called my son" (Matt. 2:15). At last, by calling His begotten son out of Egypt, Jesus became the "firstborn of many brethren," the captain of those brethren who would follow Him out of Egypt (Rom. 8:29). And we are the many brethren, but only if we follow Him out of Egypt.

We now understand the nature of the curse of the Law. But to whom does the curse apply? Who stands in covenant position with God? The tendency is always to think, *Well, that was Israel!* Or, *I know, but that was Jesus.* Isn't that human nature? We are so prone to sidestep responsibility, to shift the burden. We can make it all sound so religious. Psychologists might call this part of our defense mechanisms. Yet it is, in reality, an ongoing revelation of fallen human nature. Human nature has always been the same, and the Israelites were no exception. So God had to deal with Israel on this issue through Moses. He spoke to them directly to remind them of their personal responsibility to respond to the Covenant.

> These are the words of the covenant, which the Lord commanded Moses to make with the children of Israel in the land of Moab, beside the covenant which He made with them in Horeb (Deut. 29:1).

> **Keep therefore the words of this covenant, and do them, that ye may prosper in all that ye do** (Deut. 29:9).

God's desire and intention for His people has always been that we prosper. That theme is echoed in 3 John 2: "Beloved, I wish above all things that thou mayest prosper and be in health, even as thy soul prospereth." That is merely a restatement of what God said to Israel after they had so recently walked out of Egypt: "Keep the words of the covenant and do them that you may prosper in all that you do."

> That He may establish thee today for a people unto Himself, and that He may be unto thee a God, as He hath said unto thee, and as He hath sworn unto thy fathers, to Abraham, to Isaac, and to Jacob. **Neither with you only do I make this covenant** and this oath; **But with him that standeth here with us this day before the Lord** our God, **and also with him that is not here with us this day** (Deut. 29:13–15).

There were folks who had come in to live among the children of Israel, as if they were Israelites. To use our terminology, we would say that they had "confessed Jesus Christ as Savior." So they were **standing before the Lord**, with the Israelites, as Israel. And God made provision for those people.

When Israel celebrated Passover, God said that if there were any stranger among them who would participate, then they should go through exactly the same Passover preparation and activities that Israel went through, and they would be involved in the same blessing (Exod. 12:48–49). Of a truth, it is only because Pharaoh refused to receive the blood of the Passover that he lost his firstborn son. And it is because the Egyptians did not receive the blood on their doorposts and did not take, by faith, the action to put the blood over the doorpost, that they failed to receive the redemption.

What should this mean to you or to me? The covenant is not just with the children of Israel, but it is with those who will stand with them (Deut. 29:14). Today that includes anyone who will confess Jesus Christ as Lord. Yet the covenant extends on, even to "him that is not here with us this day" (Deut. 29:15). The covenant extended to future "believers."

> For ye know how we have dwelt in the land of Egypt: and how we came through the nations which ye passed by; And ye have seen their abominations, and their idols, wood and stone, silver and gold, which were among them: **Lest there should be among you man, or woman, or family, or tribe, whose heart turneth away this day from the Lord** our God, to go and serve the gods of these nations; lest there should be among you a root that beareth gall and wormwood..." (Deut. 29:16–18).

> **...and all the curses that are written in this book shall be upon him, and the Lord shall blot out his name from under heaven** (Deut. 29:20).

God says that the covenant that He made through Israel is made to any man, any woman, any child who will elect (or choose) to walk in it. The covenant is to everyone. Does **everyone** include you? Again the apostle Paul made this clear:

> For there is no difference between the Jew and the Greek…. For whosoever shall call upon the name of the Lord shall be saved (Rom. 10:12–13).

We understand that in Jesus Christ there is neither Jew nor Greek, bond nor free, male nor female, but we are all one in Christ Jesus (Gal. 3:28). But Jesus Christ is the same yesterday, today, and forever. The promises were not just to the Israelites. Why do you think the apostle Paul emphasized that "they are not all Israel, which are of Israel," but "he is a Jew which is one inwardly; and circumcision is that of the heart, in the spirit…" (Rom. 9:6; 2:29)? The answer is clear, both historically and futuristically. There were people back then who were not, by birth, Israelites, but who were, nonetheless, "circumcised in the heart," and chose to walk in the ways of God. They believed God, and the covenant was to them, as well.

So the covenant is to each one of us. It is to you and to your seed after you. Even if we have not spoken the name of Christ and elected to walk in His ways, the covenant is still working. It is a spiritual law that God has spoken. It cannot be retracted.

> So shall My Word be that goeth forth out of My mouth: it shall not return unto Me void, but it shall accomplish that which I please, and it shall prosper in the thing, whereto I sent it (Isa. 55:11).

The word went forth from God's mouth. It was the covenant. The covenant consisted of a blessing and a cursing. It has continued in operation to this day, and it will always continue in operation until the final redemption of mankind and the Second Coming of Christ.

Why Does God Warn His People?

God issues a warning to those who think that the curse does not apply to them. To those who say, "That was for Israel" or "That was for somebody else, or another generation, or another dispensation." His warning is unmistakable:

> **Lest there should be among you man, or woman, or family, or tribe, whose heart turneth away** this day from the Lord our God…**The Lord will not spare him**…and all the curses that are written in this book shall lie upon him (Deut. 29:18, 20).

I want to ask you a rhetorical question. If the curse does not apply to me, does not apply to you and all mankind, then why did the apostle Paul remind the Galatian church that "Christ hath redeemed **us** from the curse of the Law..." (Gal. 3:13)? If the curse does not apply to us, why would Christ have to redeem us from it? Obviously, it did apply. And that is precisely why Christ had to die for all of us. Because it applied to all. The Covenant, rich with blessing and recoiling with curse, continues to this very hour.

Moses' charge is to all of us:

> The secret things belong unto the Lord our God, but **those things which are revealed belong unto us and to our children for ever**, that we may do all the words of this law (Deut. 29:29).

There are a lot of people who make excuses. They say, "I do not understand it. It does not make any sense to me. I do not understand how there could be a curse of the law that was made back then and still apply to me. Therefore, it does not apply." God disabuses us of our defenses. The secret things, the things that you do not understand, belong unto the Lord our God. But those things that are revealed, that are scripturally opened to us, obligate us to the Covenant in black and white, whether we understand it or not, whether I can figure out how it works or not. What I do not yet comprehend, I must leave to the Lord our God, but those things which are revealed belong unto me and to my children forever, that I and they may do all the words of this law.

Moses continues to explain God's viewpoint on the Covenant.

"And the Lord thy God will circumcise thine heart."

"And the Lord thy God will make thee plenteous in every work of thine hand, in the fruit of thy body...for the Lord will again rejoice over thee for good, as He rejoiced over thy fathers" (Deut. 30:6,9).

And then Moses reminds the "Israel of God" that God desires us to serve Him with all our heart, soul, mind and strength. The Covenant blessings are conditional. "IF you, then I," says the Lord.

"**If** thou shalt hearken unto the voice of the Lord thy God, to keep His commandments...and **if** thou shalt turn unto the Lord with all thine heart and with all thy soul..." (Deut. 30:10).

The purpose of the covenant, in God's heart and mind, was to bring us into the place of circumcision of the heart. Verse 6 declares, "the Lord thy God will circumcise thine heart." That was really God's desire and intent, that we would walk in circumcision of the heart. We must cut away the flesh of Egypt and walk in the spirit.

How Was Christ Made to Be the Curse?

Jesus Christ was made the minister of the circumcision to us, according to the apostle Paul (Rom. 15:8). This ties the New Testament together with the Old Testament, the Old Covenant with the New Covenant. We can understand, then, why Paul boldly expressed, in Galatians 3:13–14, Jesus' redemptive ministry in terms of covenant and curse.

> **Christ hath redeemed us from the curse of the law**, being made a curse for us: for it is written, cursed is every one that hangeth on a tree: **That the blessing of Abraham might come on the Gentiles through Jesus Christ;** that we might receive the promise of the Spirit through faith.

Christ, as the minister of circumcision, has redeemed us from the curse of the law, that we might be circumcised in the heart and receive the blessings of Abraham. How were we redeemed? Galatians 3:13 tells us: Christ was made the curse of the Law. What does that mean?

"He became sin for us who knew no sin, that we might be made the righteousness of God in Christ Jesus," stated the apostle Paul (2 Cor. 5:21). Jesus was made sin for us. That is the most important way in which Christ was made the curse of the Law. That is the overriding thing. But that is not the only way in which Christ was made the curse. Isaiah clearly reported,

> Surely He hath borne our griefs, and carried our sorrows: yet we did esteem Him stricken, smitten of God, and afflicted. But He was wounded for our transgressions, He was bruised for our iniquities: the chastisement of our peace was upon Him; and with His stripes we are healed (Isa. 53:4–5).

That scripture was picked up by Matthew in the New Testament. Under the inspiration of the Holy Spirit, he wrote,

> When the even was come, they brought unto Him many that were possessed with devils: and He cast out the spirits with His word, and healed all that were sick: **That it might be fulfilled which was spoken by Esaias the prophet, saying, Himself took our infirmities, and bare our sickness** (Matt. 8:16–17).

He was made sickness and disease for you and me, that we might be redeemed from the curse of sickness and disease described in Deuteronomy 28. He was made sin. He was made sickness and disease. But that is not all! The apostle to the Gentiles stated:

> For ye know the grace of our Lord Jesus Christ, that though He was rich, yet for your sakes He became poor, that ye through His poverty might be rich [or have full supply] (2 Cor. 8:9).

How was Jesus made the curse? He was made the curse in every respect that the curse of Deuteronomy 28 impinged upon humankind. SIN...SICKNESS...POVERTY...FEAR.

> For ye have not received the spirit of bondage again to fear; but ye have received the Spirit of adoption, whereby we cry, Abba, Father (Rom. 8:15).

We have not received the spirit of bondage again to fear. That is why Paul advised Timothy, "God hath not given us the spirit of fear; but of power, and of love, and of a sound mind" (2 Tim. 1:7). Jesus Christ took upon Himself all of the fear of the curse of the Law, being made that fear, that we might walk in faith, in love, and in peace.

And the last enemy that shall be conquered is death (1 Cor. 15:26). That enemy, or element of the curse, is not presently conquered for us, in the sense that we will not experience that victory until the resurrection. The last enemy that shall be conquered is death.

God has not given **us** the spirit of fear. Who is the "us"? The **us** is anyone to whom the covenant has been made. We have already seen that the covenant was made to all people, because God is not a respecter of persons. It extends to "whosoever shall call upon the name of the Lord."

How Can I Move from Curse to Blessing?

Why redeem from the curse? Because the curse applies to all men. But in the same manner, the blessing is available to all who will walk free of the spirit of Egypt and in the "bond of the covenant...."

> That the blessing of Abraham might come on the Gentiles through Jesus Christ; that we might receive the promise of the Spirit through faith (Gal. 3:14).

What is the blessing of Abraham? Genesis 22 records the culmination of a series of promises to Abraham, at the time when Abraham offered his son on Mount Moriah. God spoke directly to the "father of faith" and said:

> By myself have I sworn, saith the Lord, for because thou hast done this thing, and hast not withheld thy son, thine only son: That in blessing I will bless thee, and in multiplying I will multiply thy seed as the stars of the heaven, and as the sand which is upon the sea shore; and thy seed shall possess the gate of his enemies; And in thy seed shall all the nations of the earth be blessed; because thou hast obeyed my voice (Gen. 22:16–18).

Ultimately, because God found a man who was willing to offer his only son, God was then free to enter planet earth with His only Son, to redeem us. But it was Abraham's faith concerning his only son that prepared the way. God then could send His only Son, who was perfect, to redeem us from the curse of the Law. The Jews loved to claim the fatherhood of Abraham, but Jesus rebuked them for claiming the name but refusing to walk in the

Covenant (John 8:37–47). Jesus said, "He that is of God heareth God's words: ye therefore hear them not, because ye are not of God" (vs. 47).

Abraham was blessed because of his faith (Gen. 24:35). He chose to believe God's every word. He did not pick and choose. He was blessed materially as well, by the testimony of his own son Isaac when he went out to find himself a wife. Isaac testified as to the wealth of his father, because God had blessed his father mightily. We find that the blessing of Abraham was passed down to his son Isaac, and God confirmed it to Isaac (Gen. 25:11).

Then God warned Isaac, "Go not down into Egypt" (Gen. 26:1–5). God was saying, "If you go down to Egypt you will not be blessed. But if, in the context of this famine, you will not go down into Egypt, but will trust me, then I will bless you." God's warning was clear: "Stay out of Egypt. Do not go down to Egypt. If you will trust Egypt instead of me to be your provision, I cannot bless you. But if you do not go down there, even though you are tempted to go down because it looks like a land of plenty, then I will bless you."

The blessing of Abraham, passed to Isaac, was confirmed in Jacob (Gen. 28:1–4). Jacob (surnamed "Israel") led his children back into Egypt where they became enslaved for four hundred years. Abraham left Egypt. His grandson took Israel back to Egypt. It takes only one generation to move from blessing back to curse. Just look at America!

What is the root of the curse of the Law? It is the spirit of Egypt. The spirit of the city, which is walking out from under the covenant. Even though you have confessed Jesus Christ as your Savior, you can still be walking in Egypt, because you do not understand or fully discern either the Lord's body or His covenant. Consider again the promise of the Passover.

> Thou shalt keep the feast of unleavened bread [Passover, Communion, the Lord's Supper]:…for in it thou camest out from Egypt: and none shall appear before me empty. But **if thou shalt indeed obey his voice** [the voice of the Lord through the angel], and do all that I speak; then I will be an enemy unto thine enemies, and an adversary unto thine adversaries. And ye shall serve the Lord your God, and He shall bless thy bread, and thy water; and I will take sickness away from the midst of thee. There shall nothing cast their young, nor be barren, in thy land: the number of thy days I will fulfill (Exod. 23:15–26, selected verses).

How Does the Curse Come?

We are told "the curse causeless shall not come" (Prov. 26:2). There is a reason why many of the evils we experience come upon us. If we sow to the wind, we shall reap the whirlwind (Hos. 8:7). Perhaps Jeremiah captured the spirit of the curse better than any other:

Cursed be the man that trusteth in man, and maketh flesh his arm, and whose heart departeth from the Lord. For he shall be like the heath in the desert, and shall not see when good cometh… (Jer. 17:5–6).

When we begin to shift our trust away from God, when we no longer take God at His Word at every point, we are headed back to Egypt. The curse knocks at the door even if we call ourselves "Evangelical" or "Charismatic" or even "Fundamentalist"!

How Can I Walk Free from the Curse?

To "make flesh your arm" means going back into Egypt. So how can we walk free from the curse? First we must walk in obedience. Every passage we have reviewed that talks about the curse also speaks about obedience. Jeremiah's words are uncompromising and clear.

Cursed be the man that obeyeth not the words of this covenant, Which I commanded your fathers in the day that I brought them forth out of the land of Egypt (Jer. 11:3–4).

Jesus' standard was even greater. "If ye love Me, keep My commandments" (John 19:15). And keeping the commandments, from Jesus' viewpoint, required not only conforming to the letter but also to the spirit…with joy and without compulsion (Matt. 5:17–48).

Second, Paul stated that the blessings of Abraham will come upon us by faith, which means we have to walk by faith (Gal. 3:13). That means we must take God at His Word, whether we understand it or not, and act on it accordingly. This involves a battle without and a war within.

For though we walk in the flesh, we do not war after the flesh; (For the weapons of our warfare are not carnal, but mighty through God to the pulling down of strongholds;) Casting down imaginations, and every high thing that exalteth itself against the knowledge of God, and bringing into captivity every thought to the obedience of Christ (2 Cor. 10:3–5).

The word *imaginations* in the Greek means "reasoning and thoughts." And men and women, since time began, including the Israelites, were constantly exalting their own reasoning and thoughts above the knowledge of God. Every time God said, "I will deliver you. I will provide manna. I will provide your food. I will not make your shoes wear out. I will heal you. I will save you," they said, "No, we do not believe that. We see with our eyes. We see the giants in the land. We cannot go in and take them. We do not have any food. We do not have any water. You cannot provide. We are going back to Egypt."

We must cast down imaginations! These are the temptations that cause us to wander from taking God at His Word. When we yield to the temptation to exalt our thinking or our denomination's thinking over God's Word, it becomes treasonous thinking that leads us to rebel against God's Word, authority, and governance in our lives. It is pure pride, exalting the mind and thoughts of the creature above the thoughts of the Creator.

Choose Life!

It is not a vain thing to follow God's Word. God repeats, ad nauseam, "If you will do what I say, you will get what I say. If you do not do it, you will not get it." Period! Obedience is the defining measure of true faith and trust. There are only two reasons why we don't obey God. Either we do not trust Him to keep His Word, or we are in rebellion. That is why coming out of Egypt is God's end-time message to His end-time church. **We are not ready for Christ's return. We either do not truly trust, or we are in rebellion. Either way, we are as unacceptable to be welcomed to the presence of a holy God as Israel was to enter God's Promised Land. We must come out of the spirit of Egypt, and we must choose life.** That involves a deeper heart-and-life commitment than repeating the "magic words" of a "sinners prayer" that enables some evangelist to notch his belt with another spiritual scalp. It adds nothing to "faith alone in Christ alone." Rather, it defines "faith" more precisely and in active terms. **Faith and trust are opposite sides of the same coin, and they are wedded together in obedience.**

> I call heaven and earth to record this day against you, that **I have set before you life and death, blessing and cursing: therefore choose life, that both thou and thy seed may live:** That thou mayest love the Lord thy God, and that thou mayest obey His voice and that thou mayest cleave unto Him; for He is thy life, and the length of thy days: that thou mayest dwell in the land which the Lord sware unto thy fathers, to Abraham, to Isaac, and to Jacob, to give them (Deut. 30:19–20).

For thirty years I have been walking away from Egypt and its curse. God beckons me to His blessing. He gives me not-so-subtle hints like He gave Moses: "…choose life." He said, "I am your life. I am your health. I am your strength. I am your salvation. I am your righteousness. I am your peace. I AM." I am often tempted to toy with the lure of Egypt. It requires spiritual diligence—sometimes a kind of spiritual violence of faith—to "seek first the Kingdom of God." But in the Book of Revelation, seven times Jesus said that the Promised Land will be entered only by "he that overcometh." And Jesus' instruction to us today continues to be: "He that hath an ear, let him hear what the spirit saith unto the churches" (see Rev. 2–3, concluding with Revelation 3:22). Do you have an ear?

Pray with Me

Father, thank You for the life of Your Word. It is a living Word, for Jesus told us that the words that You speak to us are spirit and they are life. I believe that, Father, and I ask that You will help me in my unbelief. I am Your child. But I have often exalted my own words and thoughts above Yours. I have often refused to obey You. I know I have experienced parts of the curse due to my own rebellion. I see the curse unfolding across our entire nation now. We seem to have an infirmity in our spirit. We have clearly gone back to Egypt. It is hard for me to admit these things and even to talk openly with You about them. Please pray through me by Your Spirit with "groanings which cannot be uttered" (Rom. 8:26). Reveal and manifest to my heart how I have wrongly claimed Your grace while spurning Your law of liberty. I want to receive and walk in all of Your covenant blessings. Thank You for redeeming me from the curse so that the blessings of Abraham may come upon me, my family, and Your church by faith. In Jesus' holy name, I pray. Amen!

Chapter Fifteen

Violent Faith

End-time faith will require end-time choices. Are you
prepared to choose? Do not answer too quickly!

FAITH IS A CHOICE OF HOUSEHOLDS! Will I choose to live
according to the ways of God's household or according to the ways of
Satan's household? Jehovah declared to Israel:

> I am the Lord thy God, which brought thee out of the Land of Egypt, **from**
> **the house of bondage** (Deut. 5:6).

God reminded Israel, "When I brought you out of Egypt, I brought
you out of one household into another household. I brought you out of the
house of bondage." Obviously, if I am not living in one house, I must be living in the other house. Otherwise, I am just a vagabond. For there are only
two households from God's viewpoint. For this reason, Jesus bluntly told the
religious leaders of His day, "Ye are of your father, the devil" (John 8:44).

Everyone has a father. In God's eyes you are either of the father, the devil,
or you are of the Father, God. And if you are living in the spirit of Egypt,
you are living in the spirit of the household whose father is the devil. **Many**
professing Christians claim to hold a key of entrance to God's household,
but they actually live in or frequent Satan's household.

You Must Choose Your Household!

The apostle Paul informed us that, in addition to "the house of bondage,"
there is also a "household of faith." In Galatians 6:10 we are told,

As we have therefore opportunity, let us do good unto all men, especially unto them who are of **the household of faith**.

You see, there are only two households. There is the household of Egypt or bondage and there is the household of faith. To come out of Egypt means that you and I have a choice. We have a choice of which house we are going to live in. My wife and I have purchased three homes during our married life. God gave me the freedom to choose where I would live. Not once did He compel me to breach my free will to choose.

God is not going to tell me, "Chuck, you have to live there" or "You have to live over here." He is going to let me make the choice. He is a gentleman. I want to be sensitive to His leading. I do not want to be filled with the lust of the flesh, the lust of the eyes, and pride of life, because all that is of the world and not of the Father. Yet God has promised to meet all my needs. So I must carefully evaluate whether a given choice meets the needs for the specific purposes God is presently calling me to fulfill.

I must carefully evaluate whether I am walking in the spirit of Egypt, in the spirit of my former father, Satan, or whether I am now walking in the spirit of that new household to which I have been called by Father God, where I can cry unto Him, "Abba, Father! Daddy, Daddy!" Do I really cast my care on the Lord and trust Him in every arena of life? That is the issue.

The spiritual choice is for a household—the household of Egypt or the household of faith. We are going to look at one man who made that choice. And we are going to see what God said about him. That man happens to be the man whom God chose to lead His people out of Satan's household in Egypt and into the household of faith in the Promised Land. Let us explore what God said about that one man, and perhaps why God made the choice of that man. It has everything to do with Moses and his choices.

How Do Your Choices Line Up?

By faith Moses, when he was born, was hid three months of his parents, because they saw he was a proper child; and they were not afraid of the king's commandment. By faith Moses when he was come to years, refused to be called the son of Pharaoh's daughter; Choosing rather to suffer affliction with the people of God, than to enjoy the pleasures of sin for a season; Esteeming the reproach of Christ greater riches than the treasures in Egypt: for he had respect unto the recompense of the reward. By faith he forsook Egypt, not fearing the wrath of the king: for he endured, as seeing him who is invisible. Through faith he kept the Passover, and the sprinkling of blood, lest he that destroyed the firstborn should touch them (Heb. 11:23–28).

Moses refused to be called a "Prince of Egypt": "By faith Moses, when he was come to years, refused to be called the son of Pharaoh's daughter." He made a

198

choice of family. He could either choose to live in the family of Egypt, of which Pharaoh's household was the symbol. Or he could choose to live in the family of God. He made the choice for God's family and God's fatherhood.

Moses, "**when he was come to years**, refused to be called the son of Pharaoh's daughter." Will we refuse to be called a "Prince of Egypt"? Will you, like Moses, reject the pomp, power, and position of worldly titles? Moses gave up the perks of power by faith. He counted them unworthy as compared to becoming a prince with God. What choice are you making? What does the evidence of your life testify regarding your alleged choice?

For those of us who are church leaders, has the title of "Rabbi... teacher"—the title of "Father," "Bishop," "Deacon," "Reverend," or even "Pastor"—placed us firmly in Pharaoh's court? Answer this one prayerfully. Before glibly dismissing such a question as radical, you might want to reread Matthew 23:5–12. In this passage, Jesus, a day before His crucifixion, excoriated the "religious right" for their claim to titles by which they sought to confirm their positions, power, and perks. Though dressed in their religious garb, they were actually wielding the scepter of Pharaoh. Jesus did not revile the function; rather He rebuked the prideful pecking-order and the use of titles that co-opted His church, turning His people into peons. Do we indeed share a grotesque Body with more than one "HEAD"? If Christ is the Head of His church, then of whose church do we claim headship?

In casting his lot with the "people of God," Moses chose to endure a kind of suffering that he otherwise would not have faced.

> Choosing rather to suffer affliction with the people of God, than to enjoy the pleasures of sin for a season (Heb. 11:25).

Moses also made a choice of treasure. He determined what he would value in this life. Was he going to value the treasure that Egypt offered: the lust of the flesh, the lust of the eyes, and the pride of life? Or was he going to esteem the values of Christ? He chose to esteem reproach and servant leadership:

> Esteeming the reproach of Christ greater riches than the treasure of Egypt (Heb. 11:26).

As you know, we have given considerable focus to deliverance from sickness, poverty, and fear—deliverance from the curse—and also to the concepts of redemption and atonement. It would be easy for someone to ask, "What you are teaching? Isn't it the lust of the eyes and the pride of life: the "prosperity gospel"—the idea that everyone should go out and drive a Rolls Royce and live in a million-dollar mansion.?" No! That could not be further from the truth. God is not the least interested in having His blessings and provision consumed upon our lust. But God does want His children to be fully supplied.

The psalmist said, "I shall not want" (Ps. 23:1). God does not want you to be so concerned about survival that you have no freedom to care for others and to minister the Word of God. We need a new vision of holy hospitality, a new vision of our role in works of ministry. We must be transformed from Kingdom reservoirs to Kingdom conduits.

God does not want you to be so concerned about your health that you have no strength to go out and do battle in this world to bring men and women to Jesus Christ. He does not want you so beaten down that you have nothing to give. But that is what the devil would have you believe. He would have you believe that if you are walking in sickness, then God is going to teach you a lesson, and it is going to be a great blessing in your life. You may experience a blessing in your life when you are sick, but it may be due to the fact that God could never get your attention until you were knocked down and dragged out. He has been trying to get your attention for years and years and years, and you were just too self-sufficient to ever listen. That may well be the case.

We must get this clear. Sickness and disease do not glorify God. There is not a single scripture to support such a proposition. There is only one passage that comes close. It is John 9. Jesus saw a man blind from birth. Jesus told his disciples that this particular man's blindness was not due to his or his parents' sin, "but that the works of God should be manifest in him" (John 9:3). In verse 4, Jesus promptly declared that he was doing "the works of Him that sent me" and then healed the man. His healing caused such stir among the priests and pastors—carriers of religious tradition—that they kicked the healed man out of the temple.

You may find yourself, like that once-blind man, having to choose to "suffer affliction with the people of God" than to enjoy the pleasures of religious tradition or to enjoy being a prince, pastor, or prominent leader in your denomination. **If you must forsake being a prince of man's religious structures and institutions in order to be a "prince with God," are you willing to make the choice?**

Moses refused to fear man or the powerbrokers of his day, be they political or religious. He was motivated by faith. He took God at His every word. He did not pick and choose those portions that lined up with his traditions, experience, or any other "high thing that exalts itself against the knowledge of God" (2 Cor. 10:3–5).

> By faith he forsook Egypt, not fearing the wrath of the king: for he endured, as seeing him who is invisible (Heb. 11:27).

By faith Abraham went out looking for a city with foundations whose builder and maker is God (Heb. 11:10). Moses did the same thing. And he did not do it because he saw how it was going to work out. Remember, at the burning bush, Moses thought he was totally inadequate for the job. He cried and whined before the Lord, and God told him to shut up. God said, "I will be your mouth. Stop talking all that nonsense about how inadequate you are. That is false humility. I am your Father. You are my son. And I am commissioning you, as my son, to do a job. Do not tell me you cannot do it if I have called you to do it." And yet, how many of us (writer included) have tried to tell God, "I cannot do it." Whatever it is that God calls you to do, you can do it. That is what grace is for...for divine enablement. Moses had to forsake Egypt "by faith." You and I must do the same.

"Through faith he kept the Passover..." (Heb. 11:28). Moses made a choice to be covered by the blood in all respects. We, too, must make that choice. Do you know that you can make the choice to be covered by the blood for the deliverance from your iniquities and yet never receive the rest of the blessing of the covering of the blood, because you do not receive it by faith? You have to receive deliverance from your iniquities by faith, don't you?

> For by grace are ye saved through faith; and that not of yourselves: it is the gift of God: Not of works, lest any man should boast (Eph. 2:8–9).

If salvation from sin comes by faith, do not the rest of the blessings come by faith the same way? Then why do we think that they should come some different way, such as waving a magic wand, or saying "abracadabra"? God does not work that way. He is a God of faith. He said that the just shall live by faith. God lives by faith (Rom. 3:3). If I am His son, I must live by faith, because I am living in the household of faith. The kids emulate the father. It all comes by faith. By faith Moses left Egypt, and by faith he kept the Passover.

Recall our discussion on atonement and redemption. We looked at 1 Corinthians 11:29–30, in which Paul informed us that there are many who are sick among us and die because they fail to discern the Lord's body. What do you think He was talking about? By faith Moses kept the Passover so that he could receive the completeness of the redemption. And when the Passover came, God said there would be no sick among them, and He would provide all their needs. He became poor that we, through His poverty, might have a full supply. By the stripes of Jesus we were healed. He became sin that I might be made righteous...and so on.

Faith Is an Act

Let us return now to Hebrews 11. We will shift our focus to another aspect of Moses' life and response to God. Moses acted on his professed belief. His actions revealed the fact of his faith.

- "**By faith** Moses when he was come to years, **refused to be called the son of Pharaoh's daughter**" (vs. 24). It was an act of his will, but it was an act.

- "**Choosing rather to suffer...**" (vs. 25). Another act of his will. He had to act with his will. He decided to choose.
- "**Esteeming the reproach of Christ...**" (vs. 26). That is yet another act of the will. It is a choice, a value choice. He had to gird up the loins of his mind and decide what he was going to value. He acted by adjusting his will.
- "**He forsook Egypt...**" (vs. 27). He actively turned and left. My Bible tells me that I am to flee from evil (2 Tim. 2:22). Implicit in this word *forsook* is the idea of fleeing. Moses had to actively gird up the loins of his mind, decide what direction he was going to go, and then literally put feet to his will and flee, or forsake.
- "**He endured...**" (vs. 27). Moses' endurance was borne of faith, not of physical stamina. He chose to persevere even to persecution, seeing by faith "him who is invisible." He refused to allow circumstances or denominational or congregational pressures to deter him. He did exactly what God said because God said it.

And that is precisely what faith is. Faith is acting on the Word of God. God had given Moses a word. He said, "Moses, you are the man. You are going to bring my people out of Egypt." And so Moses acted on the word of God, not because he saw how it was going to work out, but because God said it. And that is what you and I are required to do. **This is end-time faith. We must act on what God says, whether or not we understand it,** just because He is the Father. Father knows best.

How Can I Inherit the Promises?

God has called and is calling you out of Egypt for a purpose. Moses has told us the purpose:

> But **the Lord hath taken you**, and brought you forth out of the iron furnace, even **out of Egypt, to be unto him a people of inheritance**, as ye are this day (Deut. 4:20).

God called His people out of Egypt so they would be people of inheritance. Who are the people of inheritance? They are children of the Father. You inherit through your parents. That is why, in my former law practice, as I conferenced with a client regarding a will to be drafted, I told the client, "Generally a parent will leave most of the property equally among the children. But if one of the children should not survive the distribution of the estate of that parent, that deceased child's share shall be divided among those of his own children who survive the distribution of the estate—equally by right of representation." What does that mean? It means that they are the children of the inheritance. Children inherit though their parents. What the parents have, the children receive. God called His people into the position of being children who are entitled to an inheritance.

But I want you to know that it is also possible to be disinherited. Do you know that there are children who are legitimate children in families, but who do not walk according to the ways of those families. They do not understand the ways of the father, and for all practical purposes, they are as bastard children. They walk and live as if they had no father and mother. They walk as urchins in the world. Christians often walk as urchins in the world, because they have never seen the blessing of the household of faith. God **said** they are children of the inheritance, but they refuse to walk in the ways of the household of faith. To inherit the promises, I must walk by faith. Faith requires obedience. **It is not the talk, it is the walk.**

> Then Joshua commanded the officers of the people, saying, Pass through the host, and command the people, saying, Prepare you victuals; for within three days ye shall pass over this Jordan, to go in to possess the land, which the Lord your God giveth you to possess it (Josh. 1:10–11).

Jordan was the line of demarcation between receiving the promises of God and not receiving the promises of God. It is a symbol in the Word of God of the line of demarcation between leaving Egypt and receiving the promises. You can come out of Egypt—you can be "saved"—and never receive the promises of God, in total. You can be delivered from Egypt. There is no doubt in that. You might even squeak into heaven on your "confession of faith" in Christ. But you will never walk in victory in this life, because you refuse to "cross over Jordan."

God gave the Promised Land, but they were not in it yet. God said, "I give it to you," but they did not have it. They were not experiencing it in their life. They had to do something to experience it. And so they had to make a decision to cross from where they were, over to where the promises were in order to get them. They had to go over Jordan. And you must go "over Jordan" as well, to claim ALL the promises of God. This may, again, fight with some folks' preboxed theology, but it remains a continual theme from Exodus to Revelation.

Why Does My Faith Not Work?

There is an element of "violence" to faith. That is why Jesus declared, "…from the days of John the Baptist until now the kingdom of heaven suffereth violence, and the violent take it by force" (Matt. 11:12). There is a forceful "pressing in" that must be done before the shout of victory can be heard.

Joshua really understood what it means to take the promises of God by faith. You have never seen anyone who is a better example of violent faith than Joshua. Consider the famous account of Jericho in Joshua 6:

Now Jericho was straitly shut up because of the children of Israel: none went out, and none came in (vs. 1).

Jericho was a mighty fortress. Jericho was the first obstacle met as God's people, having come out of Egypt, entered the Promised Land. It had great walls all the way around it. Thick walls. High walls. Impenetrable walls. Just like the walls of sin, sickness, poverty, fear, persecution, and religious tradition that the enemy throws at us. They seem impenetrable, unconquerable, so we just sit down and accept them.

And the Lord said unto Joshua, See, **I have given** into thine hand Jericho, and the king thereof, and the mighty men of valor. And ye shall compass the city, all ye men of war, and go round about the city once. Thus shalt thou do six days (Josh. 6:2–3).

God said, "I have given." But then He said, "You are going to have to be the one to go get it. Not me. I am not going to lay it on you. You are going to have to go get it." So the promise is already given. The promise is to us.

And Joshua rose early in the morning, and the priests took up the ark of the Lord (Josh. 6:12).

What did Joshua rise up early to do? He did not mull it over. He did not wait to see what others would do. He did not take a poll. He did not check to see if he had denominational or congregational support. He rose up early to do everything that God had told him they were going to have to do to claim the promises.

Let's get really personal. Are you rising up early in the morning to go after God's promises? Are you "seeking first" the kingdom of God? Be honest! Joshua did not wait around to see what was going to happen. He did not wait around to see which way the wind was blowing that day. He did not wait around to see how many giants were going to come running after him, nor did he evaluate the difficult circumstances he would face. He did not wait to see if his denomination agreed with God. He got up early in the morning so he could get a head start on it.

And that is the spirit of violent faith. It is the faith that takes. It is acting with compelling force and purpose, getting up early to go after it. **If you are truly out of Egypt, you are going to pursue the Promised Land with a vengeance.** You will allow nothing to deter you. But you will not selfishly run over God's people to get there, for the Kingdom consists of people. Some, pursuing personal agendas, run rough-shod over everyone in their path to fulfill their own ambition, claiming the mantle of "holy cloth" as divine mandate. Such wield the scepter of Egypt, drinking deeply of the powerbroker-nurturing waters of a spiritual Nile.

> And it came to pass at the seventh time [that they went around the city], when the priests blew with the trumpets, Joshua said unto the people, Shout; for the Lord **hath given** you the city (Josh. 6:16).

I want you to know that at the time Joshua made that order, they still did not have the city. God said He had given them the city, but they still did not have it. Have you prayed and wanted to believe God for healing, for deliverance from financial troubles, or from a habit that grips you, or from any of a host of other threats? (I just point out those items because, if you listen, every time you have a prayer meeting those are the main things people pray about, except for salvation.) Have you gotten to the point where you say, "God promised it, I believe it, but I do not see it yet?"

Joshua did not see it either, at least not with his natural eyes. He saw it by faith. He told God's children, "There is one last act you must do. You must give a great shout." Can you imagine how stupid that seemed? What kind of a battle plan is that—to shout? But there is power in agreement. And that is what shouting was all about. I want you to take note that Joshua had ordered the people not to say a thing (vs. 10). We will talk more about that in the next chapter. Why did Joshua order the people not to say anything? Here is a hint. What is your mouth tempted to say when you do not see the promises of God manifested immediately, right in front of your eyes?

> So the people shouted when the priests blew with the trumpets: and it came to pass, when the people heard the sound of the trumpet, and the people shouted with a great shout, that the wall fell down flat (Josh. 6:20).

Why did the walls fall down flat? Hebrews 11:30 says that "by faith the walls of Jericho fell down" flat. But what was the faith? Was it a feeling, some free-floating thing out there in the wild blue yonder? No. It was taking one step at a time, seven times around the city walls, without saying a word. Why? Because God said to do it. **The first step of faith is radical obedience.** Each successive step is more of the same. Faith does not "work" for many, if not most, Christians because we fail to believe God and do what He says. We are going to need this kind of faith born of obedience for the end-time battles ahead. It must be more than theological, more than rhetorical; it must be operational.

Do You Have the Faith of God?

Faith is acting on the Word of God, one step at a time, whether you understand it or not. Whether you can see how it is going to work, or not. It is acting in what may seem to be "ruthless" obedience and trust, purposing in your heart to recognize you have a Father who loves you, who knows more about your situation than you do. Remember, "we walk by faith, not by sight" (2 Cor. 5:7).

There are two kinds of faith. Moses spoke of the "chosen people" (whom God delivered from Egypt) as "children in whom is no faith" (Deut. 32:20). How could they be children who had no faith if they were God's kids? They believed **in** God. They really did believe in God. So how could they be children who had no faith? Let me tell you why: because there are two kinds of faith.

> Therefore, leaving the principles of the doctrine of Christ, let us go on unto perfection; not laying again the foundation of repentance from dead works, and of **faith toward God**. Of the doctrine of baptisms and of laying on of hands, and of resurrection of the dead, and of eternal judgment (Heb. 6:1–2).

These are the elementary things of God's Kingdom. These comprise the "milk" of the Word (Heb. 5:12). Yet this is the primary focus of much of our "church talk"—foundational things. Paul has said, "Let us not lay the foundations over and over and over again, when we have no superstructure on top. It gives the illusion of having a structure, but it is only foundation steps—one on top of the other." He said, "Let us leave the principles of the doctrine of Christ...**not** laying again the foundation of faith **toward** God." Israel had faith **toward** God, but there is another kind of faith they did not have.

Do you remember Jesus' cursing of the fig tree? His disciples came to Him after returning from Jerusalem. They saw that the tree Jesus had cursed the day before was withered from the roots up.

> And Peter calling to remembrance saith unto him, Master, behold, the fig tree which thou cursedst is withered away. And Jesus answering saith unto them, **Have faith in God** (Mark 11:21–22).

The King James says, "Have faith **in** God." But the Greek New Testament says, "Have the faith **of** God." In other words, have the God kind of faith.

What is the difference between faith **toward** God and the faith **of** God? That is perhaps one of the most important questions we could answer. The practical implications are vast. What is the difference between those two kinds of faith?

Abraham was a man of faith. In fact, he is seen as the "father of faith" (Rom. 4:11). The Bible says he was justified by faith, and his faith was imputed to him for righteousness (Gen. 15:6). The apostle Paul, in a rather complex, analytical style, discussed why God was able to impute righteousness to Abraham by faith. In the middle of a lengthy discourse on Abraham, we find these words: "…God…who calleth those things which be not as though they were" (Rom. 4:17). Why is that so important? The writer to the Hebrews has given us some insight.

> Through faith we understand that the worlds were framed by the Word of God, so that things which are seen were not made of things which do appear (Heb. 11:3).

The same apostle Paul wrote to the church at Ephesus, admonishing, "Be ye therefore followers of God, as dear children; And walk in love" (Eph. 5:1–2). People tend to miss the full impact of the biblical message. Paul's exhortation here is just one illustration of what God is trying to communicate to His sons and daughters. What He is really saying is, "Be ye therefore imitators of God." He wants His kids to be like Him. One aspect of that is walking in love. Another major aspect of that is walking in faith—the God kind of faith.

How did God walk in faith? By calling those things that were not yet, as though they were. We must not ignore what is, but speak what God says. We must put what God says about the circumstances in our mouth, so that we are speaking what God sees and not what we see. **The end-time church must move from faith IN God to the faith OF God.** It may be essential for your physical and even spiritual survival. It will certainly be essential if you intend to be among those who "endure to the end" (Matt. 24:13).

Faith Is Present-Tense

They had been freed from Egypt. God called the children of Israel to the Promised Land, and He instructed Moses to send out twelve spies to "…search the land…which **I give** unto the children of Israel" (Num. 13:2). Note the present-tense. "I give you the land." Faith is present-tense. It was because the people understood faith to be future-tense that they never embraced nor received the promise of God.

Recall with me. When the ten spies returned from searching the land of promise, God said they gave an "evil report" (Num. 13:32; 14:37). Why did God see their report as "evil"? They spoke the truth of what they saw and what they heard, interpreted through their feelings. Yet they brought back an evil report because they misunderstood the nature of faith. They thought faith was future-tense. That somewhere in the "sweet by and by" God would lay the land, all nice and peaceful, in their laps. God said, "No! I gave you the land. Now you go in and take it."

But they disagreed. The ten spies and an entire nation of accountable adults exalted their thoughts, opinions, and perceptions over the very words of God. And they said, "No. We cannot do that. We cannot take this land. There are giants in there and we are like grasshoppers in their eyes." They had faith **toward** God, but they did not share the faith **OF** God. They refused to embrace present-tense faith—the God kind of faith.

The God kind of faith is as foreign to the church today as it was to the Israelites as they came came out of Egypt. And their refusal to agree with God and act on His Word cost them the Promised Land. Only Joshua and Caleb entered, by order of God Himself (Num. 14:28–36).

Let us return now to Jericho. What did God say to Joshua? He said, "I already gave you Jericho. I have given it to you." What God has given, He has given. And what He has given, He does not have yet to give. He already has given it. Therefore, I must receive and embrace what He's given me. If God gave me salvation through Jesus Christ by faith, how am I going to get it? By faith. I must presently embrace or claim what has been given. An offer made is worthless unless it is received and acted upon.

If God gave healing by faith, how am I going to get it?

If God gives freedom from financial despair, how am I going to get it?

All the promises of God come the same way. They are grasped and brought to fruition only by faith. If I refuse to believe them, I will never receive them. There will always be "giants" to intervene—feelings, experience, religious tradition, doubt, and fear. Yet the Word of God does not change.

> For all the promises of God in him are yea, and in him Amen, unto the glory of God by us (2 Cor. 1:20).

How Is Faith Violent?

Are you wondering, perhaps, where we get this idea of violent faith? We must return to Jesus' observation of the Kingdom.

> And from the days of John the Baptist until now the kingdom of heaven suffereth violence, and the violent take it by force (Matt. 11:12).

Now that is a troubling and puzzling Scripture. Have you ever heard anyone preach on it? Yet it means something. And what it means is that faith is a violent thing. It is not physically violent but spiritually violent. It requires you to gird up the loins of your mind. You must set your heart like a vector force, not deviating to the left or the right.

You must agree with what God's Word says, whether or not you feel like it, whether or not your tradition or experience agrees with it. Like Joshua, you must say, "We will compass the wall seven times and after the seventh time, we are going to give a great shout; the trumpets will sound; and the walls will fall flat. And here we go!" The violent shall take it by force, not at the point of a sword but by the power of faith.

Seven times in the Book of Revelation God gives a warning and admonition to His end-time church: "To him that overcometh." Seven different expressions are set forth, calling us to be overcomers. How are we to overcome? By the violence of faith! "By the blood of the Lamb and by the word of our testimony" (Rev. 12:11). We do not overcome just by the blood of the Lamb. That is what a lot of people think. No! If there is not the word of testimony acknowledging what the blood of the Lamb has done, we are not discerners of the blood and the body of the Lord Jesus, and for this reason many are sickly and weak among us and many have died (1 Cor. 11). All of the promises of God must be testified by the tongue. You may have to do violence to your feelings to do it, but you must do it! To do otherwise or to fail to intentionally and forcefully place God's word in your mouth, is to disagree with God. It is pure arrogance. And it will keep you from the Promised Land just as it did ancient Israel.

Can Faith Be Evil?

Sight faith is evil faith. After the children of Israel had already left Egypt, "when Pharaoh drew nigh, the children of Israel lifted up their eyes, and behold, the Egyptians marched after them; and they were sore afraid...." I want to tell you, now: if you lift up your eyes and look at the circumstances around you, you will always be struck with fear. You will always be struck with fear! That is the faith of Egypt.

The faith of Egypt is sight faith. Always looking to what I see and feel and not to what God tells me. It is sense knowledge. James called it devilish knowledge (James 3:15). Sense knowledge is devilish knowledge. It is premised on feelings. It is the operative mode of the American church in our generation. It is the faith of Egypt.

> And Israel saw that great work which the Lord did upon the Egyptians: and the people feared the Lord, and believed the Lord, and His servant Moses (Exod. 14:31).

Jesus said, "You have seen and have believed. But more blessed is he who has not seen and yet believed" (John 20:29). They believed only because they saw with their eyes, not because God told them. Sight faith does not endure. It does not "take" in the time of trouble. And it will not hold as end-time trials and persecutions advance.

Do you remember the story of the brazen serpent? After Israel left Egypt, they were bitten by deadly snakes. The Scripture states they became "discouraged because of the way" (Num. 21:22). And when they became discouraged because of the way, their mouths started to flap. And what did they begin to say? They spoke contrary to what God already had said. God had said, "I have given you the Promised Land." But they said, "Wherefore have you brought us up out of Egypt to die in the wilderness? Our soul loatheth this light bread." So what happened? They suffered consequences. The Lord sent fiery serpents that bit the people. Then, and only then, did the people confess their faith defect.

> We have sinned, for we have **spoken** against the Lord (Num. 21:7).

God in His mercy provided healing and deliverance through a brazen serpent, a type of Christ. But the people were only healed if they looked, by faith, on the brazen serpent rather than on their pain and circumstances (Num. 21:9).

Violent Faith Is End-Time Faith!

The beloved apostle Paul's words call us today to agree with God at every point:

> For we walk by faith, not by sight (2 Cor. 5:7).

> While we look not at the things which are seen, but at the things which are not seen: for the things which are seen are temporal; but the things which are not seen are eternal (2 Cor. 4:18).

But then Paul moved "from preaching to meddling." He moved from exhortation to warning:

> Moreover, brethren, I would not that ye should be ignorant, how that all our fathers were under the cloud, and all passed through the sea; And were all baptized unto Moses in the cloud and in the sea; And did all eat the same spiritual meat; And did all drink the same spiritual drink: for they drank of that spiritual Rock that followed them: and that Rock was Christ. But with many of them God was not well pleased: for they were overthrown in the wilderness (1 Cor. 10:1–5).

They all ate of the same spiritual meat. They all drank of the same spiritual drink. But they did not receive the blessings of God. Only two men received the blessing of God because they had the audacity, the tenacity, and the violence to walk by faith.

This is an end-time message to an end-time church. The apostle Paul minced no words in addressing us:

> Now all these things happened unto them for ensamples: and **they are written for our admonition, upon whom the ends of the world are come.** Wherefore let him that thinketh he standeth take heed lest he fall (1 Cor. 10:11–12).

Let me join with the apostle Paul in urging you on to violent faith. Faith **toward** God is infantile faith. You and I must embrace and begin to walk consistently in the faith **OF** God. We must live the God kind of faith that agrees point-for-point with God's written Word and "calls those things that be not, as though they were." Your tongue is the key to activating faith.

Let God be true, but every man a liar; as it is written, That thou mightest be justified in thy sayings, and mightest overcome when thou art judged (Rom. 3:4).

Chapter Sixteen

Taming the Tongue

Truth can make you free, but it can also make God angry.
Can your tongue discern the difference? Could
"grasshopper eyes" be affecting your tongue?

FAITH IS DIRECTLY TIED TO THE TONGUE. In the previous chapter, we discovered that to truly come "out of Egypt," we must learn to live a kind of "violent faith." We gained insight into the nature of faith. We came to realize that faith is not just saying you believe, but it actively, even violently, pursues and grabs the promises of God.
We heard Jesus' own words in the Book of Matthew:

> And from the days of John the Baptist until now the kingdom of heaven suffereth violence, and the violent take it by force (Matt. 11:12).

This is a very unusual passage, yet it has serious and practical implications for us today. We are told that we are supposed to live by faith. And, indeed, God requires us to live by faith. "The just shall live by faith." "Without faith it is impossible to please God." But very seldom are we ever told **how** to live by faith. How do you go about doing that?

It is not enough to tell a child that he must do something. You must also give him the wherewithal, some sort of leading as to how he is going to accomplish what you are telling him he has to accomplish. And God does not let His children down here. He is not a Father who requires us to live the God kind of faith without specific guidance on how to do it.

In this chapter, we will attempt to translate into action the requirement that we live by faith. God has provided the means. And it has to do with taming the tongue.

Take a moment now to pray with me: Father, I ask that You will quicken my heart and my ears now to receive Your Word, that it will live in my heart and come out on my tongue. I want to live by faith—vigorously, violently, and lovingly at the same time. I yearn to be able to take the promises that You have given to all of Your children, that I might live a full and complete life here on earth, that I might be a more effective servant, discipling other men and women into the kingdom. I long to walk in the God kind of faith. I want to please You. So open my understanding now, in Jesus' name. Amen!

What Is the Tongue of Egypt?
What does coming out of Egypt have to do with the tongue?

And the pride of Israel testifieth to his face: and they do not return to the Lord their God, nor seek Him for all this. Ephraim also is like a silly dove without heart: they call to Egypt, they go to Assyria. When they shall go, I will spread my net upon them; I will bring them down as the fowls of the heaven; I will chastise them, as their congregation hath heard. Woe unto them! For they have fled from me: destruction unto them! Because they have transgressed against me: **though I have redeemed them, yet they have spoken lies against me.** And they have not cried unto me with their heart, when they howled upon their beds: they assemble themselves for corn and wine, and they rebel against me. Though I have bound and strengthened their arms, yet do they imagine mischief against me. They return, but not to the most High: they are like a deceitful bow: their princes shall fall by the sword **for the rage of their tongue**: this shall be their derision in the land of Egypt (Hos. 7:10–16).

Israel was not in Egypt when the prophet, Hosea, declared, "this shall be their derision in the land of Egypt." Whom was the prophet addressing? He said, "the pride of Israel testifieth to his face." Who was Israel? Israel was the children of God. The called ones. They were the seed of Abraham.

So God was not speaking to some outsider here. He was talking to the insiders. He was and is addressing those who, in the church age, confess Jesus Christ as Savior. He is talking to the church. He is talking to those who claim to be believers, and He has said that "the pride of Israel testifieth to his face."

Notice first that **the tongue of Egypt is a prideful tongue** (vs. 10). What are the characteristics of a prideful tongue? A prideful tongue will always speak what seems right to the person who speaks: what "seems" right to the person who speaks, as determined by his or her own will and opinion, or by the significant relational or organizational forces in the person's life.

Therefore, if God says, "I give you the Promised Land," but then I see giants in the land, and so I say, "Nevertheless there are giants in the land, and I am not able to overcome them," that is a prideful tongue. Why? Because it chooses to speak what I see—to elevate my opinion and viewpoint over what God says about the circumstances. Whenever I make the choice, as a Christian, to speak what I think, to speak what I see, to speak what I hear or what somebody else tells me, and it is contrary to what God says, it is a prideful tongue. This is true even if I am following men or organizations that I otherwise deeply respect. **My tongue is the true indicator of who is in authority in my life: God, or men.**

Ignorance of what our Father God has said is no excuse in the "household of faith." We, as His children, are accountable for what God has said, whether or not we remember it or have paid attention. That is why the apostle Paul exhorted Timothy to "study to show thyself approved unto God, a workman that needeth not to be ashamed, rightly dividing the word of truth" (2 Tim. 2:15).

"The pride of Israel testifieth to his face: and they do not return to the Lord their God, nor seek Him for all this." What do they seek? They seek everything but the Lord. I must confess that despite being a Christian, having grown up in the church, and having confessed Jesus Christ as my Savior at five years of age, nevertheless, I lived "in Egypt" for twenty-seven years as a Christian. I lived in Egypt because I spoke the things that I saw, the things that I heard, the things that made sense to me. If my experience was different than what God's Word said, then I chose to follow my experience or somebody else's experience or denominational tradition rather than what God said. I returned invariably to Egypt while purporting to believe the Bible.

Notice secondly that **the tongue of Egypt is controlled by and speaks of power outside of God's power and authority:** "they call to Egypt, they go to Assyria." We have encountered those two powerbrokers earlier when we discussed the "spirit of the city." And we saw that the spirit of the city is the spirit of man. It is the spirit of Antichrist, which says, "I am." Not "God is." I am. I am in control of my circumstances. I am going to do what I am going to do, and I am going to rely on my power and the might of my hand. It is the might of my hand that has gotten me this wealth. I forget the Lord my God, and I go after Egypt and I go after Assyria. The tongue of Egypt is a tongue characterized by the spirit of the city. The power of man. Man in control.

The modern mind of science is rebellious. It refuses to agree with God. The spirit of science wars against the spirit of the city of the living God. There is nothing wrong with science in and of itself, so long as science is the servant and not the master. But the problem in our world is that the spirit of science is part and parcel of the spirit of the city. It rules rather than serves. So we must make a choice. Believe me, there are times when God's Word contravenes our experience. Science is based on experience. It is empirical. It is cause and effect. If I do not see it, I do not believe it. That is the spirit of science. It is the spirit that dictates to and empowers the tongue of Egypt. It paralyzes the Western mind from truly believing.

Woe unto them! For they have fled from me: destruction unto them! Because
they have transgressed against me: **though I have redeemed them, yet they
have spoken lies against me** (Hos. 7:13).

The tongue of Egypt is a tongue against God. Notice! God says, "they
have spoken lies against me." And we will see further how God understands
lying. "They have spoken lies against me," declares the Lord. As a tongue
against God, the tongue of Egypt becomes also a deceitful tongue against
others, reaping destruction.

They return, but not to the most High: they are **like a deceitful bow:** their
princes shall fall by the sword for the rage of their tongue: this shall be their
derision in the land of Egypt (Hos. 7:16).

The tongue of Egypt is a tongue of rage and self-destruction. The Bible
says,

There is a way which seemeth right unto a man, but the end thereof are the
ways of death (Prov. 14:12).

The tongue of Egypt is a tongue that speaks the ways of death. Most
Christians do not realize that they speak with "Egyptian" tongues. They do
not intend to be speaking the ways of death. They merely walk in rebellion
and ignorance of what God has said about His Word and His Ways. Ways
other than God's ways are the ways of death. We will look further at what
God has to say about "the ways of death."

Would You Lie Against God?

We must take a closer look at what God has to say about a lying tongue.
Other than obvious untruth, what does God really understand a lying tongue
to be? Listen to these warning words from Isaiah:

Behold, the Lord's hand is not shortened, that it cannot save; neither His
ear heavy, that it cannot hear: But your iniquities have separated between
you and your God, and your sins have hid His face from you, that He will
not hear (Isa. 59:1–2).

God can make a choice as to whether He will hear or whether He will
not hear, and there are many things that God will not hear. In fact, I wrote
a little book entitled *Getting the Ear of God.* It deals with this very subject,
prompted by these astounding words from Isaiah. Why won't God hear His
kids? Is He mean or capricious? You might ask, "Well what is the use of
praying, then?"

You may have had children or have children now at home. Have you ever had the experience of having your children come to you and ask you a favor when they were in disfavor with you at the time? Perhaps they had been disobedient or rebellious. They had refused to do or listen to what you told them. They had refused to act on what you had asked them to do. And they came to you and asked you a favor, but you turned a deaf ear. You heard them in the physical sense, but you did not respond.

The word *hearing,* in the Word of God, is not used in the sense of hearing sounds. It is used in the sense of hearing that produces action. If there is no action, there has been no hearing, as far as God is concerned. So if God turns a deaf ear, that means there is something wrong with the way I am living. Perhaps I am not walking in the ways of the household of faith. He is my Father, and if I am not walking in the ways of His household, He is not going to treat me with an open ear as one of His children at that time.

That does not necessarily mean I am not saved. But it may mean I am not going to get the blessings of walking in His household. Think about it! You can be adopted into a natural family here on earth and never choose to walk in the ways of that family. Your name will still be the same. You are still a member of the family. But you will never reap the benefits of the household until you make a decision to submit yourself to the father of the family and walk in the ways of that household. The same is true in the family of God. And God was talking to his own children here in Isaiah 59 when He said,

> For your hands are defiled with blood; and your fingers with iniquity; **your lips have spoken lies, your tongue hath muttered perverseness** (vs. 3).

Remember, Isaiah was talking to God's kids. He was talking to members of God's family here, not to outsiders.

What does it mean when God says that "your tongue has muttered perverseness"? Let me direct you to the dictionary definition of the word *perverseness*. It comes from the root word *pervert*. The verb form of the word is defined as follows:

> To lean or turn from the right way or from the truth; give a wrong meaning to; use for wrong purposes; change from what is natural or normal; a perverted person; to misinterpret, distort, misuse or misapply.

Would you lie against God? Has your tongue muttered perverseness? Do you do it regularly, perhaps even as a matter of course? Do not answer too quickly.

Can a Truthful Report Make God Angry?

We are now going to see how God views the perversion of His own people, as evidenced by their tongue. To do so, we must turn to Numbers 13 and 14.

God has continued going back to Numbers 13 and 14 throughout His Word. You will find its theme repeated in 2 Corinthians 10 and in Hebrews 3 and 4. The echoed theme has always been that God wants His people to walk in true faith and not in the spirit of Egypt. We are now going to learn how to "mix" faith with the Word of God. This may be one of the most important and practical principles you will ever learn as a Christian.

> For unto us was the gospel preached, as well as unto them: but **the word preached did not profit them, not being mixed with faith** in them that heard it (Heb. 4:2).

In order for God's Word to profit me, I must "mix it with faith." But how can I do that? Everybody tells me I am to live by faith, but how can I get a handle on it? Let us go now to a visceral display of perverse tongues in Numbers 13:

> And the Lord spake unto Moses, saying, Send thou men, that they may search the land of Canaan, which **I give** unto the children of Israel: of every tribe of their fathers shall ye send a man, every one a ruler among them (Num. 13:1–2).

Here are those present-tense words again: "I give." Remember, faith is now. "Now faith is the substance of things hoped for" (Heb. 11:1). Not tomorrow. Not yesterday. But now. Faith is now. It is taking God totally at His Word—now!

Present-tense. When God speaks He usually speaks in "now" terms. When He has spoken, He expects that what He has spoken will continue to be in force and effect and will operate from the moment He speaks. Here are God's own words declaring this God kind of faith.

> So shall my word be that goeth forth out of my mouth: it shall not return unto me void, but it shall accomplish that which I please, and it shall prosper in the thing whereto I sent it (Isa. 55:11).

Back in Numbers 13 God said, "I give unto the children of Israel" the Promised Land. So Moses sent out twelve spies into the Promised Land to check out the land. He wanted to know what they would be faced with there, so they could go in and grab hold of the promises of God. The spies returned from searching the land after forty days and delivered this message:

> And they told him, and said, We came unto the land whither thou sentest us, and surely it floweth with milk and honey; and this is the fruit of it (Num. 13:27).

How did they communicate that message to Moses? With their mouth. They spoke it. But they continued with their report:

Nevertheless the people be strong that dwell in the land… (Num. 13:28).

How did they get that message across to Moses? With their mouth. They spoke it.

…and the cities are walled, and very great: and moreover we saw the children of Anak there. And the Amalekites dwell in the land of the south: and the Hittites, and the Jebusites, and the Amorites, dwell in the mountains: and the Canaanites dwell by the sea, and by the coast of Jordan. And Caleb stilled the people before Moses, and said, Let us go up at once, and possess it; for we are well able to overcome it (Num. 13:28–30).

Notice that Caleb "stilled the people." The only time you can get faith out is by stilling unbelief. Can you see why Jesus, in the story of Jairus's daughter, when He went into the house, put them all out of the house except Peter and James and the mom and dad of the little girl? Why do you think Jesus put them all out of the house? Because faith cannot function in an environment of unbelief. What generally produces an environment of unbelief? A flapping, perverse tongue.

But the men that went up with him said, We be not able to go up against the people; for they are stronger than we (Num. 13:31).

"But…" Our lives are filled with buts. "But you do not understand **my** circumstances, Lord," we whine. "That was good for them, but it is not good for me. You do not understand the economy today. You do not understand the problems in my family."

And they brought up an evil report of the land…" (vs. 32).

God said it was an evil report, and yet they spoke what appeared to be the truth. They were sincere. They spoke the truth as they saw it from their natural eye. They spoke the truth as they heard it with their ears. There were definitely giants in the land. The Word of God reports that the bed of one of those giants was thirteen feet long. Now that is some kind of bed. They were huge dudes! They would have made our football hulks look like midgets. There was no denying the reality of the situation.

Caleb and Joshua did not deny the reality of the giants. Whenever you start talking about speaking the Word of God by faith, you can count on somebody saying, "But how can you deny the circumstances?" You do not deny the circumstances. You focus on what God says instead of focusing on what you see. It is a choice. Faith is a choice. And that is what Joshua and Caleb had to do. They had to make a choice. "Am I going to look at the giants or am I going to look at what God said?" Joshua and Caleb made a choice, and the other ten spies made their choice. But God called the majority report an "evil report."

Then God said, "How long shall I bear with this evil congregation, which murmur against me?" (Num. 14:27). God makes it clear that when I speak contrary to what He says, I am murmuring against Him.

"Say unto them, As truly as I live, saith the Lord, as ye have spoken in mine ears, so will I do to you" (Num. 14:28).

How do you speak? You speak with your mouth, with your tongue, don't you? What had they done with their tongue?

> And **all** the congregation lifted up their voice, and cried; and the people wept that night. And **all** the children of Israel murmured against Moses and against Aaron: and **the whole congregation** said unto them, Would God that we had died in the land of Egypt! (Num. 14:1–2)

God goes out of His way to inform us that "all…the whole congregation" were perverse. **The majority may rule in America, but it does not rule with God. Only faith rules.** There are a lot of people in God's family who are effectively saying, "Would God that we had died in the land of Egypt!" or "Would God that we lived in the land of Egypt!" Why? Because it is tough rolling out of bed every day to walk on the cutting edge of faith. It goes contrary to human experience. It is work. It is violent faith!

There are many people in the kingdom of God who have not yet understood that. Most! Those who will take the promises of God must take them by violence. A violent kind of faith. It is a faith that takes. It is a faith that reaches out and walks around Jericho one step at a time, when you cannot see any way that those walls will ever fall down, because they appear impenetrable. But you walk because God said to. You put one step in front of the other—by faith, not seeing with your eyes, not hearing with your ears, but taking God at His Word. How many marriages would have been saved if we had demonstrated a tongue of faith?

We see, then, that a perverse tongue in God's eyes is a tongue that speaks contrary to what God has said. God said, "I give you the land." They said, "There are giants there. We are not able to overcome it." And God called it an evil report. What would God say about the report coming from your lips each day? Do you agree with God? What do you do when your feelings or experience or other voices, even religious voices, advise you contrary to what God has said? Do you find yourself trying to find "escape clauses" to release you from areas of God's Word that disagree with your desires or feelings or with what the majority seem to say? This lies at the root of America's divorce-and-remarriage debacle. God has spoken clearly on these essential issues. But modern American pastors and parishioners arrogate their own opinions over the simple words of the Scriptures. We manipulate words to suit our personal or collective fancy.

And God said, "I will not listen to or hear those people. They are perverse." Not only that but, "as ye have spoken in mine ears, so will I do to you" (Num. 14:28). And that is a spiritual law. Your tongue speaks faith (in agreement with God) or a contrary faith (in agreement with the spirit of Antichrist). Our contrary faith has enabled Fundamentalist Christians in America to religiously justify a divorce rate higher than the nation as a whole, and produced a 50% higher rate in America's "Bible Belt" (per Barna and Rutgers University reports). Death has resulted to millions of purportedly "Christian" families, desecrating the name and Body of Christ.

Your Tongue: A Matter of Life and Death

The matter of the tongue is a matter of life and death! It is desperately serious! As an issue of life and death, it behooves us to listen very carefully so that we can avoid death and choose life. As a matter of fact, God said exactly that to Israel after they came out of Egypt and just before the survivors of unbelief entered the Promised Land.

> I call heaven and earth to record this day against you, that I have set before you life and death, blessing and cursing: therefore choose life, that both thou and thy seed may live (Deut. 30:29).

But we have to make the choice. No one can make it for you. Neither your pastor nor priest can choose for you. In fact, you cannot necessarily rely upon their choices either. They may be bringing up a "majority report" that sounds good and feels comfortable but that also may disagree with God. You cannot exercise faith vicariously through a "holy man." You must believe God. And you must conform your tongue to agree with His Word. Consider for a prayerful moment these potent words. They could change your life.

> A man's belly shall be satisfied with the fruit of his mouth; and with the increase of his lips shall he be filled (Prov. 18:20).

It is not the fruit of your ears, by sitting in church, but the fruit of your mouth by speaking the word of God, that will satisfy. You will be filled, not with the increase of your ears, but with the increase of your lips.

> Death and life are in the power of the tongue: and they that love it shall eat the fruit thereof (Prov. 18:21).

Did the children of Israel "eat the fruit" of what they loved? Yes. Every one of them missed the promise of God but for two men. Every one of them. To their refusal to tie their tongues to God's truth, God responded, "How shall I bear with this evil congregation, which murmur against me?...**as** *ye* **have spoken** in my ears, so will I do to you" (Num. 14:27–28).

Faith is not a matter of democracy. It is not majority rule. It is faith rule. That is tough stuff, I know. It is tough stuff for me, because I realize that just because I belong to a church or profess Christ does not mean that I will get the promises of God. The majority of God's kids are not operating in the promises of God because they are following the report of the ten spies. Their tongues tell the tale of their testimony. "It does not seem right," we say. "It goes against my experience, what I see with my eyes, what I hear with my ears, what science is telling me, what my bankers tell me."

It was the tongue of the children of Israel that continually got them into trouble. They had loose lips that flapped with their feelings, unformed by faith. This matter of the tongue is truly a matter of life and death. "Life and death are in the power of the tongue, and they that love it will eat the fruit thereof" (Prov. 18:21).

The serpent will speak unbelief. It was the "serpent" whose persuasive tongue sowed the seeds of unbelief in the heart and mind of our forebears, Adam and Eve. His question tests our own tongues continually to this very day: "Hath God said...?" (Gen. 3:11). As God's children were tested in the wilderness, having come out of Egypt, the serpent plied his trade of challenging their trust. He used discouragement as the vehicle.

> And they journeyed from mount Hor by the way of the Red Sea, to compass the land of Edom: and the soul of the people was much discouraged because of the way (Num. 21:4).

Think with me for a minute about what that means: "because of the way." What happened along the way? There were giants. They craved food. And they thirsted for water. They came to a place where the water was bitter. Then they became bitter against God and Moses. Not only did they cry out for water, but also for Egypt. "Wherefore have ye made us to come up out of Egypt," they whined, "to bring us unto this evil place?" (Num. 20:5).

Moses was beside himself with frustration. The people refused to believe. Now they even called God's path to the Promised Land "evil"! Each time when they cried out, instead of responding in faith, they responded in unbelief, longing for the ease of Egypt. "Why didn't you leave us in Egypt? At least there we could be Christian cruisers. We would have leeks and onions and garlic. We did not have to do this faith thing. It is too hard to trust God." They never got the gist of what the experience of walking by faith was all about. Only two men—Joshua and Caleb—really picked it up. And the Word says in Numbers 14 that they had "a different spirit." I want you to remember that as we progress further.

What happens when people get discouraged? They look at the circumstances. It is an invariable rule of life. It is human nature.

> The people spake against God, and against Moses (Num. 21:5).

The people spoke against God and against God's appointed leader. That is what happens when people get discouraged because of the way. The temptation is to flap the jaw and wag the tongue and to say whatever we jolly well please.

When the serpent strikes through unbelief, the tongue tangles with temptation. Death—spiritual and even physical—results. Thousands of Israelites became dead proof to this problem plaguing God's people. Fiery serpents bit the people and many died. Finally, in agony of flesh and spirit, the people begged Moses for deliverance. Their confession reveals both their sin and ours as our tongues refuse to be tamed to speak in agreement with what God has said.

> We have sinned, for **we have spoken against the Lord**... (Num. 21:7).

God provided a remedy. He told Moses to put up a brazen serpent around a pole, and anyone who would look at the brazen serpent would be delivered from death brought about by those poisonous snakes. Notice! The people were not delivered just because Moses put up the pole. The Scripture says that a person bitten had to intentionally look at the brazen serpent in order to live. An act of faith was required.

Have you become discouraged because of the way? Most do. Circumstances cripple belief. Giants grasp for the last vestiges of faith. Needs prevail over promises. The Israelites' tongues spoke the circumstances. And death followed. It was a tongue of death. What do you do with your tongue? Do your words generally voice God's declaration, or do they speak of circumstantial dictates? Does your tongue most resemble the masses of Israel, or the men of "a different spirit": Joshua and Caleb?

The tongue of Egypt is a tongue of perverseness and it is the tongue of death. It may seem right. It may even seem religious. But it will prove to be the tongue of death.

Grasshopper Vision Lubricates Egyptian Tongue

Let us look further at the Egyptian tongue. The children of Israel had come out of Egypt and were standing before the Red Sea. They had just come out. They had just been "saved." They had just been delivered in the Passover from the death angel. They were included among the children of Abraham—by faith, God's chosen. Then came the first temptation. Look at it!

And when Pharaoh drew nigh, the children of Israel lifted up their eyes…
(Exod. 14:10).

What did they lift their eyes up to? Was it God? No! It was the Egyptians:
"behold, the Egyptians marched after them." And any time you and I lift up
our eyes to the Egyptians, to the giants, to the circumstances of life, we will
have strong temptation to speak what we see. We must choose where we put
our eyes, where we put our ears. What do you listen to day and night? Do
you listen to the news day and night, or do you listen to the "Good News"
day and night? I am not suggesting that you be ignorant of what is going on
in the world. But how much of that junk do I put in? How do you renew
your mind? Do you renew it with the news or with the Good News?

> And they said unto Moses, Because there were no graves in Egypt, hast thou
> taken us away to die in the wilderness? Wherefore hast thou dealt thus with
> us, to carry us forth out of Egypt? (Exod. 14:11)

Israel was under tremendous bondage in Egypt. It was awful. Yet no sooner
did they come out, than they wanted to go back in. At their first chance to
use faith, they blew it royally. They spoke what they saw instead of what God
said.

God said, "I give you the Promise Land."

God said, "I delivered you out of Egypt."

And they said, "You did it then, but we do not believe You will do it
now."

We say that Jesus Christ is the same yesterday, today, and forever (Heb.
13:8). But most of us have difficulty truly believing it, don't we? It is intellectual
knowledge but seldom becomes applied truth. If we really believed it, it would
radically change the way we view life. It would also dramatically change the way
we apply God's Word. The problem is clear. Circumstances loom larger than
Christ. We speak of what we see and feel rather than what God has said.

This is how the great serpent, the deceiver, steals victory from you and
from most of God's kids. Israel's experience reveals this viscerally. Listen to
their words as the spies return from the Promised Land: "There **we saw** the
giants, the sons of Anak…and we were in our own sight as grasshoppers, so we
were in their sight" (Num. 13:33). They had "grasshopper vision." They were
so intensely focused on their problems on the near side, that God's promises
were totally out of focus on the far side.

What has Paul told us in the New Testament about the nature of faith?
"We walk by faith, not by sight." Do you see why these two chapters, Numbers
13 and 14, are so important to God in His Word? They are a fulcrum over
which much of the rest of the Word of God turns, in presenting life application
of faith. Through this account, God is attempting to communicate a way of

life. While all of the Word points to Christ, the bulk of the Scriptures reveal how to please God by living and walking the life of faith victoriously. Very little of the Bible is actually devoted to discussing how to be saved from sin. Most Scriptures deal with living the saved life.

Can the Tongue Destroy Nations...and You?

Let us see how Joshua dealt with this matter of faith and the tongue as he led the children of Israel into the Promised Land.

> Now Jericho was straitly shut up because of the children of Israel: none went out, and none came in. And the Lord said unto Joshua, See, **I have given** into thine hand Jericho… (Josh. 6:1–2).

The Lord said, "I have given…." This is a past-tense declaration. It is past-tense because God told Moses to send spies to the land, which "I give to the children of Israel" (Num. 13:1–3). What God gives, He has given. But the men to whom the gift was given all died in the wilderness without receiving the gift because of their unruly tongue of unbelief.

Joshua was one of only two men who heard and believed the promise of God and was allowed to enter the Promised Land. Now Joshua was leading the surviving children of those loose-tongued unbelievers (from Numbers 13 and 14) who all died in the wilderness. Joshua knew the commandments delivered through Moses. He was well aware that the sins of the fathers are visited upon the third and fourth generations (Exod. 20:5).

Joshua knew who he was dealing with, and I want you to see how Joshua treated them in order to accomplish the fulfillment of the promise of God in taking Jericho.

> And Joshua had commanded the people, saying, **Ye shall not shout, nor make any noise with your voice, neither shall any word proceed out of your mouth**, until the day I bid you shout; then shall ye shout.

Why do you think Joshua refused to let the people speak? Because he knew as soon as they saw the walls of that city, as soon as they considered the seemingly ridiculous nature of their walking around the fortress seven days, as soon as they considered "the way," they would begin to mutter and complain among themselves. They would lose the city over unbridled tongues of unbelief. So he ordered them to keep their unbelieving mouths shut. That was the best he could do, because he knew he could not trust them to speak by faith. This incident is not alone in cementing this principle.

Let every word and principle be confirmed by two or three witnesses. Consider Hezekiah's action under similar circumstances. Rabshakeh, ambassador of Sennacherib, king of Assyria, came to challenge the southern Israelites,

Judah, who were under King Hezekiah. Hezekiah requested Rabshakeh to speak in another tongue so that the common people of Israel, who were on the wall, would not understand what was being said. Hezekiah feared an insurrection of unbelief. But the ambassador refused to comply. And he began to yell with a loud voice saying, "Who do you trust? How can you trust Hezekiah? The Lord will not deliver you. You know that Sennacherib is going to come in and wipe you all out. Look what he has done to all these nations around. He is going to destroy you." Second Kings 18:36 records these words:

> But the people held their peace, and answered him not a word: for the king's commandment was, saying, answer him not.

Why would Hezekiah order his people to keep silent? He was not ignorant of Israel's history. He was a godly king who knew the deadly power of an unbelieving and unbridled tongue even among God's own children.

James reaffirmed this principle in the New Testament. He was brutally honest: "If any man offend not in word, the same is a perfect man, and able also to bridle the whole body."

Consider the powerful implications of these words. If you can control your tongue, you can keep your entire body in control *and* be a "perfect" man or woman before God. A "perfect" man is one whose tongue is tied to his faith, not with glib confessions but with godly convictions. A "perfect" man is a man whose tongue agrees with God and who conducts himself accordingly:

> Behold, we put bits in the horses' mouths, that they may obey us; and we turn about their whole body. Behold also the ships, which though they be so great, and are driven by fierce winds, yet are they turned about with a very small helm, withersoever the governor listeth. Even so the tongue is a little member, and boasteth great things. Behold, how great a matter a little fire kindleth! And **the tongue is a fire, a world of iniquity: so is the tongue among our members, that it defileth the whole body, and setteth on fire the course of nature; and it is set on fire of hell** (James 3:3–6).

How many of the members of the Body of Christ are defiled by your own tongue? How many are walking in continual sickness, disease, poverty, and all kinds of bondage, destruction and fear because of their own tongue? How many in the church are walking in fear and destruction and misery because of the tongues of other members of the Body of Christ? How many walk in defeat or totally lose the promises of God due to unbelieving tongues? How many husbands or wives live defeated lives or have destroyed marriages because of undisciplined tongues that refuse to agree with God.

Can the Tongue Be Tamed?

The tongue is a world of iniquity, but it can also be the engine of faith. James further reveals the desperate seriousness of our tongues:

> For every kind of beasts, and of birds, and of serpents, and of things in the sea, is tamed, and hath been tamed of mankind: But **the tongue can no man tame**; it is an unruly evil, full of deadly poison (James 3:7–8).

We are talking about coming "Out of Egypt: Taming the Tongue." James was unrelenting in his diagnosis. The tongue is unruly, wicked, full of iniquity, and sets on fire the course of nature, even in our own bodies. "The tongue can no man tame," he stated. What kind of silliness is that? If the tongue cannot be tamed, then why are we talking about it?

There is only one who can control the tongue: the Holy Spirit. A thoughtful rereading of Acts 2 reveals why God had to send the Holy Spirit, the promise of the Father at Pentecost. It sheds light on why the 120 disciples spoke with other tongues "as the Holy Spirit gave them utterance." Note! It was not the disciples who gave themselves utterance, but the Holy Spirit gave them utterance. Why was this so important? Was it just so others could hear them speak in their own language? I think not. It is the tongue that is the key to the man, and God cannot get hold of the man until He gets hold of his tongue.

Look at the apostles—all of the apostles. Those cowards who all ran away from Jesus in Gethsemane, who denied the Lord three times—as soon as their tongues came under control of the Holy Spirit, from that moment on they spoke with boldness the Word of God. There was not one vacillation after that. The Holy Spirit is the only one who can tame the tongue. Only He can truly tame your tongue and mine. This is perhaps why the issue of "tongues" is the fulcrum of a bitter division in the church. If Satan can keep you from releasing control of your tongue to the Holy Spirit, he can continue in many ways to control you. Similarly, if those exercising "tongues" do so in "fleshly" displays, Egypt knocks at the door. The tongue of God's people can only be tamed when God's people decide to come out of Egypt. Tongues never divided a congregation. Only fleshly demonstrations or refusal to believe divide. Truth both divides and unifies.

Let me ask you. Are you stiffnecked, resisting the Holy Spirit, rejecting the clear words of Scripture to preserve and protect your own tradition or position? It is exceedingly dangerous! Such a heart position resulted in the leaders of God's people turning "back into Egypt" and slaughtering Stephen, the first martyr of the true church (Acts 7:39, 51, 57–60). Unbiblical traditions and beliefs die hard, don't they? But freedom lies on the other side! You may have to die to some sincerely held unbiblical beliefs in order that your spirit may live. We may have to ask with Peter, "What was I that I could withstand God?" (Acts 11:15–17).

It is not that which goes into a man that defiles a man, but that which comes out of his mouth, reasoned Jesus (Matt. 15:11). "For out of the abundance of the heart the mouth speaks" (Matt. 12:34). That is the reason why a man cannot control his tongue. Because out of the abundance of his heart, the mouth speaks. And what is the abundance of the heart? What is the abundance of the heart in most Christians? Not the Word of God, but the word of men: the word of their bishop or denomination, the word of their experience or lack thereof. Circumstances reign supreme. The circumstances of life. That is the abundance of the heart. And it is out of the abundance of your heart that your mouth speaks, whether pastor or people.

I have the same problem. We are all tempted with the circumstances of life. We struggle to believe God. And that is why we must have violent faith. We must gird up the loins of our minds while submitting wholesale to the Holy Spirit. We will have no end-time power, no end-time authority, and no end-time endurance without it. This is serious business! Your tongue holds life and death. And your tongue, according to Jesus, is tied to ultimate judgment. Listen carefully to the Lord of the church pound on this point:

> But I say to you, that **every idle word that men shall speak, they shall give account** thereof in the day of Judgment. For **by thy words thou shalt be justified, and by thy words thou shalt be condemned** (Matt. 12:36–37).

Do You Agree with God?

We find that when the Holy Spirit did get hold of the disciples' tongues, they were all amazingly in one accord. How is it they came into one accord? The prophet asked rhetorically, "Can two walk together, except they be agreed?" (Amos 3:3). The answer is an obvious, NO!

God has said, "How can I walk with you? Your tongues are muttering perverseness. You are speaking contrary to almost everything I tell you in my Word. I tell you by the stripes of Jesus you are healed, and you say how sick you are or that My healing is not for today. I tell you how much I have provided all your needs and you tell me how poor you are. I tell you that I have made you the righteousness of God in Christ Jesus and you tell me what a worm you are. I tell you to forbid not to speak with tongues, but you pass an edict directly opposing my Word (1 Cor. 14:39). I tell you I hate divorce, but you do it anyway, claiming My approval. Whose church is it? I am the Father, here. I told you what I did and what I will do for you, and you just keep speaking to the contrary. You do not really believe anything I say, do you?" How would you feel as a parent? God is fed up!

Can two walk together, unless they be agreed? (Amos 3:3)

A fool's mouth is his destruction, and his lips are the snare of his soul (Prov. 18:7).

Death and life are in the power of the tongue: and they that love it shall eat the fruit thereof (Prov. 18:21).

How do I agree with God? Since God called His people out of Egypt, we ought to find His answer recorded from the time He first called His children out until now. And that is precisely what we find. Listen to Moses, the former prince of Egypt.

"And thou shalt shew thy son in that day, saying, This is done because of that which the Lord did unto me when I came forth out of Egypt.

And it shall be for a sign unto thee upon thine hand, and for a memorial between thine eyes, that **the Lord's law may be in thy mouth**: for with a strong hand hath the Lord brought thee out of Egypt (Exod. 13:8–9).

Where should God's Word be? In my what? In my mouth! Not in my head. Not under my arm. Not on my coffee table. Not in my ear, but in my mouth. That is the key. Say it now! "God's Word must be in my mouth, on my tongue." Moses cast the mantle of authority on Joshua to lead the people into the Promised Land. What did Joshua have to say about living victoriously?

This book of the law shall not depart out of thy mouth; but thou shalt meditate therein day and night, that thou mayest observe to do according to all that is written therein: for then thou shalt make thy way prosperous, and then thou shalt have good success.

There is a condition for spiritual prosperity and victory. I must agree with God on every point. To do that, the very words of God must not depart out of my mouth.

What happens, then, when we run into circumstances in which we are strongly tempted to believe what we see? What do we do when our senses or current theories of science or theology scream at us contrary to what God says? What should I do when even spiritual leaders seem to exalt their own ideas and opinions over what is clearly stated in Scripture? Paul's instruction gives us aid:

For though we walk in the flesh, we do not war after the flesh: (For the weapons of our warfare are not carnal, but mighty through God to the pulling down of strongholds;) **Casting down imaginations, and every high**

thing that exalteth itself against the knowledge of God, and bringing into captivity every thought to the obedience of Christ (2 Cor. 10:3–5).

If you inspect the Greek, the word *imaginations* means "reasoning and thoughts." So Paul has advised you to cast down your reasoning, your thoughts, your traditions, and all those things you feel are so important to you. Our reasoning and our thoughts are the most important things that we have. And Paul has said, "Cast them down." Cast down also the reasoning and thoughts of others who, despite their education or position, disagree with God. Then bring every thought into captivity to the obedience of Christ. That is how violent faith works. It is directly linked to your tongue. "But how can I do it?" you ask.

First, you plug in the Word of God. You can not get enough of it by just sitting in a church service. Your mind will be renewed the other six days a week in the world. So you have to plug the Word into your heart every day. How? By putting it in your mouth. You must memorize it. You must speak it quietly to yourself. Massage it into the membranes of your mind and heart. Meditate on it. Speak it. Mutter it continually. It will enter your ear, be planted in your heart, and out of the increasing abundance of your heart your mouth will continue to speak. Faith will come. It will come by hearing, from your own lips, and hearing by the Word of God" (Rom. 10:17).

Let's pray. Father, I thank You that in the days of famine I shall be satisfied. I thank You, Father, that I can do all things through Christ who strengthens me, regardless of how it looks. Father, I thank You that I do not have the spirit of fear, but of power and of love and a sound mind. Father, I thank You that by the stripes of Jesus I am healed. Father, I thank You that You have made me the righteousness of God in Christ Jesus. I thank You, Lord, that you are taming my tongue.

And you do not acquire a tamed tongue merely by looking at and listening to somebody who has been doing this for ten or fifteen years. Because then you may get discouraged. How did they walk around Jericho? One step at a time. Take one verse out of the Word of God. Put it onto your tongue. As you begin to meditate on one verse or passage at a time, the Holy Spirit will reveal that one to you. It will explode in your heart, in your mind. The Holy Spirit will take that verse, bind it upon your heart, and then you will get another one. One upon one upon one, line upon line, and before long Jericho falls.

Years ago, on an auto-parts business in Pasadena, California, I saw a little sign that caught my attention: "We speak and stock foreign car parts." So I ask you. What do you speak and stock? You cannot speak what you do not stock. What do you speak and stock of the Word of God? Life is on the line!

Pray again with me. Father, I commit myself today, in the name of Jesus, that I will stock the Word of God in the membranes of my heart and my mind, that I may walk by faith and not by sight. Lord, I need this God kind of faith in these days. I see the end-time pressures building and the trials of life pressing in. I commit this to You, in Jesus' name. Father, I will agree with You at every point. And help me to cast down my own reasoning and thoughts that exalt themselves against You. Forgive me for my unbelief. Tame my tongue by Your Holy Spirit. In Jesus' name. Amen!

Chapter Seventeen

Anointed for Deliverance

Have you found your place in God's end-time purpose?
The real issue is not who I am, but who God is.

WE STAND AT THE MOMENT OF TRUTH in the valley of decision! Will we come out of Egypt or will we not? Will we continue to straddle the heavenly fence, fraternizing with the Spirit of God on Sunday but fornicating with the spirit of Egypt on Monday? There has never been a more profound moment in history for the Word of God to pierce the deepest recesses of our minds and hearts. This is the moment of truth for those who profess the name of Christ.

The Word of God is sharper than a surgeon's scalpel, seeking to cut away the flesh of Egypt. We are poised on the cutting edge of that Word. Will you and I yield to the radical procedures needed to prepare us, as a pure Bride, for the Second Coming and the difficult days ahead? The Great Physician stands ready to do His part.

> For the Word of God is quick, and powerful, and sharper than any two-edged sword, piercing even to the dividing asunder of soul and spirit, and the joints and marrow, and is a discerner of the thoughts and intents of the heart (Heb. 4:12).

We are beyond desire at the point of decision. That is where we are. The point of decision. It is a spiritual travesty to come out of Egypt and sit in the wilderness. That is what happened to Israel. They came out of Egypt but sat in the wilderness for forty years, while the Promised Land was just a few miles in front of them. They refused to see themselves in the Word of God. They refused to agree with God. Their undisciplined tongues of unbelief brought death. Do you want that to be your lot? I rather doubt it.

God Winces over Our Bondage

In this chapter we ask a probing and provocative question: How can I see myself in the Word of God when I come out of Egypt?

The goal God had for His people then, is still God's goal for His people now. We must remind ourselves again. It is God's people who are in Egypt. God is not talking to the world here. When we read His addresses to people coming out of Egypt, generally He is not talking to those we think of as the "world" or the nonbeliever or the person who has not confessed Jesus Christ as Savior and Lord. He is speaking to and about those who have come into a knowledge of the truth, who claim to be His children, but who are still living in the ways of the old household. They live at least part time in the household of Pharaoh, under the household of Satan, rather than having stepped fully into the household of God. That, I am convinced, includes the majority of American Christians today.

We talked earlier about daring to live in the spirit of adoption. God's kids can be adopted into God's family and still live in the ways of the old family. Do you realize that? You can have your Father's name and never live according to your Father's ways. You can see that in the natural. You can have a natural child who is called by his father's name yet never lives according to his father's way, by choice. Therefore, he does not receive the blessings of living in that household. In fact, he may be disinherited. We can disinherit ourselves, as children of God, from receiving the promises of God by refusing to walk by faith in the ways of our Father's household. With that review, we find God wincing over the bondage of His children in Egypt.

What Does a Deliverer Look Like?

And the Lord said, I have surely seen the affliction of my people which are in Egypt, and have heard their cry by reason of their taskmasters, for I know their sorrows; And **I am come down to deliver them** out of the hand of the Egyptians... (Exod. 3:7–8*a*).

God will deliver His people. He has promised. But He seeks a human hand and a human heart through whom He can work, since He has given dominion to man in the earth (see Ps. 8:4–6).

I am come down to deliver them out of the hands of the Egyptians, and to bring them up out of that land into a good land... (Exod. 3:8).

Come now therefore, and I will send thee... (Exod. 3:10).

Join me in taking a closer look at the call of Moses:

> Now Moses kept the flock of Jethro his father in law, the priest of Midian… (Exod. 3:1).

Moses was a shepherd. The great leader that God called for deliverance was a nondescript shepherd. He, like David, was a nobody at the time of his calling. The shepherd David was so puny, so insignificant, that his own brothers, when he brought bread and cheese to where they were fighting the Philistines, looked at him with disdain and said, in essence, "What are you doing out here, you punk kid?" (1 Sam. 17:28). Saul tried to arm David with his own armor. Israel's military tried to cloak David with the garments of "Egypt." But David had a different spirit about him, boldly confronting Goliath:

> Thou comest to me with a sword, and with a spear, and with a shield: but I come to thee in the name of the Lord of hosts, the God of the armies of Israel, whom thou hast defied (1 Sam. 17:45).

The puny shepherd kid turned big . It was not because of who he was, but because of who God is, and because of who David understood himself to be in relationship to his Father, God.

So here is Moses, a measly old shepherd. Not exalted among the people. Not a fearless leader. But an unknown shepherd of forty years experience. Let me ask you. How do you see yourself? Are you a mere shepherd in society? Shepherds were despised by Egypt but are prized with God. God specializes in raising simple people to raise His arm of deliverance. Shepherds are despicable to the Egyptian mind but dear to God's heart (Gen. 46:34).

There is yet more that God saw in the man, Moses.

> By faith Moses, when he was come to years [the age of accountability], refused to be called the son of Pharaoh's daughter (Heb. 11:24).

Moses was a man of faith. He made a decision of households. Would he live in the household of Satan—man's way of doing things symbolized by Pharaoh—or would he live in the household of God? He made a life decision to dwell in the household of God, so he refused, by faith, to be called the son of Pharaoh's daughter.

There is something else that Moses did by faith:

> By faith he forsook Egypt, not fearing the wrath of the king: for he endured, as seeing him who is invisible (Heb. 11:27).

Moses acted in faith. He had to engage in two acts. The first act was to make a decision of households. He refused to be called the son of Pharaoh's

233

daughter. Some people think that when you make a decision to receive Christ, you have automatically walked out of Egypt. It is not so. God is continuing to call **His** people out of Egypt. If they were already out of Egypt, why would He be begging them to come out? Most of God's people are in Egypt. That is why He is calling them out. Many professing Christians continue to claim identity in the ways of the world, in Pharaoh's household.

So Moses had a two-step process. The first step was to make a choice of family, God's or Satan's. The second step was to decide whether he would walk out of the ways of Egypt altogether. He did that by faith, just like you and I must do it. By faith. We must join Abraham and Moses in looking for that city with foundations whose builder and maker is God.

Is This Holy Ground?

"And the angel of the Lord appeared unto him [Moses] in a flame of fire out of the midst of a bush…" (Exod. 3:2). God appeared to Moses in a flame of fire. What does fire generally symbolize in the Word of God? It symbolizes purification, does it not? But it also symbolizes the agent of purification, the Holy Spirit. Now, Scripture does not say it in so many words, but I believe that God manifested Himself to Moses by the Holy Spirit in the burning bush. The fire was a manifestation of the Holy Spirit. Think back. When the disciples were sitting around for fifty days, waiting for the "promise" that had been given them by Jesus, the Holy Spirit came with cloven tongues "as of fire" (Acts 2:3). The passage does not say it **was** fire. It says "as of fire."

I want you to see here, in Exodus 3:2, that the bush never burned. It was "as fire" but it never burned. Neither the bush nor Moses were burned. But Moses' heart was lit aflame. The Holy Spirit had come to bring God's call to Moses. Who is calling us? Who is calling you? Who has already called you and me? Is your heart yet burning within you, perhaps even at this very moment?

> And when the Lord saw that he turned aside to see, God called unto him out of the midst of the bush… (Exod. 3:4).

You see, God manifests Himself in the earth by His Holy Spirit. That is the role of the Holy Spirit. The purpose of the Holy Spirit is to be the arm and voice of God to men in the earth. When Jesus was here, the Holy Spirit worked through Him. But when He left, He said, "I will send the promise of the father." The "promise" is the Holy Spirit who speaks, guides, and empowers men and women to exercise God's dominion and to do His will in the earth. For this reason Jesus' parting words to all who would follow Him were these: "As my Father hath sent me, even so send I you" (John 20:21). His very next words were "Receive ye the Holy Ghost" (John 20:22). You can receive the Holy Spirit, or you can reject Him. It is a serious matter to reject the Holy Spirit.

And when the Lord saw that he [Moses] turned aside to see, God called unto him out of the midst of the bush, and said, Moses, Moses. And he said, Here am I (Exod. 3:4).

I have to ask myself the question, "What am I saying when God calls?" Then again, "Do I even hear when God calls?" That is the threshold question. Most American Christians are intensely busy about the cares of life and this world. We are not spending quiet and quality time daily in the Word of God. How, then, can our hearts be truly open? How can the fallow ground of my heart be broken up to receive the seed of the Word of God, so that when it is planted there by the Holy Spirit, it does not wash away or blow away with every wind of doctrine and with the troubles of life? Is my ear, is your ear open to truly hear when God calls? How else can we know our personal responsibility in the Kingdom of God?

Once you hear Him, do you say, "Here am I"? Say the words right now: "Here am I, Lord!" Say them! Out loud! Let God work through your faith. Faith is NOW! **"Who am I?" must become "Here am I!"**

Moses had an awesome, holy respect for God. He did not run around in life with a half-baked, cavalier attitude toward God. "Oh yeah, I believe in God. I go to church." His was not a user-friendly God. He had an awesome, holy respect, such that when God spoke to Him, he hid his face from Him. He understood that God is a holy God, that he was on holy ground.

Moreover he said, I am the God of thy father, the God of Abraham, the God of Isaac, and the God of Jacob. And Moses hid his face; for he was afraid to look upon God (Exod. 3:6).

Are you on holy ground in your living room, in your bedroom, in your office, or wherever it is that God is ministering His Word to you? Are you conscious that when you sit there at that desk, or at the table, or wherever you are, that your feet are on holy ground? This is a personal faith transaction. Only at that point does the Word of God become alive and real. Only at that point are you and I conscious that there is a genuine transaction taking place between our Father and His son or daughter. We must see ourselves in our Father's Word. That is faith. Anything less is mere religion.

Who Am I?

Now comes the moment of truth for Moses. **Religion must become reality, or it is futility**: Come now therefore, and I will send thee unto Pharaoh, that thou mayest bring forth my people the children of Israel out of Egypt." God has been discussing with Moses the problems of the children of Israel. The need is great! The time is now!

Now therefore, behold, the cry of the children of Israel is come unto me: and I have also seen the oppression wherewith the Egyptians oppress them (Exod. 3:9).

Most of us are adept at seeing all the problems, all the needs, and all the difficulties. We could write volumes on the circumstances around us and our perceptions. But when it comes down to being the agent of deliverance, somehow the "I" just seems to slip away. I? Me? Where do I fit in the picture?

God first discussed Israel's problem. Moses saw the problem. Deep in his heart he knew about the problem. That is how he got into the wilderness in the first place. He saw the problem forty years earlier. But it is not enough to see the problem. You must see the solution.

It is still not enough to see the solution. You must see yourself as part of the solution. I have to see myself as part of the solution. And I must discover what God has in mind for me to do as part of that solution. Most of us, though, are like Moses. We want God to send anyone other than us. "Send Aaron, God. He is a much better speaker. He has far more training."

And Moses said unto God, Who am I, that I should go unto Pharaoh, and that I should bring forth the children of Israel out of Egypt? (Exod. 3:11)

This was Moses' response to God's choice. First there was God's general expression of need and urgency. Suddenly God pointed His finger and declared, "You are the one I want." It is like sitting in the church service and having your pastor point his finger at you, or at least you feel like he is pointing his finger at you, because the message comes home. How does the message come home? The Holy Spirit whispers in your ear, "That's you." Then your heart begins to pound!

So Moses had the message come home to him, and he responded "Who am I?" He quivered and shook in his boots. "Why are you pointing at me, Lord?" he whined. "I am just an old shepherd out here in the wilderness."

Have you ever asked the "Who am I" question? I have. Maybe not in words, but in my attitude. In my response or the lack thereof. If there is no response to the call, then I have done one of three things:

- I have just completely turned God off;
- I have rebelled openly against Him and said, "I won't";
- Or I am saying, "Who am I? You have the wrong person, Lord. You made a big mistake."

Just like He made a "big mistake" with Moses, God made a "big mistake" with Gideon. He made a "big mistake" with David. He made a "big mistake" with Jesus. Don't forget! Jesus was born in a stable. Israel was looking for a strong king on a white stallion but was given a suffering servant born in a manger.

God's response never changes to our artful dodging and excuse making. He merely declares His sufficiency in the face of our insufficiency. That is true grace. And God did just that for Moses.

> And God said unto Moses, "I AM THAT I AM…" (Exod. 3:14).

God forcefully admonished, "Moses, you see yourself through your own eyes, but you are my son. I am your Father. I can see a picture broader than you can. You are my man, and I will be everything that you need to accomplish what I give you to do as my son. I AM. I am your strength. I am your mouth. I am your voice. I am your hands. I am your feet. I am your mind. I am everything you need. I AM THAT I AM."

This was the call of Moses, the way God singled him out. Moses' response? Does Moses sound like a great deliverer? Does he infuse you with confidence? Hardly! And is such a response not just as typical of you and me? We could call Moses "Mr. Everyman." He is just like us. "Who am I, Lord?" It all sounds so humble, doesn't it? Yet God did not think so. His anger was aroused at Moses' excuse making (Exod. 4:14). Why? **The real issue is not who I am but who God is.**

What Is Man?

Before we go further, we must understand something about the nature of dominion and authority in the earth. God made His plans and intentions known from the beginning:

> And God said, Let us make man in our image, after our likeness: and let them have dominion… (Gen. 1:26).

Dominion over what? What was man's role? He was to exercise dominion over the whole earth as God's hand extended. For that reason, God created man in His very own image:

> So God created man in His own image, in the image of God created he him; male and female created He them. And God blessed them, and God said unto them, Be fruitful, and multiply, and replenish the earth, and subdue it: and have dominion over the fish of the sea, and over the fowl of the air, and over every living thing that moveth upon the earth. (Gen. 1:27–28).

"I have given you everything," God said. "Now you, Adam, go out and exercise this dominion. Do it in my name. Do it under my authority. Do it as my son. I give you authority."

I want you to see that once God told Adam to exercise dominion, God did not come down to exercise dominion in this earth. Adam operated with dominion over the earth, with the delegated authority from his Father. His Father did not come down to meddle with it. He let Adam do it. God had forever committed Himself to working exclusively through men in the earth.

That is how Adam got all messed up. Adam had a free choice. He could act with his authority, with total responsibility the way God had given it to him, or he could mess it up. And he messed it up. In essence, he transferred or forfeited that authority to Satan when he sinned. Because Adam's action involved "kingdoms," Adam actually committed treason against God. He turned dominion in the earth over to Satan. Satan became "the god of this world," the "prince of this world," and the "prince of the power of the air" that "now worketh in the children of disobedience" (2 Cor. 4:4; John 14:30; Eph. 2:2).

David clearly understood the nature of the dominion that God had granted. His oft-quoted words established man's dominion from the beginning, as elementary to God's design:

> When I consider thy heavens, the work of thy fingers, the moon and the stars, which thou hast ordained; What is man, that thou art mindful of him? And the son of man, that thou visitest him? (Ps. 8:1–4)

David was asking the question that men always ask. It is a traditional man-oriented question that says, "What is man? We think, *Who am I? Small peanuts. What is man? God does not think much about me. He is up there on His great white throne, and I am puny, little me down here. God really does not care about me. Woe is me.*

But David did not leave it there. I want you to see what David understood about your role and mine in the earth:

> For thou hast made him [man] a little lower than the angels, and hast crowned him with glory and honour (Ps. 8:5).

The Revised Version does not use the word "angels" in verse 5. It reads, "For thou has made him a little lower than God." A direct Hebrew-to-English translation taken from Green's Hebrew lexicon gives a similar rendition:

> What is man that you remember him and the son of man that you visit him **and made you him have lack a little from God**, and with glory and honor.

The word translated *God* here is the Hebrew word *Elohiym*, which is the most majestic word for God in the Scripture. It means, "The most high God," or "the Supreme God." Could David actually be saying here "**thou hast made man a little lower than the most high God** and hast crowned him with glory and honor"?

238

What did the psalmist mean when he wrote, "God standeth in the congregation of the mighty; he judgeth among the gods" (Ps. 82:1)?

Remember, "Every word of God is pure" (Prov. 30:5). So what is the psalmist talking about? Is he talking about the idols of the world? Other religions? No! He goes on to say:

> ...all the foundations of the earth are out of course. I have said, **Ye are gods; and all of you are children of the Most High**. But ye shall die like men... (Ps. 82:5).

Jesus offered this understanding in a verbal spar with the Jews. He quoted directly from Psalm 82 when accused of blasphemy:

> Is it not written in your law, I said ye are gods? If He called them gods unto whom the Word of God came and the Scripture cannot be broken... (John 10:30–39).

What does this mean? Are Jesus and the psalmist saying that we should exalt ourselves and walk around saying "I am god"? Was this laying the foundation for the New Age movement? No! The New Age movement is a counterfeit of the real. Neither Jesus nor the psalmist was saying we ARE God or will become God. What they are saying is that we are to understand ourselves as having been placed in an extraordinarily high position in the eyes of God.

Look at it this way. If Elohim, the Most High God, is my Father, and I am His son, what should we expect of the kids of the "Most High God"? Do the children not take on the characteristics of their parents and the parents' household? "Be ye therefore followers [imitators] of God, as dear children," instructed the apostle Paul (Eph. 5:1). So it means that I am somehow to see myself in a radical change. I am not to walk in the selfishness of my own pride, but I am to walk in the full knowledge of what it means to be a son of Elohim. "Beloved, **now** are we the sons of God...," wrote John the apostle (1 John 3:2).

Only when I see myself in that position, will I ever be able to truly fulfill the call of God in my life. This is precisely what Jesus declared as the "last Adam."

> For as the Father hath life in Himself; so hath He given to the Son to have life in Himself: And hath given Him [Jesus] authority to execute judgment also, **because He is the Son of Man** (John 5:26).

Authority? Where? In the earth. Jesus was the Word incarnate, made flesh, in the earth. And Jesus testified He was given authority in the earth as a man to execute judgment because "He is the Son of Man." His authority in the earth came not because He was the Son of God, but because He was the Son of Man. This does not deny or undermine His deity. Rather, it confirms His mission.

Jesus had authority in the earth because He became as man. God had given dominion to man, and man alone, in the earth. God does not break His word. Man still has dominion in the earth. God expects His sons to reclaim that dominion from Satan, to whom the first Adam forfeited authority. That is why God is calling His people to stand up in righteousness, to see themselves in the Word of God, and to begin to fulfill their responsibilities. We must rightly exercise that dominion and authority in the earth before Christ returns. Either we are Christ's Body, or we are not!

Again, the Scriptures clearly state, Jesus Himself had authority in the earth, not because He was the Son of God, but because He was the Son of Man. He was truly "God the Son," but He emptied Himself of all the perks of being God, humbled Himself, and became obedient just as you and I must (Phil. 2:7–8). He became a "high priest" that could be "touched with the feelings of our infirmities" because He was "tempted [tested] in all points like as we are" but without sin (Heb. 4:15). Because of this, Jesus "was given a name above all names" (Phil. 2:9–10), and we can "come boldly" before God (Heb. 4:16). Humbly, yet boldly! **We must not only accept our position of righteousness IN Christ but we must also accept our position of responsibility THROUGH Christ in the earth.**

It would be foolish to ignore the tremendous tension of traditional religious thinking over this very issue. We must remember that Jesus was a man on the earth. He was God. But He was also fully man, and He was tested with **all** of the problems of man. He was touched with **all** of our infirmities, just like we are, yet without sin (Heb. 4:15). So we cannot and must not remove His true manhood. To do so is to both destroy His mission and subvert His message.

Religious people always want to piously stick "deity" alone on Jesus and strip away His manhood so they can explain away their responsibility. Then we can blithely say, "Well, that was Jesus, and He is God." In so doing, we cleverly and religiously wash our hands like Pontius Pilate did, thinking we have absolved ourselves of full accountability and responsibility. In so doing, we truly deny the power of God in order to protect our own exalted thinking and tradition, making the Word of God of none effect (see Mark 7:7–13; 2 Tim. 3:5).

We see this tension revealed in a confrontation between Jesus and the religious leaders of His day who knew the Scriptures backward and forward.

> And, behold, they brought to Him [Jesus] a man sick of the palsy, lying on a bed: and Jesus seeing their faith said unto the sick of the palsy; Son, be of good cheer; thy sins be forgiven thee (Matt. 9:3–5).

Listen to the way traditional religion responds to this issue:

> And, behold, certain of the scribes said within themselves, This man blasphemeth. And Jesus knowing their thoughts said, Wherefore think ye evil in your hearts? For whether is easier, to say, Thy sins be forgiven thee; or to say, Arise and walk? (Matt. 9:3–5)

Jesus said, "I have authority in the earth to do all of them, **because I am the Son of Man**. So which one is easier? Take your choice. I do not care. I am here under authority to do all of them. Then He said,

> But that ye may know that the **Son of Man** hath power [in the Greek this is "authority"] on earth to forgive sins, (then saith He to the sick of the palsy), Arise, take up thy bed, and go unto thine house (Matt. 9:6).

This kind of talk infuriated the scribes and Pharisees. It may trouble you, too. They thought "this man blasphemeth," and the penalty for blasphemy was death (Matt. 9:3). They envied His power (Matt. 27:18). That was their heart motivation for ridding Jesus from the earth. But they crucified Him for blasphemy (Matt. 26:65–66). That was the official religious justification for death. And religious people still "crucify" as blasphemers men and women who own up to what God has declared of His sons and daughters. Sometimes we call it "pride." But which is more prideful, to come into agreement with what God has said, or to arrogate your opinion over what God has said, in order to preserve the required stamp of religious approval?

If, as the apostle Paul warned, I am "not to think more highly than I ought to think," then how highly ought I to think (Rom. 12:3)? Has it become "prideful" to humbly agree with God, or do we prefer the false humility of religious tradition that denies what God has said, declaring, "That is blasphemy." Is not the heart of blasphemy verbalizing our disagreement with God? W o u l d   I contest God Himself? That is arrogance of the highest order. It is, in effect, declaring myself equal with God, under the guise of humility. Furthermore, can two walk together unless they be agreed?" (Amos 3:3).

Please Note! That does not mean that you or I are perfect or that we can cleanse a man from sin. That would be a faulty understanding of what Jesus was saying in Matthew 9. On the contrary, Jesus was saying here, "I have put men, my children, in the earth as my agents to agree with me so that when I say to men their sins are forgiven (that is, when my Father says 'your sins are forgiven'), my children can turn to the same person and declare, under authority, 'your sins are forgiven if you repent and turn away.'" He was saying, "I have authority to say the same thing my Father says—to agree with Him on His conditions and to declare it so."

And He [Jesus] arose, and departed to His house. But when the multitudes saw it, they marveled, and glorified God, **which had given such power unto men** (Matt. 9:7–8).

Notice the words. God does not mince words, nor does He misspeak Himself. The passage does not say "which had given such power unto **God**." It says, "which had given such power unto **men**." You see, the tension between traditional religious thinking and true spiritual life is that people always want to try to put God in their own limited box of thinking. Religious man thinks that it is blasphemy to admit and acknowledge who I am in the family of God. For years, the church and her leaders have put down people of true faith, thinking that the way to avoid religious pride is to keep people from acknowledging the good thing that is in them through Christ Jesus. But Paul admonished Philemon, "...that the communication of thy faith may become effectual [operational, active, working] by the acknowledging [owning up to, admitting] of every good thing which is in you in Christ Jesus" (Philem. 6). You make the choice. Agree with God. To do otherwise is to declare yourself equal with Him.

How to Anger God

Moses engaged in a verbal sparring match with God. God, in no uncertain terms, told Moses he was hand-picked as deliverer of Israel. Understandably, Moses questioned, "Who am I that I should go unto Pharaoh?" To which God graciously responded, "Certainly, I will be with thee" (Exod. 3:10–12). God then went into great detail, describing what would happen as Moses embarked upon his task (Exod. 3:13–22).

Moses refused to take God simply at His Word. He reasoned, "**But**, behold they will not believe me, nor hearken…" (Exod. 4:1). Watch out for the "buts"! God does not take kindly to buts. As our Father, He expects us to take Him at His Word. After all, He IS God!

We have seen earlier how Israel's "buts" deprived them of the Promised Land. Twelve spies searched the land. Ten spies returned a report of giants. Caleb stilled the people, saying, "Let us go up at once, and possess it." "**BUT** the men that went up with him said, We be not able to go up against the people; for they are stronger than we" (Num. 13:30–31).

We think our "buts" are rational and reasonable, that we have good reason to disagree with what God has said. Eve had the same kinds of thoughts. We value our perceptions over God's plans and pronouncements. Even pastors do. We expect God to negotiate, to compromise, to see it our way. But God does not see things our way. "My thoughts are not your thoughts, neither are my ways your ways, saith the Lord" (Isa. 55:8). It was an "evil report," God declared of the spies who exalted their opinion over God's

Word. It cost them and an entire nation the joy of entering the Promised Land (Num. 13:32; 14:30–31).

God may be patient, but His anger can wax hot, yes even against His chosen people or "deliverers." Moses continued to equivocate with God. "Throw your rod on the ground," ordered the Great I AM. And the rod became a hissing snake. But Lord, "I am not eloquent," Moses retorted; "I am slow of speech." The Lord, losing patience, responded abruptly, "Who hath made man's mouth? Have not I the Lord?" (Exod. 4:10–11).

And the anger of the Lord was kindled against Moses (Exod. 4:14).

What does it take to anger God? Do you want to be the one to test Him? **These end times that are coming upon us are no time to test a God who is intent upon bringing the tributaries of history together to fulfill His eternal Word. He is looking for a remnant—a few good men and women of true faith who will dare to agree with Him, without argument.**

We think Moses was being humble. God did not think so. From the Divine viewpoint, Moses was elevating his own ideas and thoughts above those of the Almighty. And the "anger of the Lord was kindled against Moses." When God wants business done, He means business. When He speaks, He expects His servants and sons to take Him at His Word.

The Spirit of God is saying, "I AM. I will be your mouth. I will be anything you need in order to do what I want you to do. I will be with you." Will you dare to take God at His word? Will you agree with Him even if it goes against your experience, your feelings, or your tradition?

Can Your Hand Be God's Hand?

Now things are about to get exciting. True trust reveals true faith, and true faith yields tremendous transformation. The next few pages could change your life forever. I trust your vision will be expanded. I believe your heart will leap with joy in the leap of faith you are about to take.

And he [Aaron] shall be thy spokesman unto the people: and he shall be, even he shall be to thee instead of a mouth, and **thou shalt be to him instead of God** (Exod. 4:16).

What is God saying? Is God saying that He is going to step out of the picture so that Moses, or you, can take over? No. He is saying that if you or Moses is a son of God, you must act as if you are a son of God. You must know the responsibility and authority of that name and position. You have a responsibility. When you walk down the street, you must walk with the full knowledge and responsibility that you are a son of Elohim, the Most High God. That is heavy. That is not an ego trip, but a humbling responsibility.

Moses finally got the message. He decided to agree with God, to take Him at His Word. And an amazing thing happened. Here is the record:

> And Moses took his wife and sons, and set them upon an ass, and he returned to the land of Egypt: and **Moses took the rod of God in his hand** (Exod. 4:20).

Let me ask you, "How did the rod of Moses become **the rod of God?**" It was clearly Moses' rod (Exod. 4:2). Something happened between Exodus 4:2 and Exodus 4:20 to convert the rod of Moses into the "rod of God."

I want to call your attention to the story of Gideon. He also was called as a "deliverer." You see, God called Gideon to deliver the children of Israel from the Midianites. Israel was having a similar problem with the Midianites that they'd had with the Egyptians. Israel cried out. They needed a deliverer. But there was no deliverer around.

God called puny, little Gideon, who was hiding away, frightened. God called when Gideon was in a frightened state, and God said, "Go in this thy might…. Have not I sent thee?" (Judg. 6:14). What a seemingly stupid thing to say! I am sure Gideon thought the same thing. "What in the world are you talking about—my might? I do not have any might. I am running scared like everybody else." Yet the angel of the Lord called him "thou mighty man of valour" (Judg. 6:12). Something happened to Gideon. Suddenly, in the next chapter, we find him transformed. He now saw things from God's viewpoint. He was now ordering soldiers.

> When I blow the trumpet, I and all that are with me, then blow ye the trumpets also on every side of all the camp, and say, **the sword of the Lord, and of Gideon** (Judg. 7:18).

How did Gideon's sword become God's sword? God did not have a sword. So how could he say such a silly thing? Let me tell you. Gideon moved from the point where he could not see himself in his Father's word, to the point where he accepted himself in his Father's word. God said, "Surely I will be with thee…"—the same promise He gave to Moses and the same promise He gives to you (see Judg. 6:16; Exod. 3:12).

> Fear thou not, for I am with thee: be not dismayed; for I AM thy God: I will strengthen thee; yea I will help thee; yea I will uphold thee with the right hand of my righteousness (Isa. 41:10).

The Bible reports that the Spirit of the Lord came upon Gideon (Judg. 6:36). I want you to know that the Spirit of the Lord came upon Moses.

The Spirit of the Lord came upon Gideon. The Spirit of the Lord came upon Jesus. And the Spirit of the Lord will come upon you, if you will let Him.

It was not until the Spirit of the Lord came upon Jesus that He was able to work and perform the will of His Father (John 1:32–33). And the Spirit of the Lord must come upon you and upon me (Acts 1:8). When you see yourself in God's Word as did Moses, as did Jesus, and as did Gideon, you too will cry out as did formerly fearful Gideon: "The sword of the Lord and of Gideon" (Judg. 7:18).

Jesus' disciples were no different before their lives were transformed and their identity crisis was resolved. Peter had denied the Lord three times. Just a few days later, we find him preaching with boldness. And they saw the boldness of Peter and John, and they discerned that they were ignorant men, but they also discerned that they had been with Jesus. The difference? Holy Spirit empowerment, coupled with seeing themselves in God's Word. What a new and novel prayer they prayed: "Lord…grant unto thy servants, that with all boldness they may speak thy word, **by stretching forth thine hand to heal**; and that signs and wonders may be done in the name of thy Holy Child Jesus (Acts 4:29–30). They saw their hand as God's hand extended. How about you? Do you truly see your hand as God's hand extended?

Jesus followed the same pattern in Luke 4. Jesus stood up to read, as was His custom, and He found the place where it was written in the Book of Isaiah:

> The Spirit of the Lord is upon me, because He hath anointed me to preach the gospel to the poor; He hath sent me to heal the brokenhearted, to preach deliverance to the captives, and recovering of sight to the blind, to set at liberty them that are bruised. To preach the acceptable year of the Lord. And He closed the book, and he gave it again to the minister, and sat down. And the eyes of all them that were in the synagogue were fastened on Him. And He began to say to them, This day is this Scripture fulfilled in your ears. And all bare Him witness, and wondered at the gracious words which proceeded out of His mouth (Luke 4:18–22).

No sooner did they consider what Jesus had said, than they grabbed Him and carried Him out to throw Him over a cliff. The same people! Religious tradition cannot countenance true faith. They are necessarily at odds. And **when you choose to wholly take God at His Word, you too will find yourself at odds with an unbelieving Egyptian system that values form over substance and rhetoric over righteousness.** This must happen. For the spirit of the city of man is coming into final conflict with the spirit of the city of the living God. It is the conflict of the ages. You will be on one side or the other. There is no middle ground.

Stretch Out Your Rod

It was Moses' moment of truth. The children of God, having come out of Egypt, stood paralyzed before the Red Sea. Suddenly the ground trembled with the pounding of Pharaoh's horses and chariots. The people were scared spitless. They had no way to turn.. They were screaming at Moses, screaming at each other, terrified! Moses, the deliverer, said, "Lord, what in the world are we going to do?" And God said, "Why are you crying unto me, Moses? You speak to the children of Israel and tell them to go forward." "Lift thou up **thy** rod and stretch out **thine** hand over the sea and divide it" (Exod. 14:16). That sounds pretty harsh, doesn't it? Yet God only wanted Moses to exercise the authority that had already been delegated to him. Notice the specificity of the words, "thy rod" and "thine hand."

And so Moses stretched out the rod, but the Scripture says God divided the water. Moses did not divide the water. God divided the water. But God would not have divided the water had not a man—who had been delegated authority in the earth—taken the initiative to act. Moses had to stretch out **his** rod. Under authority, and by faith, it became God's rod.

In these last days God is again calling His people out of Egypt. Where do you and I fit in God's eternal plan? Have you come out of Egypt? Have you been anointed for deliverance? Do you see yourself in your Father's Word? Is it that real to you? Have you played the religious game of false humility, denying God could possibly intend such words to apply to you? Is it not time for you to take God fully at His Word? You and I must prepare for the difficult times ahead before our Lord's return. As the prophet so clearly stated, it is only "the people that do know their God [who] shall be strong, and do exploits" (Dan. 11:32).

Isaiah cast the vision so beautifully. Perhaps you, too, can see yourself in the mirror of his words, by which he declares,

> My spirit that is upon thee, and my words which I have put in thy mouth shall not depart out of thy mouth, nor out of the mouth of thy seed, nor out of the mouth of thy seed's seed, henceforth and forever (Isa. 59:21).

> Arise, shine, for thy light is come, and the glory of the Lord is risen upon thee. For, behold, the darkness shall cover the earth, and gross darkness the people: but the Lord shall arise upon thee, and His glory shall be seen upon thee. And the Gentiles shall come to thy light, and kings to the brightness of thy rising. Lift up thine eyes round about, and see… (Isa. 60:1–4a).

Lift up **your** eyes round about and see. Lift up your eyes round about, and see that the Lord has anointed **you** for deliverance. It may be for a few, for a family, or for a following. Many will need your faith. Many will require

God's hand extended through yours in the difficult days to come. Be empowered by the challenging words of Ken Medema's musical rendition of Moses' call:

Old Moses, way out there in the wilderness,
Saw some smoke, came to the bush,
And the bush was burning;
And the Lord said, "Stop, take off your shoes, Moses.
You're on holy ground.
Moses, I've chosen you to be my man.
Moses, way down in Egypt land.
Moses, I've chosen you to work for me.
Moses, you're gonna set my people free."

"Not me, Lord.
D-d-d-don't you know I can't talk so good.
I stutter all the time.
D-d-d-don't you know my brother, Aaron.
Well he can sing like an angel, talk like a preacher.
Not me, Lord.
I can't talk so good."

"And another thing, how will they know what you sent me to do?
How will they know that I've been here with you?
Don't you know in Egypt they want little Moses' head?
Don't you know in Egypt they want little Moses dead?
Don't you know they'll never hear a single word I say?
Maybe you'd better get your dirty work done some other way.
Not me, Lord."

"What's that in your hand, Moses?"
"It's just a rod."
"Well, throw it down Moses."
"D-d-d-do you mean, like, on the ground?"
"Yes. Throw it down, Moses."
"But, Lord I…"
"Throw it down, Moses."

Moses threw the rod on the ground and the rod became a hissin' snake.
Well. Moses went a runnin'.
I betcha you'd run. Well, maybe I'd run.
He was a runnin' from a hot rod.
Runnin scared from a hissin' snake.

Runnin' scared of what the Lord was gonna do.
Runnin' scared He'll get a hold of you.

And the Lord said, "Stop!
Pick it up, Moses, by the tail."

"Lord, you have not been here very long,
Lord, you've got the whole thing wrong.
Don't you know that you never pick up a hissin' snake by its…"

"Pick it up, Moses!"

"Lord, it's a rod again.
It's a rod again."

"Do you know what it means, Moses?
Do you know what I'm trying to say?"

The rod of Moses became the rod of God.
With the rod of God, strike the rock and the water will come.
With the rod of God, part the waters of the sea.
With the rod of God, you can strike old Pharaoh down.
With the rod of God, you can set the captives free.

So what do you hold in your hand this day?
To whom or to what are you bound? [Tradition, fear, false humility, unbelief?]
Are you willing to give it to God right now?
Give it up.
Let it go.
Throw it down.

Let's Pray

Father, I ask that You would reveal this word to me that I may see myself in Your Word—that I may take up the rod of God (whatever that is) that You have given to me, that I will become an effectual tool in Your Kingdom. Help me to see my hand as Your hand, my mouth as Your mouth, my mind as Your mind. Give me revelation of Your Word. Help me obey Your voice. Anoint me with Your Holy Spirit and holy boldness. I am tired of religious forms. I want to walk in the reality of faith from this day forth. In Jesus' name, I stretch forth my hand now so that signs and wonders may be done in the name of thy Holy Child, Jesus. It is not by my might, nor by my power, but by Your Spirit that anything of value shall be accomplished. Here I am, Lord. Send Me.

Chapter Eighteen

End-Time Hospitality

*Can we be raptured to Christ's home if
we refuse to open our home?*

G OD'S HEART IS BROKEN over the broken hearts of His
sons and daughters. From the church house to the White House,
America's heart is broken. There are few subjects of a more pressing, practical,
or potent nature for the church or the healing of America than that of hospitality. **Anyone who would come out of Egypt must be given to hospitality!
There is no option!**
In this chapter are seeds that will revolutionize your life. In this chapter is
preparation for heart surgery. This chapter reveals the greatest secrets of church
growth. This chapter contains a divine prescription for racial healing. Read
it prayerfully! Wince if you must when it steps on your toes or pierces your
heart. But rejoice, for a new vista of Christian life is about to be opened. It is
end-time preparation for the end-time church. We begin with Moses.

Moses, Midian, and Modern America

Stephen, first martyr of the church, spoke of a seldom-emphasized memory
of Moses, the great deliverer. Moses fled Egypt, and "was a stranger in the
land of Midian…" (Acts 7:29).

Moses, once noted and promoted by the pomp of Egypt, became a nobody,
a stranger in a strange land. Stephen told us that in his strangerhood, Moses
"begat two sons" (Acts 7:29). Forty years Moses lived as a stranger from the
comforts of Egypt. All who live godly in Christ Jesus today will live as strangers and pilgrims in "Egypt," the spirit of the city, the spirit of this world. But
must we live as strangers from each other?

Pastors and Parishioners at Risk

George Barna, in his book *Virtual America* (1994), revealed the following astounding statistics. They should break your heart but may also reveal your heart.

- Fifty-five percent of all non-Christian Americans believe it is getting harder and harder to make lasting friendships.
- Sixty-two percent of "born-again" Christians claim it is getting hard to make lasting friendships.
- Seventy-three percent of all "evangelical" Christians are finding it difficult to make real friends.

Do we dare put it in print? It appears that the stronger the apparent commitment to Scriptural authority, the more severe the problem of our relationships. Conclusion: the more RELIGION, the less RELATIONSHIP. Something is desperately wrong! Do you agree? Divided and in a state of dissolution, we stand.

On my daily broadcast, *VIEWPOINT*, I interviewed H. B. London, head of pastoral ministries for Focus on the Family. Our focus was on the topic "Pastors at Risk." He disclosed that at least 70 percent of pastors in America claim they have NO friends. One listening pastor later told me he thought the figure was really much higher.

Let me ask you a question: What ever happened to Christian community? What ever happened to the "Covenant Community" in America? Are we destined to be strangers in the "Commonwealth of Faith"?

Secular and religious observers alike are in agreement on at least one thing. The overarching social problem in America is not AIDS or abortion, but rather the total fracture of all sense of community. AIDS and abortion did not create the fracture but reflect it. Having crossed the threshhold of the seventh millennium, we are neither committed to one another, nor to life itself. It appears our increasing commitment is to SELF and self alone.

The fracture of community is also revealed in the widening chasm that divides our families. The divorce rate among Christians has long equaled or exceeded that of the nation at large. Now, the divorce rate among pastors equals that of their congregations, and divorce among fundamentalist Christians exceeds the nation at large. Christ may be our Savior, but SELF is king.

William Hendricks, author of *Exit Interviews*, also appeared on *VIEWPOINT*. He revealed that 52,000 people per week are leaving through the "back door" of America's churches. To find out why, he interviewed two dozen frustrated parishioners from coast to coast, who no longer darken church doors but remain committed to Christ.

Among the various concerns given, Hendricks confirmed three basic reasons why Christians of ten years or more of church experience are fed up. Are you ready?

- They do not believe they are being told the "gospel truth" by their pastors and leaders.
- **They do not believe the church provides true Christian fellowship and community** but is rather a "gospel country club" of Sunday back-slappers who couldn't care less about one another after the noon hour on Sunday.
- **They do not believe their individual giftedness and spiritual purpose on earth, as part of a body, is recognized** beyond the cry for tithes and offerings.

In short, American Christians increasingly feel like strangers WITHIN the church that is supposed to be a single body—the BODY of Christ.

A Cry for Community

America, from the church house to the White House, is crying out for genuine community. We cannot live without it. Jesus' cry to the Father before His crucifixion was, "That they may be one." The hallmark of the early church was, "Behold how they love one another." And our nation was born out of a vision for genuine covenant community of the New Testament variety.

Is there hope for a revival of true "covenant community" in this land where our fathers died? I believe there is. Our hope lies not in tirades against Washington but in trumpeting the truth to God's people; not in crystallized religion but in Christian relationship; not in "churchianity" but in a twenty-first-century display of "the Word made flesh," dwelling among us. It is called "hospitality."

Zipporah bore Moses a son, "...and he called his name Gershom: for he said, I have been a stranger in a strange land" (Exod. 2:22). But it was never God's intent that Moses find himself a stranger among his own people.

In the Congregation, but Not OF It!

IT'S TOUGH TO BE A STRANGER

It is estimated that three million Israelites fled, as cries of anguish pierced the Egyptian night for her firstborn. Four hundred years the Israelites had languished as slaves and strangers in a pagan land. As they came out, Moses delivered the warning word of the Lord:

> Thou shalt neither vex a stranger, nor oppress him: for ye were strangers in the land of Egypt (Exod. 22:21).

Six hundred thousand adult male descendants of Abraham, besides women and children, fled from Pharaoh's dominating grasp (Exod. 12:37). Most found identity and comfort among their twelve tribes. "Strangers" also joined Israel's march, believing the God of Jacob but being alien to the sons of promise (Exod. 12:38). Gentiles. Apparently God expected such strangers to join the children of Israel by faith or fellowship (though not by lineage), for He specifically included them (see Exod. 12:48–49).

It is fascinating to note that exactly seventy times the "I AM" spoke to the stranger through Moses during Israel's sojourn from Egypt to the Promised Land, in Exodus, Leviticus, Numbers, and Deuteronomy. In Moses' final instructions to Israel (in Deuteronomy) before they crossed over Jordan, he spoke of God's heart for the stranger twenty-four times—twice for each of the twelve tribes.

Interestingly, Moses expressed Yahweh's heart for the stranger, even in declaring a believing stranger as being one in covenant with the congregation:

Keep therefore the words of this covenant, and do them, that ye may prosper in all that ye do. Ye stand this day all of you before the Lord your God…men of Israel, your little ones, your wives, and **thy stranger that is in thy camp**…. That thou shouldest enter into covenant with the Lord thy God… (Deut. 29:9–12).

Israel knew what it was like to be a stranger. It's tough! And God would not let Israel forget it. He commanded Israel to open her heart, her hand, and her home in hospitality. Hospitality reaches to strangers. And all of us are susceptible to strangerhood in an alienated sea of crowded loneliness.

CRISIS OF LONELINESS

"He died of a broken heart" is a phrase often heard, but it is difficult to grasp the mechanism of how such a thing might occur. If a man can die of a broken heart, how about a family, the church, or even a nation?

My attention was captured by two letters to the editor of *Time* magazine in response to a feature article "Twentieth-Century Blues." A Michigan woman lamented, "What we crave is people—the closeness of relatives…a neighbor…an unexpected guest. These are not Darwin's social instincts…. They are gained by reaching out." But a New York man cut the festering sore of loneliness amidst Twentieth-Century Blues wide open: "Feeling miscast in our own lives, we experience depression almost as a moral stand, a protest against a world we do not understand."

I interviewed author and commentator J. Kerby Anderson on my daily broadcast, *VIEWPOINT.* In discussing his excellent book *Signs of Warning—Signs of Hope,* he warned that the "baby boom" generation is headed for a crisis of loneliness. Since the "baby boomers" (those born between 1946 and

1964) comprise the single largest generation in American history, our entire society is in for a revelation of the consequences of fractured community, a revelation beyond anything yet experienced or even comprehended.

The children of baby boomers provide an early taste. Although referred to as "baby busters," more commonly they bear the label "generation X." They have been crossed out by their parents and crossed off by society, rooted neither in family, culture, nor community. They are the "alone" generation. Strangers.

LEGACY OF LONELINESS

Loneliness can truly break the heart. A Harvard sociologist warned that, emotionally, one of the social consequences of the fragmentation of social groups would be loneliness and a legacy of coldness. Another consequence is insecurity and the nagging question, "Who cares for me?"

In *The Broken Heart: The Medical Consequences of Loneliness*, James Lynch has documented, "The price we are paying for our failure to understand our biological needs for love and human companionship may be ultimately exacted in our own hearts and blood vessels." According to studies at both the University of California and the University of Michigan, adults who do not belong to nurturing groups or relationships have a death rate twice as high as those with frequent, caring contact.

SMALL-GROUP INCLUSION

As church congregations increasingly shift toward megachurches, the most nurturing relationships outside the family increasingly fade into "crowded loneliness." Small groups, relationally based rather than organizationally driven, can be wonderful bridges for the Body. But often such groups, when organizationally driven, create the illusion of satisfying relational needs, but are lacking in underlying covenant commitment, since they often serve more the needs of organization management than the needs of relational ministry. Organizational programs will never resolve relational pain and emptiness. The church house in America faces a crisis of loneliness, and our hearts are bleeding and broken. Where can we find hope?

The Covenant Connection

John Winthrop (1588–1649) was the most prominent of the first Puritans to land on our shores. As a godly attorney, he described the "city set on a hill" that he and his fellow Puritans intended to found. His words have remained a model for what life in America was intended to be:

> **We must delight in each other, make others conditions our own, rejoice together, mourn together, labor and suffer together, always having before our eyes our community as members of the same body.**

Before the Puritans landed at Massachusetts Bay in 1630, John Winthrop penned perhaps the clearest expression of the "American vision" ever penned. He called it "A Model of Christian Charity." A few short excerpts should be sufficient to set the tone.

> We are a company professing ourselves fellow members of Christ...we ought to account ourselves knit together by this bond of love, and live in the exercise of it....

Reflecting on the weakness of Christians in implementing true Christianity, Winthrop declared, "That which most people in churches only profess as a truth, we bring into familiar and constant practice. We must love...without pretense...with a pure heart and fervently; we must bear one another's burdens; we must not look on our own things but also on the things of our brethren." What a vision!

But Winthrop also warned, "Nor must we think that the Lord will bear with such failings at our hands as He does from those among whom we have lived...." He sounds like Moses warning Israel.

THE PRICE OF BROKEN COVENANT

The early Puritans believed the gospel was truly good news. But they were equally convinced that toying with God's plan was bad news. "If we neglect to observe these articles," wrote Winthrop, "and—dissembling with our God—shall embrace this present world...seeking great things for ourselves...the Lord will surely break out in wrath against us...and make us to know the price for the breach of such a covenant."

And so we have it! We have seen the great blessing that flowed for two hundred years from the fountain of our fathers' holy faith, expressed in a covenant community. Yet in the same fashion, we have reaped the devastating whirlwind of our own progressive rebellion against that covenant in this last century—a century that has been euphemistically called, "The American Century." We have exchanged the covenant community for independence and individualism. We are now totally free—free from God and free from each other—and America's heart is broken. What can repair the breach?

WHAT'S HAPPENED TO AMERICA'S HEART?

The pastor of a seemingly vibrant church lamented about how, in a single week, he had buried three of his congregation. The cause of death: suicide. Why would three Americans who were attending a growing, active church commit suicide in a single week? There was no suicide compact and no terminal illness. The stock market did not crash. And to my knowledge, there was no marital breakup. So why? What could motivate a person to such a drastic action?

The answer is written in the hearts of millions of men and women across our land. It is a plague that eats at the heart. It gnaws like cancer at the innermost being. It haunts the memory and scrapes at the mind. It is a living death. But for many, there is little or no relief. It is loneliness. Its cause: *selfishness*. Truly America's heart is broken. We are strangers!

The Book of Proverbs declares, "The curse causeless shall not come." The curse of loneliness and the fracture of America's heart issue from a deep fissure running through the American Experiment for at least two centuries. Having gone unattended, the fissure has only widened. Now, two entire generations are tumbling into its yawning chasm. We have, in effect, gone back to Egypt.

Back in 1835, French observer Alexis de Tocqueville warned us as a people that a plague which he called "individualism" was beginning to eat at the heart of the nation. "Individualism," he said, "is a calm and considered feeling which disposes each citizen to isolate himself from the mass of his fellows…he gladly leaves the greater society to look after itself."

Then he warned us with a vivid picture of individualistic destiny: "Such folk owe no man anything.…. They form the habit of thinking of themselves in isolation and imagine that their whole destiny is in their hands." Finally they "forget their ancestors." They isolate themselves both from their descendants and their contemporaries. "Each man is forever thrown back on himself alone, and there is danger he may be shut up in the solitude of his own heart."

Was he a prophet? Robert Bellah, et al, in the best seller *Habits of the Heart*, concluded, "Tocqueville saw the isolation to which Americans are prone as ominous for the future of our freedom." The same isolation threatens both the message and the mission of American Christians.

HOPE FOR A BROKEN HEART

America's only hope includes a restored covenant community. We must again become a people committed to active, sacrificial relationship with one another, as a demonstration of our covenant with God. It begins at your home and in the church. It begins with holy hospitality. It is formed in an open heart, an open hand, and an open home. With broken homes, come broken hearts. With divided church, comes divided community. A nation divided against itself cannot stand.

A people committed only to themselves will starve physically, emotionally, and spiritually. Similarly, church congregations committed only to their own programs, without active commitment to the body at large in their own city, are incubators of isolationism. God is calling you and me to a renewed understanding of Christian covenant and a restored commitment to Christian community. It is our only hope! And it is born in a heart of hospitality.

The Hope of Hospitality

Hospitality means to reach to strangers. A stranger is anyone who is unknown, unfamiliar, unacquainted, not admitted to fellowship. Our world and our churches are packed with strangers. At least seventy percent of our pastors admit to being strangers in the midst of the crowd. A holy disillusionment is brewing from pulpit to pew. Jesus is coming back. He is ironing out the wrinkles in the Bride's gown. He expects us fully reconciled—ONE!

The hope of our healing is rooted deeply in the Father's heart of hospitality. The very gospel is good news precisely because it tangibly translates God's heart of hospitality. We are all estranged—sinners, strangers from God. The Father's open heart of hospitality opened His divine hand, sending His only Son "across the tracks" into a sinfully unpleasant place called earth, to extend an invitation to join Him for an eternal marriage supper in His home. For Christ declared, "In my Father's house are many mansions: I go to prepare a place for you...that where I am, there ye may be also" (John 14:2–3).

Reconciliation began in Egypt. God called Moses and then Israel to flee Egypt as strangers so that He could welcome them to His Promised Land.

God loves strangers! "Cursed be he that perverteth the judgment of the stranger...," warned Moses (Deut. 27:19). God's heart never changed. Malachi closed the Old Covenant, declaring:

> I will come near to you to judgment; and I will be **a swift witness against those that...turn aside the stranger**, and fear not me, saith the Lord of Hosts. For I am the Lord, I change not (Mal. 3:5–6*a*).

Jesus was hospitality incarnate. Watch Him reach to the outcast, to the poor, to the tax collector, to the sinner. Peter, apostle to the Jews, warned, "The end of all things is at hand" (1 Pet. 4:7). In that end-time plea, he commanded, "Use hospitality one to another without grudging" (1 Pet. 4:9). The great apostle to the gentiles, Paul, drove home the same message:

> **Let love be without dissimulation**: Be kindly affectioned one to another with brotherly love,...**given to hospitality** (Rom. 12:9–10, 13*b*).

Notice! Paul did not say "gifted in" hospitality. We are told to give ourselves TO hospitality. So elementary and foundational is this principle in the Kingdom that Paul required each person in leadership to be "a lover of hospitality" (Titus 1:8).

Hospitality is the tangible translation of agape love we talk so much about. It is the key that unlocks the door to genuine Body life. It is the single most powerful evangelistic tool, since statistics clearly reveal that over 70 percent of all persons come to Christ, not through crusades or programs but through relationships.

Hospitality is the "grease" that lubricates and activates all legitimate ministry. There is no true ministry without hospitality. Hospitality is the nondelegable, unavoidable essence and manifestation of true Christian love. Purported ministry without it, regardless of appearances, is a cheap organizational counterfeit.

Truth without relationship born of hospitality is void of reality. God could have sent a flying scroll, but instead He send a suffering servant to "flesh out" the truth. Jesus declared Himself to be "the Truth" (John 14:6). "The Word was made flesh, and dwelt among us" in divine hospitality, so that "we beheld His glory…full of grace and truth" (John 1:14). That is what will bring integrity to our message. **Preachment without hospitable relationship is a perversion of God's plan and purpose.**

Preaching, teaching, and living biblical hospitality will revolutionize the church as we know it. It gives the necessary "handle" to effectuate and activate the love of God we profess to offer. It is the window through which we can reach an alienated world of strangers from the "commonwealth of faith." Jesus will not return until we give ourselves to hospitality. Until then, we will remain in Egypt.

Hospitality Will Conquer Racism!

Racism is a reality! It has no place in Christ's church and is repugnant to our covenant with God and our fellow man. But fundamentally, racism is not a problem that can be remedied by legislation or finger-pointing. It can be accomplished only by "heart surgery."

Let's face it. Racism is rampant in both White and Black America. It began with Whites, and now, surprisingly, many Black pastors across the nation are calling for segregation and Black separation. Racism has become a two-way street, if not a multihubbed intersection. It defies solution by coercion or ingenuity. It is a matter of the heart. And "habits of the heart" must be dealt with in the realm of our faith under the authority of God Himself. The exaltation of color, culture, and tradition over oneness in Christ is idolatry. It is time we cast down our fleshly idols. As Dr. Tony Evans has so poignantly said, " God has not come to take sides. He has come to take over!"

The first two great spiritual awakenings in our nation resulted in massive social impact and in the cleansing of many social evils. Slavery was confronted by revivalists in each. Our response has been a legal response: first an Emancipation Proclamation, then a Civil Rights Act. We are long overdue for another revival in America. This time, the Lord of the church is looking for a heart response.

America faces her greatest crises ever in this precipitous moment of her history. A mournful cry issues from saint and sinner alike, amidst the agony of the tearing of the flesh and fabric of our society. Prayer goes up from churches across the land as Christians plea for revival. Yet the God who gave us liberty will no longer tolerate a church that, in both Black and White congregations, not only tolerates but perpetuates America's national sin of racism. Our iniquity has not only separated us from each other, but our iniquities have separated us from our God "that He will not hear" (see Isa. 59:2).

The time has come for judgment to begin at the house of God. We are praying for revival with unclean hands. God has not winked at our failure to cleanse the stain of racism from His church in America in our two previous "awakenings."

The reconciliation of Black and White believers in American Christendom remains a condition to be met before we see the great move of God's hand and Spirit, so desperately sought and so drastically needed across the face of these United States. It will require holy hospitality.

The Supreme Ruler of Nations will not tolerate or send His Son for a church with spot or wrinkle or any such thing (see Eph. 5:27).

So how can this socially enforced strangerhood of racism and separation be healed? **Relationship is the only biblical path to reconciliation**. Both Black and White believers must be intentional about the opening of our homes and hearts in genuine hospitality. Hospitality means to "reach to strangers." If it were natural, we would not have to reach.

It is time for us to take "Kingdom risks." We must love God enough to love our brothers. **We cannot love congregationally until we love individually**. Do not wait for the other guy. Invite someone across the color barrier to your home today. Do it again the next week and the week following. Do it. Perfect love will cast out your fear. The healing of America will only begin in your home. **If we break bread together, we will break barriers together.** Do not wait for the other guy to do it. You do it! Do it now! Pick up the phone now. Write the note now. Discuss your plans with your spouse now. Talk is cheap. The walk will cost you your time. Forget organizations. Forget programs. Build relationships.

If we would enter the Promised Land, we must leave Egypt. All who leave Egypt open their homes to "strangers" in Christ, including those of different color. **Holy hospitality will conquer racism!**

Institutionalized Strangerhood

A Stern Reprimand for Israel

God loves strangers! Israel suffered strangerhood in Egypt for four hundred years. God heard their cry and their groaning. And He sent Moses to deliver them. But they were a tough bunch. They were perpetually tempted to enforce strangerhood on those journeying with them.

After a generation of wilderness wandering—out of Egypt in the flesh but groveling there in spirit—Israel received a stiff rebuke from Moses.

Circumcise therefore the foreskin of your heart, and be no more stiffnecked (Deut. 10:16).

Now what attitudes and behaviors does this language conjure in your mind as meriting such a stern reprimand? Adultery? Thievery? Idolatry? These would certainly have earned God's wrath. Yet those were not God's concerns here. Prayerfully listen to Moses' pronouncement. Read it out loud.

For the Lord your God is God of gods, and Lord of lords.... He doth execute the judgment of the fatherless and widow, and **loveth the stranger**, in giving him food and raiment. **Love ye therefore the stranger: for ye were strangers in the land of Egypt.** Thou shalt fear the Lord thy God; Him thou shalt serve (Deut. 10:17–20).

A FINAL CALL TO THE CHURCH

Our God is unchanging. He still loves the stranger. His message to His children has never changed, neither have His children. For we are still stiff-necked. For at least seventeen centuries we have developed traditions and practices to institutionalize strangerhood, in the church, even in the name of Christ.

The very way we "do church" has, in effect, become institutionalized strangerhood. We have developed it into an art form. And Yahweh, Jehovah—the Lord of lords and God of gods—addresses His children, wooing and warning before the Second Coming of Christ: "LOVE THE STRANGER!" "Grieve me no longer!" "Come out of Egypt." Could this be His final call?

A CLEVER SLEIGHT OF HAND

Satan is very clever. By the third century, he found a way, in religious disguise, to build a box that would paralyze the effectiveness of the church for seventeen centuries. The Roman emperor Constantine converted an empire to Christianity by imperial fiat. Within the apparent blessing that eliminated rampant persecution, came a curse.

Politically decreed faith replaced personally conveyed faith. Cathedrals relegated the church to boxes with four walls. An open heart's door was replaced by a massive "church" door. The haven of the home took a backseat to the haven of the "sanctuary."

Stained glass replaced clear windows. The church could not see the world, nor the world the church. Beautiful buildings stole the beauty of the Body of Christ. "Come see our building" became the Kingdom cry, casting a deep shadow over the natural haven of the heart in homes where body life had once thrived. Men bowed in shrines of wood and stone while the life of "living stones" that make up the church was smothered in ecclesiasticism and all but snuffed out.

Men and women who had worshiped from house to house in the first century were now relegated to "God's house." Once accountability thrived as they looked each other in the eye, breaking bread from home to home. Now the cold pallor of strangerhood hovered over the spirit of hospitality. Worshipers gathered in rows rather than in relationship. The collective effect was devastating.

Hierarchies heralded the demise of elders and servant pastors, who had made tents by day and loved the brethren, not by trade but by a living truth that constrained them. Instead of the Lord "adding to the church such as should be saved," the church added such as should become members of glorified country clubs. Back-slapping churchgoers replaced warm-hearted, hugging families.

"Come to my church" obscured "Go into all the world." The building obscured the Body. Programs of the church obscured the people of God. The corporeal body became a corporation. Big became better. Love was largely lost in the lurch. Institutionalization paralyzed the people. The heart was left at home. Men became strangers to their brothers in Christ and were isolated even from their own flesh, as families became divided by age and sex for the "efficient propagation of the gospel." It was a clever sleight of hand—all so religious. Deception is still deception.

FEELING STRANGE, ACTING STRANGELY

The sense of the covenantal community disintegrated. The back of men's heads in pews structured out the glory of God to be seen on faces. Strangerhood was now structured in the church. And the Spirit of God was grieved.

Home remains where the heart is. And God still calls us to leave Egypt. When we "leave Egypt," we must again open our hearts to the "strangers" among us. But in many respects, the entire Body of Christ has become a "stranger." We feel strange with one another and treat each other strangely. From congregation to congregation and even within our own congregations, we do not know one another. Most neither care nor know how to care for one another.

Love has become "organizational" rather than organismal. Our programmed style of caring often renders faceless the objects of our care. The Master still yearns for us to bring the poor to our own house and to feed the hungry with our own food (Isa. 58:7). He wants to eradicate strangerhood at the table of His truth. He yearns for us in the final moments of history to truly come out of Egypt.

Where Is Your Heart?

The "I AM" is stirring by His Spirit to create a holy disillusionment with institutionalized "churchianity." He is calling His church home, for "Home is where the heart is." Through small-group and cell ministry, touching one another's lives "from house to house," he is breaking us out of the "house of bondage" of institutionalized worship. His purpose is to restore the relational gospel of a Savior who was the "Word made flesh"—the very incarnation of the divine heart of hospitality that "dwelt among us"—that we might again "behold His glory, full of grace and truth." The Father's heart will not allow His Son's prayer to go unanswered: "Father, that they all may be one; that the world may believe that thou hast sent me" (John 17:21).

It is time to come out of Egypt. It is time to restore a spirit of holy hospitality. Integrate your faith, your hope, your love. Let there be no more strangers among the true "household of faith." Open your heart; then open your hand; and open your home. It will change the way you think and live! It will revolutionize the way we "do" church. And it will profoundly impact our nation and the world.

Mary and Joseph found no room in the inn. Will your brother and sister find room in the inn of your heart and home? Remember! Home is where the heart is. Where is your heart? Have a heart. Open your hand and home!

Can we be raptured to Christ's home in the heavens if we refuse to open our homes on earth? Do not answer too quickly. For if we do not love those we can see, how can we say we love God whom we cannot see? (see 1 John 4:20–21). The Father asks you today, "Do you love me?" His response echoes through the centuries: "Then love the stranger. Leave Egypt, forever!"

Want to Read More on Hospitality?

Chuck and Kathie Crismier have authored an entire book to equip you, your cell or small group, and your congregation with essential tools exhorting you to begin or expand the incredibly life-changing ministry of hospitality. Ask for *The Power of Hospitality,* endorsed by 17 national Christian leaders. Elijah Books, 2005, ISBN: 0-9718428-2-5.

For further information on seminars and materials, contact Charles Crismier c/o SAVE AMERICA Ministries, P.O. Box 70879, Richmond, VA 23255, or call (804) 754-1822.

Chapter Nineteen

Obey My Voice

Could our lawless society be a public expression of the private abandonment of God's law by His own church?

"WHO IS THE LORD, THAT I SHOULD OBEY HIS VOICE?" cried Pharaoh. And that is the cry of America today from the church house to the White House.

What Is the Censored Word?

Obey is a "four-letter word" and is despised as such. It is a censored word in our national spiritual parlance. The spirit of independence has given way to the spirit of rebellion. "I'll DO IT MY WAY" has become our cultural anthem. Polls have replaced principles. The will of the people has supplanted the will of God.

Since America's bicentennial in 1976, a cry for revival has echoed from sea to shining sea. Pastors, parishioners, and parachurch promoters have chanted 2 Chronicles 7:14, while paving a path to the White House as if the seat of power resides in Pharaoh's court. Yet Pharaoh continues to mock, "Who is the Lord, that I should obey His voice?"

Solemn Assemblies have multiplied. Christians cry over the consequences of our collective rebellion, while refusing to recognize that Pharaoh is now a member of most American congregations. Political power prevails over purity. Pragmatism reigns over principle.

Conservative Christians wring their hands in despair as truth is trampled in the streets, sighing with ancient Israel "by reason of the bondage" (Exod. 2:23). The pain is palpable. "Who will deliver us?" we cry! The cacophony of our groaning obliterates the unchanging words of the great I AM, "OBEY

MY VOICE" (Jer. 7:23). We would rather pray than obey. We would rather rejoice than repent.

We say, "The problem is THEM! It is the Congress. It is the White House. It is the president. It is Egypt. It is Pharaoh." Here ye the word of the Lord! The problem is rooted in the church house. We are wallowing in Egypt and are fornicating with Pharaoh. The words of the ancient prophet are as piercing and profound to the inhabitants of the proverbial American promised land as they were to the inhabitants of the Promised Land six centuries before Christ.

To Whom Is God Making His Plea?

Jehovah ordered Jeremiah, "**Stand in the gate of the Lord's house, and proclaim there this word…**" (Jer. 7:2). "Pray not thou for this people, neither lift up cry nor prayer for them, neither make intercession to me: for **I will not hear thee**" (Jer. 7:16). "Do they provoke me to anger? saith the Lord: do they not provoke themselves to the confusion of their own faces?" (Jer. 7:19).

Do you get the sense that the patience of the "I AM" is taxed beyond its limits—beyond mere provocation? "Behold my anger and my fury shall be poured out upon this place, upon man, and upon beast, and upon the trees," saith the Lord (Jer. 7:20). "Put your burnt offerings unto your sacrifices, and eat flesh" (Jer. 7:21). In modern vernacular, Yahweh almost sarcastically retorts, "Your religious forms, your worship, your fastings, your prayers, sacrifices, and solemn assemblies are a sham. They are substitutes for the substance I desired. Would you play games with God?"

> For…in the day that I brought them [your fathers] out of the land of Egypt…This thing commanded I them, saying, **obey my voice**, and I will be your God, and ye shall be my people (Jer. 7:22–23).

How did **God's people** respond? Here is God's opinion. It is the only opinion that counts:

> But they hearkened not, nor inclined their ear, but walked in the counsels and in the imagination of their evil heart, and went backward, and not forward. Since the day that your fathers came forth out of the land of Egypt unto this day I have sent unto you my servants the prophets…Yet they hearkened not unto me… (Jer. 7:24–26).

Grace or Disgrace?

You may say, "Well, what does that have to do with me? What does all this have to do with the church in this enlightened moment at the end of the American century? Are you implying something? Surely you are not suggesting that God's people today are stubborn and rebellious like Israel was? Besides, don't you know this is America? We are under God. We have a Christian heritage. Besides which, that Egypt business is all in the Old Testament. We are not under that legalistic stuff now. We are under grace."

Truly we are under grace. Grace is not mercy. Grace is divine enablement to do what God expects of us. It is the ability God gives us to conform to His will, His ways, and to the image of the "Word made flesh." **We have spurned His grace to do as we ought, replacing it with license to do as we want. That is not grace. It is disgrace. And God is not pleased.**

Why Is God Furious?

It grieves God when His own children stray from the ways of their Father. It angers Him when they blithely ignore His kind remonstrances. But it infuriates Him when His very own children—the people who call themselves by His name—repeatedly, continuously, notoriously and rebelliously refuse not only His wooings but also His warnings.

God knows that His righteousness and holy character demand justice and judgment in the face of continuous and unrepentant disobedience. His holy heart agonizes over the necessity of promised judgment. His love requires consequences for lascivious living. His mercy mandates repentance to avoid penalty. His holiness demands humility from those who would claim to be His sons and daughters. His kingly righteousness is satisfied only by right-ways-ness among those who profess to be His subjects.

So what does God see? How does He view America? How do American Christians line up with the divine plumb line? Are we in Egypt? Or have we entered the Promised Land? Here are some brief skeletal facts:

- Ninety-plus percent of America believes in God, but 91 percent of us lie regularly, conscious premeditated lies. According to secular advertisers Patterson and Kim, "Lying has become an integral part of the American character" (*The Day America Told the Truth*).
- Seventy-eight percent of America believes we are in severe moral decline, yet 96 percent of American parents believe they are doing a good or excellent job in teaching their children moral values (*Los Angeles Times*).
- Thirty percent of all fundamentalist Christians ever married are divorced, while only 23 percent of all **non**-Christians ever married are divorced (premier issue of the *Barna Report*).
- The divorce rate among pastors now equals their congregations' divorce rate (*Ministries Today* per Hartford Seminary research project).
- Weekly church attendance has dipped to the lowest level in a half century (George Gallup's *Emerging Trends*).
- Divorce of pastors has risen 65 percent in the last twenty years—second highest of all professions (INJOY Ministries Report).

- Twenty percent of pastors admit to having an affair while in the ministry (INJOY Ministries Report).
- Cohabitation has increased 1000 percent since 1960.
- Ministers join in collective rebellion against the Scriptures to marry same-sex couples or to bless remarriages of heterosexual persons which Jesus called "adultery."
- The "Bible Belt" of America has a divorce rate 50% higher than the nation as a whole and new AIDS cases 9 times the national average.
- Over one-third of all American births are illegitimate. Half of all American children will soon be born out of wedlock" (Sen. Daniel P. Moynihan).
- Forty percent is the approximate number of adulterers and fornicators (by biblical standards) sitting in America's church pews on any given Sunday morning.

Newsweek captured the truth succinctly, asking, "Are you a believer? Provocative new surveys reveal a nation where most claim to be religious but few take their faith seriously" (Nov. 29, 1993, p. 80).

What Should God Do?

What is your response? How do you feel about this picture? Where do you fit? If you were God, what would you be thinking? Just imagine how a holy God is viewing this moral carnage…this orgy of moral and spiritual rebellion. And then we turn around and justify much of this evil, calling our willful disobedience an extension of God's grace to us. We have truly convinced ourselves that God is winking jovially at our promiscuity, declaring from pulpit to pew, "God wants me to be happy."

Twenty- and thirty-year marriages are dissolved with impunity on the authority of such twisted theology at the altar of the almighty SELF—the new millennium's "I AM."

Is God dead? Did He change His mind? Does He shed His character with our ever-changing moral fashions and frolicking fornication? Did He not say, "Be ye holy, for I am holy" (Lev. 20:7)? Did he not declare that "he hateth putting away [divorce]" (Mal. 2:16)? Did not Jesus declare unequivocally, "Whosoever shall put away his wife, saving for the cause of fornication, causeth her to commit adultery: and whosoever shall marry her that is divorced committeth adultery" (Matt. 5:32; 19:9)?

Did not the apostle Paul twice drive home the inviolability of the marriage relationship, saying, "The woman that hath an husband is bound by the law to her husband so long as he liveth: but if the husband be dead, she is loosed from the law of her husband. So then if, while her husband liveth, she be married to another man, she shall be called an adulteress…" (Rom. 7:2–3; 1 Cor. 7:39)? It no longer matters when we "do it our way," does it? We declare "I have peace" while we pervert God's law. We claim His grace as enablement to *dis*grace His creation covenant. Hedonism reigns supreme, as pastors pander to the whim of the people rather than preach the will of God. Jesus lamented, "Moses because of the hardness of your hearts suffered you to put away your wives, but from the beginning it was not so" (Matt. 19:8).

We wince with righteous anger at the report of Pharaoh's exterminating all Israel's boy babies to prevent a deliverer from arising. We gasp with horror at Herod's edict that all Jewish boys under two be impaled on Roman swords to prevent the "King of the Jews" from rising to the throne. Yet America has exterminated nearly 50 million of her own sons and daughters since 1973 on the altar of personal pleasure. Forget the pursuit of power. Our children died by the hedonist sword their own mothers, fathers, and physicians, in pursuit of pleasure.

Divorce and remarriage are to the church what abortion is to the nation. Abortion kills the kids. Divorce kills the whole family. Each is "politically and pastorally correct" in its own sphere. "I'LL DO IT MY WAY" is more than a pop-culture anthem, it is a way of life—a life of unmitigated rebellion from the church house to the White House. And the God who is a "consuming fire" is furious at such pernicious lifestyles among the very people who claim to be expecting the soon-return of His Son (Heb. 12:29). What should God do?

Is There a Word from the Lord?

Hear the Word of the Lord, America. Listen, you who profess His name in the "land of the free."

> The Lord hath a controversy with the inhabitants of the land, because there is no truth, nor mercy, nor knowledge of God in the land. My people are destroyed for lack of knowledge: **because thou hast rejected knowledge, I will also reject thee**...seeing thou hast forgotten the law of thy God, I will also forget thy children...therefore will I change their glory into shame. And there shall be, like people, like priest: and I will punish them for their ways, and reward them for their doings...**they shall return to Egypt.** For [America] hath forgotten his Maker... (Hos. 4:1, 6–9; 8:13–14).

This is strong medicine! But God is not finished. We have forgotten that God is the great "I AM." He will not be mocked (Gal. 6:7). The cup of His judgment is full. "Behold therefore the goodness and severity of God" (Rom. 11:22). "For if God spared not the natural branches [Israel], take heed lest He also spare not thee," American Christian (Rom. 11:21).

> This is a nation that obeyeth not the voice of the Lord their God, nor receiveth correction: truth is perished, and is cut off from their mouth. No man repented

him of his wickedness, saying, What have I done?...my people know not the judgment of the Lord...for every one from the least even unto the greatest is given to covetousness, from the prophet even unto the priest every one dealeth falsely. Were they ashamed when they had committed abomination? nay, they were not at all ashamed, neither could they blush: Shall not my soul be avenged on such a nation as this? (Jer. 7:28; 8:6–11; 9:9)

"Who is the wise man, that may understand this?" asks the Lord. The land perishes "because they have forsaken my law...and **have not obeyed my voice...**" (Jer. 9:12–13).

For I earnestly protested unto your fathers in the day that I brought them up out of the land of Egypt, even to this day...protesting and saying, **Obey my voice.** Yet they obeyed not...therefore I will bring upon them all the words of this covenant which I commanded them to do; but they did them not (Jer. 11:7–8).

Judgment is sure, unless we repent. Judgment will begin FIRST at the house of God (1 Pet. 4:17). It may begin in your house. It could begin in mine. But it will begin. In many ways it has already begun. What can we do? Are we without hope? Is there a remedy?

Will It Be Doom, Gloom, or Glory?

Thus saith the Lord, American Christian:

At what instant I shall speak concerning a nation...to pluck up, and to pull down, and to destroy it; If that nation; against whom I have pronounced, turn from their evil, I will repent of the evil that I thought to do unto them (Jer. 18:7–8).

When Israel was a child, then I loved him, and called my son out of Egypt...for I am God, and not man; the Holy One in the midst of thee: and **I will not enter the city** (Hos. 11:1, 9).

Sow to yourselves in righteousness, reap in mercy; break up your fallow ground: for it is time to seek the Lord, till He come and rain righteousness upon you. Ye have plowed wickedness, ye have reaped iniquity, ye have eaten the fruit of lies: because thou didst trust in thy way, in the multitude of thy mighty men (Hos. 10:12–13).

I am the Lord thy God from the land of Egypt, and thou shalt know no God but me: for there is no savior beside me (Hos. 13:4).

The Prophetic Voice

"By a prophet the Lord brought Israel out of Egypt, and by a prophet was he preserved" (Hos. 12:13). America shall be no different.

Never has there been a greater need for the voice of the true prophet on American shores than in this generation poised on the cusp of a new millennium awaiting the impending Second Coming of the Holy One of Israel—the Messiah. The nation is weighed in the balances and found wanting. We are neck deep in the spirit of Egypt. The nation faces imminent judgment. Professing Christians face eternal judgment for rebellion from which they have not repented. God's mercy and patience is stretched to its penultimate. There is no further room for delay.

How does God call a nation or His church to repentance? He sends a VOICE! The true prophetic voice woos and warns. It does not pander to personal predilections or pastoral proprieties. It pierces through the murky fog of perverted tradition, pragmatic religion, and promised (yet unfulfilled) contrition. It is a loving God's final act of mercy before judgment.

How will you respond to the VOICE? There may be many messengers, but if they are true prophets, they will speak with one VOICE. There are many "prophetic" voices today, saying sweet nothings in the people's ears, luring money for programs, projects, and personal gain. And then there is the VOICE of the Lord. The true prophetic voice cries on behalf of the great I AM: "OBEY MY VOICE!"

God Tried to Kill Moses

God tried to kill the "Prince of Egypt." That's right! Exodus 4:24–26 records the story. On the way from the wilderness of Sinai back to deliver Israel from Egypt, "the Lord met Moses and sought to kill him." Why? Why would a loving God seek to kill the great deliverer before he had a chance to begin his challenge to Pharaoh?

Moses had failed to circumcise his son. Moses well knew God's covenant with Abraham. After all, it was because of His covenant with Abraham that God was committed to deliver Israel from Egypt, the house of bondage (Exod. 2:23–25). Circumcision was the "everlasting earthly sign confirming God's covenant with Abraham; as it is written, "…My covenant shall be in your flesh for an everlasting covenant" (Gen. 17:13). To Abraham and his seed, Yahweh ordered,

> This is my covenant, which ye shall keep, between me and you and thy seed after thee; Every man child among you shall be circumcised (Gen. 17:10).

Moses had not circumcised his own son. He was in disobedience. In actuality, it was a sin of **omission** rather than a sin of **commission**. We tend to treat omission as a lesser offense and even "wink" at such things. But God is God.. And it came to pass as Moses traveled by the way of the inn, that "the Lord met him, and sought to kill him" (Exod. 4:24).

Zipporah saved Moses' life. His wife, who was not of Israel, "took a sharp stone, and cut off the foreskin of her son, and cast it at his feet, and said, Surely a bloody husband art thou to me" (Exod. 4:25). From that day forward, Moses' "obedience quotient" rose dramatically.

You do not mess with God and His Word (unless of course you happen to be an American). We Americans believe we are the exception to every rule, do we not? Even God's rule! *After all, we are Americans*, we think to ourselves. *We have a godly heritage.* Moses had a godly heritage too, and God sought to kill him.

God made it clear to Moses. The person to fear is not Pharaoh but God himself. As it is written, "The fear of the Lord is the beginning of wisdom" (Ps. 111:10). Not until the fear of the Lord is restored in the land will the love and mercy of the Lord again be revealed in the land.

The fear (or awesome respect and reverence) of the Lord is revealed in the one who "trembleth at my word" (Isa. 66:2). When the church again trembles at the Word of the Lord, we will have begun our journey out of Egypt. Obedience is your ticket to leave Egypt (Deut. 30:1–3). The price of obedience is humility.

Today Is Your Day

Prayer is no substitute for obedience. Today if you will hear His voice, harden not your heart, as Israel did, tempting and testing God. God was grieved with that generation. He said, "They do alway err in their heart, and they have not known my ways" (Heb. 3:7–10). So God swore in His wrath, "They shall not enter into my rest."

Will you enter into His rest? Will you repent? Will you obey His voice? **America is dying. The cause of death is the collective disobedience of professing Christians in the land.**

There is no kinder way to express this truth. Your decision will determine her destiny. It may also determine your eternal destiny. **To obey, or not to obey—that is the question.**

Today, if you hear God's voice, harden not your heart. With true repentance and obedience, God may yet allow America to fulfill her divine destiny to disciple the nations. With true repentance and obedience, you will be prepared for the soon return of Christ. The alternative: "they shall return to Egypt" (Hos. 8:13). Your end-time trust will be revealed in your obedience and will be strengthened by your obedience. Trust and obey. There is still no other way! Leave Egypt today.

Postscript

Ultimately it may be more difficult to live for Christ than to die for Christ. Will you pass life's ultimate test?

Chapter Twenty

Let My People Go!

Slavery is still slavery, whether in Egypt or America.

GOD'S PEOPLE ARE ENSLAVED as much today as they were three thousand years ago. Contrary to popular spiritual opinion and application, when Jehovah ordered Pharaoh, through the mouth of Moses, to "Let My people go, that they may serve Me," it was God's people, the seed of Abraham, and heirs to the promise, who were in bondage (Exod. 10:3).

To this very day God continues His eternal effort to deliver His own people from the "house of bondage." He seeks a modern Moses to stretch out his rod over the spirit of Egypt, dividing between the holy and the profane. He seeks a third-millennium Moses, submitted to God's power and authority, daring to raise a voice to the Pharaonic powers of the modern day. There may be many messengers, but they will sound with only one true VOICE.

Blow the Trumpet in Zion

God is not happy! His church is enslaved. And He will not send His only begotten Son to receive enslaved sons at His Second Coming. His is not a Bride of bondage. Furthermore, His sons have been unable to complete their assigned work as we approach the "great and terrible day of the Lord."

The Lord is "uttering His voice before His army" (Joel 2:11). He is "blowing the trumpet in Zion" (Joel 2:15). "Let the priests, the ministers of the Lord, weep between the porch and the altar…" (Joel 2:17).

> I will pour out My spirit upon all flesh; and your **sons and daughters shall prophesy**…. And **also upon the servants and upon the handmaids** in those days **I will pour out My spirit** (Joel 2:28–29).

How are God's own people in bondage today? Beyond fornicating with the spirit of Egypt and walking like an Egyptian in daily living, is there further enslavement that frustrates the plan and purpose of a God whose Word, through obedience to that Word, makes men free? Indeed there is. The spirit of the ancient Pharaohs lives today, even in the realm of the ministry. To grasp the gravity of this bondage and the burden that it casts on the end-time work of the church, we must understand that our viewpoint can determine destiny.

Viewpoint Determines Destiny

Viewpoint determines vision: what I see. Vision determines direction: the way I act. And direction determines destiny: where I end up.

Tradition often determines viewpoint. Tradition built on tradition cements a viewpoint. But what if the original tradition became skewed, was modified, or was compromised for any number of reasons? If the original tradition was correct, any adjustment, no matter how noble or seemingly practical for the moment or times, results in change of direction...and also of destiny.

Consider a great ship. The captain determines his destination thousands of miles across the Atlantic. He sets sail, and as he ventures out across time and water, the seas swell, storms threaten, differences of opinion arise with underranking officers. Decision is made to change course to avert difficulties, and the great ship plows ahead. It becomes comfortable. There are no immediate threats. Life goes on. The miles pass. Two thousand miles are now behind us. But course correction has not been accomplished. Will the ship reach its intended destination?

Such is the plight of the Christian church. Direction was set. Destination was established. But the winds of time, storms of life, and struggles of men at the helm of the great ship—the church—left the established course. Intentions were good: avert mutiny, avoid storms, achieve peace, acknowledge earthly authority and ecclesiastical position. But destiny was compromised.

Two thousand years have passed. Christ's return seems imminent. But the church is unprepared. Despite waves of modern technology, the church is not equipped. Despite rolling in the high seas of life and covering many miles, the church has not accomplished her task. And in America, despite an unprecedented deluge of books, tapes, and media bombardment of radio and television "ministries," the church remains ill-equipped. Both pollsters George Barna and George Gallop find the behavioral model, standards, and performance of the church to be indistinguishable from the world. How can this be?

Folks, we are off course. Our viewpoint changed since the church was born. As our viewpoint changed, so did our vision. And our destiny (as well as that of the nation and the world) is in jeopardy...with the exception, that is, of a recurring promise: "I will build My church." What does that mean? Where did we go wrong? What must we do to cooperate with the original plan of the Master who seeks to be placed back at the helm? Where can we start?

The Work of the Ministry

We must start at the beginning. What was the church called to do? Aside from operating in godly ways with Christlike character and attitude, the church was commanded to "make disciples," and its shepherds were required to "perfect the saints." What does it mean to "perfect the saints"? For what are the saints to be perfected? Who are the saints?

Few would question that the "saints" are the called-out ones (or Christians) who may or may not be shepherds of some sort. How, then, are they to be perfected, and for what purpose? We clearly hear the apostle Paul tell us that the saints are to be perfected "for the work of the ministry, for the edifying of the body" (Eph. 4:12). For the saints to be perfected means to be "furnished" or "thoroughly equipped." Paul went on to describe the goal of such perfecting or equipping to his trainee, Timothy: "The things that thou has heard of me...the same commit thou to faithful men, who shall be able to teach others also" (2 Tim. 2:2).

Jesus put it differently. Just before He ascended, after earlier declaring, "Ye are the light of the world...ye are the salt of the earth," He left a mantle of ministry on all who would follow Him.

Never forget these words, "...**as My Father hath sent Me, even so send I you**" (John 20:21). That is what Jesus said. Could He have meant that? Was that only for pastors, priests, and popes? If not, what practical impact does that declaration have on the way we "do church," or on the way we "perfect the saints for the work of the ministry," or on our expectations of what the "saints" should do and when? Are you ready for this? Some spiritual "deep breathing" followed by a prayer for grace to receive may be needed at this point.

Plantation Ministry

Think back with me for a moment. In the early days of our nation, and particularly as we moved into the eighteenth century, plantations began to develop, particularly in the South. A plantation, as we commonly think of it, is a large estate cultivated by people other than the plantation owner. Those other people are either sharecroppers or slaves. The plantation exists because a planter decides to plant. He believes he cannot do it by himself, however, and cannot afford to hire others to do it. The planter owns the plantation. Therefore the planter needs either slaves or sharecroppers.

A sharecropper is like a tenant farmer. He tills a portion of the plantation and delivers a portion of the crop or revenue to the plantation owner. (Might this be a protestant denomination?) With enough sharecroppers, the plantation owner can maintain his plantation.

The most common plantation, however, was served by slaves. A slave is one who is wholly subject to the will of another—one who is thought to be the property of another human being, or who is wholly under the dominion of another's power.

There are tremendous and unfortunate similarities between the plantation model and traditional ministry models in the Body of Christ. The impact is not surface but substantial on pastor, parishioner and on the entire Body of Christ as well as on their collective ability to carry out the cause of Christ in the earth.

The pastor is the plantation owner. He considers the flock that he shepherds to be **his** church. In general, he treats the flock accordingly. Although he would never voice it, the sheep exist to keep the shepherd in business. After all, the shepherd as been "chosen by God to do the work of the ministry." Sheep must therefore help him. They become his slaves. Their job is to do whatever is necessary to keep his plantation going.

What will keep the plantation going? Busywork. Of course it is all "voluntary." The sheep must mow the church lawn, polish the brass, dust the window sills, build the parish house, establish an infinite number of programs to attract guests to the plantation so that the plantation owner feels worthy of the charge of "minister." And then they must serve on an infinite number of boards, councils, and committees to perpetuate the programs that promote the public and private image of the plantation and its owner. And those who would not do such menial tasks themselves can delegate the responsibility, becoming in effect, "house slaves" or perhaps sharecroppers, by contributing sufficiently to the plantation treasury so that those more menial responsibilities might be delegated to others.

This is not biblical ministry but management by manipulation. Ministers minister with **people**, not to buildings, projects, and programs.

This may not be a pleasant picture, but the practical impact of this analogy and the implicit attitudes that accompany it are inescapable. It strikes to the very heart and soul of our conception of ministry, and furthermore, it calls into question the whole meaning of what it means to equip the saints for the work of the ministry. If the shoe does not fit, do not put it on, but do not opt out too quickly. Seventeen centuries of tradition have a vice grip on our minds and hearts. Have we, by our traditions, made the Word of God of none effect? (see Mark 7:6, 9, 13).

There are at least three serious problems with the plantation model of ministry:

1. **Pride.** Pride of ownership. Realtors talk of it often. There is a tone in these words reflective of a sense of both place and possession. And they are words that might well describe much of what plagues "ministry" today. There is a tendency to view the local flock as "my" church. There is much talk of "my" ministry. And when the thought of "my" church escapes the membranes of my mind or even passes my lips, there is implicit the sense of location—a building. Pride of ministry and focus on place of ministry snuffs the life out of the people. So did slavery.

2. **Power.** It is said that "power corrupts, and absolute power corrupts absolutely." That is as true in the church as anywhere else. The plantation model focuses on the power, place, and privilege of the pastor. And power is deeply related to pride. The more focus placed on the pastor, the less focus on the people. Many an alleged "ministry" has little to do with people. The pastor reasons, "If I am not 'in power,' I may lose 'my' ministry. My plantation will be gone. Then what will I do?"

3. **Purpose.** Pride and power are a function of distorted purpose. The plantation model distorts purpose. The purpose of ministry is, after salvation, to raise up others to do the work of the ministry and to, in effect, take joint stewardship of the plantation. But if I, as a pastor, do that, there goes "my" plantation. So, the sheep must be kept, by and large, as sheep, so that my place as shepherd or plantation owner can be preserved.

The problem: sheep are to become shepherds in God's kingdom. That means genuine equipping of the saints puts the plantation ownership (it is really stewardship) at risk.... Unless, of course, the pastor has a vision big enough to replace himself. Anything else is slavery.

My dear pastor friends, the slaves are crying to be free. God has heard their cry. And God is preparing to free them. Will you? Are you ready? "Your" ministry will never be the same. You will be freed too!

The Servant Model

Jesus came to flesh out—"put flesh on"—the Word of God. He revealed God's truth in tangible relationship with the people. Did not Jesus also provide God's ministry model? Was His ministry model appropriate only for His time? Or was Jesus' model of ministry God's only true plan and example to prepare the Bride of Christ throughout the generations?

The apostle Paul has given us a clue. He has urged us, "Let this mind be in you which was also in Christ..." What was that "mind"? Paul went on to tell us that Christ "...took upon Him the form of a servant" (Phil. 2:5–7). Jesus was a servant. He ministered as a servant. He taught as a servant. He discipled as a servant. And He gave His life as a servant. But **the true shepherd/servant is an abomination in Egypt** (Gen. 46:34).

Jesus told us that He neither did nor said anything that the Father did not teach Him. And He always did things in a way that would please the Father. He told us that He demonstrated a servant model for us as an example. And then He revealed the secret to happy and fulfilled ministry. Are you listening?

"If you have these things, happy are ye if ye do these," advised the Master pastor-teacher-shepherd. Yet we are living in an age of great discouragement and dismay in ministry. Pastors drop out in droves. They are not happy. Results are dismal. The collective Body of Christ in America has not, for the most part, grown in the last thirty years. Parishioners have merely shifted allegiances.

Faith is overcome with frustration. Pastors try to keep a "stiff upper lip" outwardly while wilting inwardly. Lack of fulfillment in ministry has reached epidemic proportions. Special counseling programs and seminars are promoted to help pastors cope with despair. Disillusionment, depression, and even disgust prevail. All the while, fifty-two thousand people a week leave through the "back door" of America's congregations.

Could it be that we are reaping the devastating consequences in Christendom of adopting false models and mentors for ministry? Have we not inverted and perverted Jesus' model? **Have we not become lords over the flock—Pharaohs rather than servants?** If the King of kings and Lord of lords did not rule and lord it over the flock, ought we to? Isn't it time to let God's people go?

You say, "But that is not true! I wear myself out for the flock. My family suffers. I am exhausted! And it is not even appreciated!" You are probably right. But the reason is that all that energy and effort is often expended under an inverted and perverted ministry model. Many have been making wrong sacrifices. Pastor and people have conspired unwittingly to undermine and frustrate God's eternal plan in the name of efficiency, and as a result, holy disillusionment grips the church from pulpit to pews.

This is a strong statement, but I believe it to be absolutely true. If we follow a "lord-it-over," top-down ministry model, we have consigned our ministry to eternal frustration and have deprived the saints of their rightful role as "ministers of our God." That yields temporal judgment in the form of ministry misery, but it leads to eternal judgment for preventing the saints from "doing the work of the ministry." If that sounds harsh, try reading God's unedited version in Ezekiel 34. But there is an alternative!

Some say the people will not commit. That is a half truth. Seventeen centuries of slavery to an Egyptian system has numbed spiritual senses, suppressed faith, and suborned indolence. Slavery breeds and secures dependency: It also promotes the plantation owner to prominence. The Jesus model raised the people to prominence. After only three years, the Lord of the church said, in effect, "I am out of here. It is up to you boys" (John 20:21). He had to get out of their way so that they could "do the work of the ministry." **If pastors truly empowered the people to prominence in people-ministry, the pastoral burden would be dramatically lifted.** Are you convinced, in your heart, that nonseminary trained people can do full-fledged kingdom ministry?

The Freedom Alternative

This may seem a shocking statement, but God did not intend for pastors to "do the work of the ministry." He intended for pastors to "perfect [equip] the saints for the work of the ministry." Would not that simplify your job? Do you dare? Do you really want to do it all? Must you be top dog? Do we need to change our "traditional" viewpoints on what it means to "be a minister" and what it means to "do ministry"?

Consider the blessed alternative. Your goal is to equip and prepare every man and woman in your care to replace you—YES, REPLACE YOU! And quickly! Is that not what Jesus did? If we truly believe Jesus is coming soon, should we not immediately repent of our unwitting frustration of His eternal purposes, and forthwith, set about to rapidly **equip** and **release** the people to end-time ministry? As the people of God, this is our calling.

Spiritual Child Abuse

With every new birth into the Kingdom, I must, as a pastor, transmit a vision of spiritual adulthood and full-fledged ministry. I must not stand over the flock but come under them, pushing them up as fast as I can. I am responsible to move spiritual infants quickly into childhood, children into adolescence, and adolescents into responsible adulthood and maturity. Why? To augment and multiply my ministry, and yes, to replace me, even before I die (or retire).

It is an utter travesty that the majority of Christians never leave infancy. Infants suck milk. And "everyone that useth milk is unskillful in the Word of righteousness" (Heb. 5:13). The majority of Christians are woefully ignorant and unskillful in the Word of God: George Gallop made this observation at the 1994 Christian Booksellers Convention. Yet we are obese with Christian information.

A parent who fails to nurture his child out of infancy is a child abuser. That is especially true if somehow the motivation is to subtly, or perhaps not so subtly, keep that child in infancy to protect and preserve the parent's role as parent. It is sick, folks, but it is done regularly under the banner of ministry. And it is the perverted result of a perverted ministry model. To say that God is displeased is an understatement.

Ball-and-Chain Ministry

Even more common, however, is the perpetuation of eternal childhood or adolescence in the Body of Christ by pastors who fear the threat to their position by mature believers. Many love their position as spiritual "parent" so much, enjoying the dependency and adulation of the people, that they do not bring the flock to the "cutting of the apron strings." This is tough to admit! But this, too, is spiritual child abuse. It is prevalent in the natural, but epidemic in the supernatural.

Refusal to cut the apron strings is the product of an inverted ministry model that has the church in a stranglehold. This is ball-and-chain ministry. It flourishes under an overextended interpretation of authority, concluding that only the **pastor**, ultimately, can do "real" ministry. It is calculated to perpetuate the "plantation" model, limiting spiritual development to the goal of serving the pastor's purposes rather than Kingdom purposes. It stifles **THE** church growth and, in the long run, it will stifle **your** congregation's growth.

Maturity is readiness for heavy-duty, real-life, full-fledged ministry. How much growth is necessary for such maturity? It will largely depend upon the vision you instill in each disciple. It will also depend upon your own maturity—your ability to see and prepare for the gradual and purposeful release of your disciple from your ministry grasp. Jesus gave His motley, uneducated crew three years. Then, with the baptism of the Holy Spirit, they turned their world upside down. Could it be that some of us do not really want our world turned upside down? Let us be about the task. Maybe God, through you, empowered by His Spirit, will turn your world right- side-up.

Until then, **slavery is still slavery, whether in Egypt or America.** Pharaohs controlled, dominated, and abused God's people for their private purposes. For four hundred years they built private kingdoms on the backs of God's sons. Theirs was SELF interest, not son's interests. The lust for power, perks, prominence, and position drove them to control, restrain, and manipulate the sons of Abraham. But the agonized cry of Abraham's seed, the sons of faith, tormented the ear of their Creator. God remembered His covenant with them (Exod. 2:23–25). God had respect unto them.

And the Lord God cries out to pastors today as He did to ancient Pharaohs:

> How long wilt thou refuse to humble thyself before Me? **Let My people go, that they may serve Me** (Exod. 10:3).

Pharaohs, or Priests and Ministers?

This is a difficult decision. It tormented Pharaoh. He had grown to love the benefits of people serving him rather than their God. It was ingrained in the culture after four hundred years. Pride, power, and prominence prevailed. Pharaoh saw himself as the anointed and appointed one. He would dare even to resist God Himself to protect and preserve the perks of power. Besides, didn't Egyptian tradition validate his position. Of course. "This is the way we do it in Egypt," he reasoned.

That may be the way Pharaoh does it in Egypt. That may be the way Western Christians have done it since Constantine. It may be the way American Christians have done it, following the top-down institutional and organizational models of American business. But it is not the way God does His ministry.

With a mighty arm God led His son out of Egypt, declaring from the beginning His holy intentions:

> **Ye shall be unto me a kingdom of priests, and an holy nation** (Exod. 19:6).

Was it Yahweh's desire that the Levitical priesthood rule the kingdom of God until Christ's return for His Bride? Absolutely not!

> For it is evident that our Lord sprang out of Judah: of which tribe Moses spoke nothing concerning the priesthood (Heb. 7:14).

Who Are the Ministers of God?

Who then are the "priests" in God's eyes? Are they pastors, popes, or potentates? No! They are ALL of God's people who will OBEY HIS VOICE. Isaiah made this clear, proclaiming the kingdom, beginning with our great high priest:

> The Spirit of the Lord is upon me; because the Lord hath anointed me to preach good tidings...to proclaim the acceptable year of our God (Isa. 61:1–2).

Yet Isaiah did not stop with Christ. He continued his proclamation of a kingdom of priests: "To appoint unto them that mourn in Zion...that they might be called trees of righteousness, the planting of the Lord, that He might be glorified" (Isa. 61:3). Those that mourn in Zion, those who are called "trees of righteousness" are ALL those who OBEY GOD'S VOICE and are reborn in Christ.

Consider now these unequivocal and profound words of Isaiah. Meditate on their implication and application for both pastor and people:

> **But ye shall be named the Priests of the Lord: men shall call you the Ministers of our God** (Isa. 61:6).

Repeat it out loud: "Men shall call me a Minister of my God. I am a Priest of the Lord." Repeat it again. Do you believe it? Mister Pastor, do you really believe those you are charged to equip are as valuable in ministry as you are—perhaps even more so? Remember, the word *pastor* occurs only once in the New Testament, not as referring to a minister but as to an equipper of those who will minister (Eph. 4:11–12).

Can you fathom the massive consequences for the effective ministry of the end-time church if we truly believed this and then conducted ourselves accordingly? It would be nothing short of revolutionary. The Protestant Reformation may have pronounced the priesthood of all believers, but it never truly promoted or practiced it. And the Lord of the church waits. "How long?" He cries. "How long will you keep My people in bondage? Let My people go!"

A Kingdom of Priests

The record is clear and the plan, plain. When the sons of God left Egypt, the I AM declared, "ye shall be a kingdom of priests..." (Exod. 19:6). Isaiah repeated the theme in his prophecy of a Messiah who would be the first Priest among many priests, the firstborn of many brethren (Isa. 61:6).

Peter understood this profound principle of the kingdom. You can almost hear him. Listen in your "mind's ear":

> Ye...as lively stones, are built up a spiritual house, **an holy priesthood**, to offer up spiritual sacrifices, acceptable to God by Jesus Christ (1 Pet. 2:5).

And Peter was not through on this subject. His words are so well known that they have been put to music. Yet somehow we do not functionally believe them.

> Ye are a chosen generation, a royal priesthood, a holy nation... (1 Pet. 2:9).

It is little wonder that Peter saw fit in the very same book to instruct and warn elders (those who would pastor, preach, and teach) to "feed the flock of God...not by constraint, but willingly, not for filthy lucre [money and perks], but of a ready mind; **Neither as being lords over God's heritage**, but being examples to the flock" (1 Pet. 5:2–3).

> Yea, and all of you be subject to one another, and be clothed with humility: for God resisteth the proud [Pharaoh and all who dominate with him], and giveth grace to the humble (1 Pet. 5:5–6).

The words of the apostle John complete the picture, from the beginning of the book to its end. This is "The Revelation of Jesus Christ" (Rev. 1:1):

> Jesus Christ, who is the faithful witness, and the **first** begotten of the dead, and the prince of the kings of the earth...**hath made us kings and priests unto God and His Father**; to Him be glory and dominion for ever and ever (Rev. 1:5–6).

> The Lamb "took the book out of the right hand of Him that sat on the throne. And twenty four elders fell down before the Lamb.... And they sang a new song, saying, Thou are worthy...and hast redeemed us to God by thy blood.... And **hast made us unto our God kings and priests**: and we shall reign on the earth (Rev. 5:6–10).

By this time you should be on your feet or on your face singing the Hallelujah Chorus...

> Blessing and honour, and glory, and power, be unto Him that sitteth upon the throne, and unto the Lamb for ever and ever (Rev. 5:13).

A Final Wooing to Pastors

The Antichrist is rapidly preparing his own demonic priesthood. It is the global democratic rule of the people. It looks good, smells good, even seems to taste good, but it is founded in rebellion and rooted in unrighteousness. His priestly adherents are multiplying rapidly from nation to nation. Democracy will soon rule the world under a resurrected and revived Roman Empire. But it is a counterfeit universal priesthood. Meanwhile, God's universal priesthood of believers remains unsubmitted to His authority. Millions are defecting, as the apostate "church" joins forces with the Antichrist's democratic priesthood. Yet millions of the remnant who remain are slaves to a religious system with Pharaonic leadership that refuses to "let them go that they may serve me" (Exod. 10:3).

Pastor, today if you will hear His voice, harden not your heart. Humble yourself. Say not, "Who is the Lord that I should obey His voice?" Joel has written, "Multitudes, multitudes in the valley of decision: for the day of the Lord is near in the valley of decision" (Joel 3:14). And also, "Egypt shall be a desolation…" (Joel 3:19).

Thus saith the Lord, "Come out of Egypt. Do not delay. Do it in haste. **Let my people go!**"

A Final Warning to Professing Christians

And to the priesthood of believers, my sons and daughters, thus saith the Lord:

Woe to the rebellious children, that take counsel, but not of Me; and that cover with a covering, but not of My Spirit, that they may add sin to sin: That walk to go down into Egypt, and have not asked at My mouth; to strengthen themselves in the strength of Pharaoh, and to trust in the shadow of Egypt! Therefore shall the strength of Pharaoh be your shame, and the trust in the shadow of Egypt your confusion (Isa. 30:1–3).

The Egyptians shall help in vain. Now go, write it…note it in a book, that it may be for the time to come for ever and ever: That this is a rebellious people…that will not hear the law of the Lord: Which say…Prophesy not unto us right things, speak unto us smooth things, prophesy deceits (Isa. 30:7–10).

Woe to them that go down to Egypt for help…and trust in chariots…and in horsemen, because they are strong; but they look not unto the Holy One of Israel, neither seek the Lord! Now the Egyptians are men, and not God; and their horses flesh, and not spirit (Isa. 31:1–3).

Thus Saith the Lord,

In returning and rest shall ye be saved (Isa. 30:15).

This is My covenant with them, saith the Lord: My spirit that is upon thee, and My words which I have put in thy mouth, shall not depart out of thy mouth, nor out of the mouth of thy seed, nor out of the mouth of thy seed's seed…for ever…. **Arise, shine; for thy light is come**, and the glory of the Lord is risen upon thee. For, behold, the darkness shall cover the earth, and gross darkness the people: but the Lord shall arise upon thee and His glory shall be seen upon thee. And the Gentiles shall come to thy light, and kings to the brightness of thy rising. **Lift up thine eyes round about, and see…** (Isa. 59:21; 60:1–4).

Postscript

This may well be your final call out of Egypt. You cannot fornicate with Egypt and be the Bride of Christ. Today, if you will hear His voice, harden not your heart. Who do you really trust? Obedience is the ultimate test of trust.

He which testifieth these things saith, Surely I come quickly. Amen. Even so, come Lord Jesus. The grace of our Lord Jesus Christ be with you all. Amen (Rev. 22:20–21).

Chapter Twenty-One

Preparing for Promised Land

"Let him that thinketh he standeth take
heed lest he fall." I Corinthians 10:12

ALL WHO WOULD ENTER the Promised Land must prepare for promised land. It is not enough to come out of Egypt. Six hundred thousand
adult descendants of Abraham, Isaac and Jacob were delivered from the bondage of Egypt, yet only two were allowed entrance to the Promised Land.

The Template

The beloved apostle Paul made it clear that you and I should be guided
from Egypt to the Promised Land by the experiences that took place over
3000 years ago. "Now all these things happened unto them for examples,"
he warned, "and they are written for our admonition, upon whom the ends
of the world are come" (I Cor. 10:11). Paul then urged us not to proudly
think we also could not be kept from the Promised Land just as God refused
entrance to the great majority of "chosen people" in Moses' day. "Wherefore
let him that thinketh that he standeth take heed lest he fall" (I Cor. 10:12).

We are blessed because God established a template of living truth to guide
us in this amazing yet challenging hour of human history. In this chapter,
we will trace that template even as we review Israel's journey Out of Egypt,
through the wilderness, and into the Promised Land. It is God's template
outline for you and me in our journey as well.

EXPERIENCE GOD'S PRESENCE

When the fulness of time had come for God's people to be delivered from
the bondage of Egypt, a leader had to experience God's presence in order to

lead others into His presence. God confronted Moses with His holy presence at the burning bush (Ex. 3:1-6).

Each of us, whether pastor, prophet or people, must have a "burning bush" experience where we encounter not merely an emotional high but are confronted with the awesome nature of the holy God we serve. We must remember that without holiness "no man shall see the Lord" (Heb. 12:14).

Holiness is essential to enter the Promised Land, yet American pastors and people alike report frustration in almost never experiencing the true presence of God as we worship regularly together. Many even try to conjure up His presence with ever louder music and beats, supposing that methods will draw the Master or that frenzied emotion is indicative of the Spirit's presence. Obviously something must change, and quickly, if we are truly in the season of Christ's return. We must now experience God's holy presence to enter His eternal holy presence.

EXODUS FROM EGYPT

To enter the Promised Land, you must leave Egypt. When God declared His intent to "bring them into a good land... flowing with milk and honey," He determined to deliver the children of Israel "out of the hand of the Egyptians" (Ex. 3:7-8). You and I cannot remain even partially "in the hand of the Egyptians" and enter Promised Land. The spirit of Egypt is contrary to the spirit of the Promised Land.

ENCOUNTER THE "I AM"

If you will enter the Promised Land, you must know the God of that land as He wants to be known. God has made it plain how He wants to be known to His people. When Moses inquired as to how he should report the God he encountered to the children of Israel who were wincing under Pharaoh's bondage, God said, "I AM THAT I AM." "Say unto them, I AM hath sent me unto you" (Ex. 3:10-15). "This," He said, "is my name forever... my memorial unto all generations."

The words "I AM" express God's entire being, character and function among His creation. If we would enter Promised Land, we must come clearly to know God both corporately and personally as "I AM," which includes but is not limited to "creator," "savior," "healer," "protector," and "provider."

ERADICATE FLESHLY EXCUSES

When God calls us to step out, to leave the "leeks, onions and garlic" of Egypt and to lead others through the unknown wilderness of pagan culture and fleshly trials, most of us are quick with excuses. Like Moses, we complain about our perceived inadequacy for the task (Ex. 4:1-16).

Many call this "humility." But God sees it differently. "The anger of the Lord was kindled against Moses" for his barrage of fleshly excuses. If you expect to enter Promised Land, you must see "man's extremity as God's opportunity." Fleshly excuses, however well intended, are a fundamental denial of God's character as the "I AM." We must eradicate the false humility of fleshly excuses!

EXTEND GOD'S ROD

Each of us is given the precise abilities and equipment necessary to fulfill God's expectations as part of His congregation marching toward the Promised Land. Unfortunately, most of us, like Moses, fail to recognize what God has put in our hand and become frustrated, feeling inadequately equipped (Ex. 4:1-20).

God asks you, as he did Moses, "What is that in thine hand?" Refusal to acknowledge what is "in my hand," what God in His wisdom has made available, is to again deny Him as my "I AM." That is serious, because "I AM" is His all-encompassing name. You and I, like Moses, must come to see our "rod" as "God's rod" and then extend it, trusting that God will do His part. That is when the journey Out of Egypt gets exciting.

ENDURE INEVITABLE REJECTION

All who follow the Master Out of Egypt toward Promised Land will suffer rejection. It is inevitable.

From the moment Moses identified his rod as God's rod, rejection began. First it was Pharaoh. Then it was God's own people (Ex. 5-Deut. 33). The same happened to Jesus. The moment he declared, "The Spirit of the Lord is upon me" and acted accordingly, all hell broke loose against the heavenly messenger. Satan began the rejection, but God's people perpetuated it (Lk. 4:1-29). The spirit of religion always seeks to suppress God's active "rod" in the hands of men into powerless religious ritual.

Yes, "all that will live godly in Christ Jesus shall suffer persecution" (I Tim. 3:12). Some of the most painful persecution or rejection comes from among the very people who profess Christ as savior and who we seek to lead Out of Egypt toward the Promised Land but who love the ways of Egypt more than the ways of God (John 16:2). Prepare to endure rejection if you truly begin to leave the spirit of Egypt.

ENGAGE THE ENEMY

God delivered Israel from Egypt with a mighty hand and an outstretched arm, yet immediately Pharaoh pursued them to undo all that God had done (Ex. 14:1-31). The people panicked and Moses cried out to God for help while telling the people, "Fear ye not, stand still and see the salvation of the Lord."

It sounded religious. It had the ring of faith. But God was not pleased. The Lord said, "Wherefore criest thou unto me? Speak unto the children of

Israel, that they go forward. Lift up thy rod, and stretch out thine hand over the sea and divide it."

God despises whining. He is looking for winners who will not sit idly by, who will engage the enemy by faith with what God has put in their hands, trusting God to do what they can't. If you are to reach the Promised Land, you must not only flee the spirit of Egypt but be prepared to resist, with spiritual weapons, the forces of the enemy who will pursue and track you down, entrapping you with seemingly impossible alternatives. That is not the time to whine, to cry, or to flounder in faith, but to engage the enemy of your soul with all that God has put at your disposal. Partner with God. You do what you can so that God, by His grace, can do what you cannot. Submit to God, resist the devil (Jam. 4:7).

ENDURE WILDERNESS TRIALS

Deliverance from Egypt does not lead straight to Promised Land. Contrary to much popular belief, only those who endure wilderness trials demonstrating true deliverance from the spirit of Egypt are eligible, by God's grace, to enter the Promised Land.

Immediately after the miraculous crossing of the Red Sea, Israel "went out into the wilderness." At the first test, they cried and complained (Ex. 15:22-25, 16:1-3). In fact, only two accountable adults who were delivered from Egypt gained entrance to the Promised Land. The others continuously cried, murmured and complained, refusing to agree with God throughout their wilderness experience, and all died in the wilderness (Numb. 13-14). Jesus was victorious, enduring the wilderness (Matt. 4:1-11). Joshua, a type of Christ, was likewise victorious despite the testing in the wilderness.

Escaping Egypt is not the goal. Entering the Promised Land is the goal. Only Joshua and Caleb were permitted entrance because they had a different spirit (Numb. 14:24). God called the rest of the congregation of "chosen" people... "evil" (Numb. 14:35). Jesus made it clear, "He that shall endure to the end shall be saved" (Matt. 24:13), "because iniquity shall abound and the love of many shall wax cold" (Matt. 24:12). But you shall be blessed and receive the crown of life if you faithfully endure wilderness trials and temptations, which "the Lord hath promised to them that love him" (Jam. 1:12).

ESTEEM THE BLOOD COVENANT

It took the blood of an unblemished lamb in Egypt to deliver the seed of Abraham from Egypt (Ex. 12). And it took the blood of the covenant to keep "chosen people" from returning to the house of bondage en route to Promised Land (Ex. 24:1-8).

Just as Moses "esteemed the reproach of Christ greater riches than the treasures in Egypt" (Heb. 11:26), so you and I must esteem the blood of Christ more highly than all the treasures of Egypt, including its ways and values.

"Behold the blood of the covenant," declared Moses, upon reading the word of the Lord to the people." And they responded, "All that the Lord hath said we will do, and be obedient" (Ex. 24:7-8).

Loving and faithful obedience to God's commands is the sole measure of the extent to which you esteem the blood of the covenant. Not feelings but faithful obedience defines eternal destiny. Grace grants remission of sin by the blood of the Lamb and grace empowers you and me to obey the Lamb. Obedience or faithful "works" reveal whether grace has, in fact, been genuinely received.

Grace was extended to all of the covenant seed of Abraham to be delivered from Egypt, to walk through the wilderness, and to enter Promised Land... yet... only two genuinely received that grace and were permitted entry. Only Joshua and Caleb truly believed God. The others merely liked to identify themselves by God's name. Though they claimed the promise of the covenantal seed, they did not inherit the promise (Heb. 3:8-19).

The Lord of the "church in the wilderness" declares today, "Not every one that saith unto me, Lord, Lord, shall enter into the Kingdom of heaven: but he that doeth the will of my Father which is in heaven" (Matt. 7:21). Jesus said, "If ye love me, keep my commandments" (John 14:15). Do you esteem the blood of the covenant?

EMPLOY ELDERS TO LEAD

The burden of leading 600,000 men plus women and children Out of Egypt through life's wilderness was beyond Moses' ability alone. The "church in the wilderness" needed to be guided by empowering and employing elders "to be rulers of thousands, and rulers of hundreds, rulers of fifties, and rulers of tens" (Ex. 18:13-26). Paul undoubtedly followed this example when he instructed Titus to "ordain elders in every city" (Titus 1:5).

The needs of people have never changed. We still need "elders" who can pastor us in small groups as the Spirit of God draws the church increasingly back to the home. Consider the qualifications: "... able men, such as fear God, men of truth, hating covetousness" (Ex. 18:21). With the oversight of apostles and prophets, we must reconsider the biblical model as well as the standard for godly leadership if we hope to shepherd a significant flock through wilderness wilds to Promised Land.

EXERCISE THE LAW OF LIBERTY

"If ye will obey my voice indeed, and keep my covenant, then ye shall be a peculiar treasure unto me above all people... and ye shall be unto me a kingdom of priests, and an holy nation," declared Yahweh to the wilderness wanderers (Ex. 19-20). God gave them ten commandments to guide them on their journey.

James, the brother of Jesus, called it, "... the perfect law of liberty" (Jam. 1:25). He ought to know, since he heard Christ himself distill their essence, summarizing, "Thou shalt love the Lord thy God with all thy heart, and with all thy soul, and with all thy mind." And "thou shalt love thy neighbor as thyself" (Matt. 22:36-40). It is *license* we should most greatly fear on the pathway to Promised Land, not the perfect law of *liberty*. Loving obedience to God and loving our neighbors, especially those of "the household of faith" in Christ, is the truest measure of our freedom in Christ by whose grace we gain inheritance to His Promised Land (Gal. 6:10). Living "in the Spirit" will never permit you to live a life loosely embracing the works of the flesh. As the beloved apostle Paul so forcefully warned, "... they which do such things shall not inherit the kingdom of God" no matter how much they profess Christ's name or include themselves in His church (Gal. 5:21, I Cor. 6:9-10)).

ESTABLISH AUTHORITY OF GOD'S WORD

What does the Lord require of you after leaving Egypt on your journey to the Promised Land? The simple answer is: (1) to fear the Lord, (2) to walk in His ways, (3) to love him and (4) to serve Him with all your heart and soul (Deut. 10:12). To "fear" the Lord is to have an awesome respect that prompts you to obey His Word when you don't otherwise feel like it. To "walk in his ways" is to obey Him in action and attitude. To "love him" is first defined by obedience rather than by emotional feelings for Jesus said, "If you love me, keep my commandments." "He that loveth me not, keepeth not my sayings" (John 14:15-24). Trust is revealed in obedience.

The strong tendency for most travelers toward the Promised Land is to claim to love and serve the Lord while either failing to or refusing to obey. Neither religious activity nor even belief in the truth of religious facts is an adequate substitute for obedience. Even prayer is no substitute for obedience. "For to obey is better than sacrifice" (I Sam. 15:22). Therefore God warns you and me, "Take heed to yourselves, that your heart be not deceived" (Deut. 11:16).

Parents, we must both teach and display the authority of God's Word in our lives and homes if we desire that our children reach the Promised Land. This is a non-delegable duty.

Preserving God's word as our authority for every aspect of our lives and obeying it out of love for our Lord will bring blessing on the journey and preserve our right to possession of the Promised Land. God's mercy forgives when we fail but truly repent. His grace enables us to do what we ought, not what we want. Only by God's grace do we enter His land of promise. But rebellion and disobedience can keep us out.

"Take heed, brethren, lest there be in any of you an evil heart of unbelief, in departing from the living God. But exhort one another while it is called Today; lest any of you be hardened through the deceitfulness of sin. For we are made partakers of Christ, IF we hold the beginning of our confidence steadfast unto the end" (Heb. 3:12-14). Remember, only two out of 600,000 covenant seed of Abraham who left Egypt were permitted entrance to the land of promise. Why?

God said, "They do alway err in their heart; and they have not known my ways" (Heb. 3:10). What proved to God their underlying unbelief despite calling themselves the "christians" of their day, as the inheritors of the covenant promises through Abraham? It was disobedience and rebellion. It was refusal to take God at His Word. They believed IN God but did not believe Him. They were excluded from the Promised Land. Don't let it happen to you, your children, or your congregation.

EMPHASIZE PROMISE OVER PROBLEM

If you will not believe God in the wilderness, He may find no affinity in you for the family of faith. Persistent murmuring for manna or money may prevent the ultimate blessing of the Master.

There are no more profound chapters in Scripture than Numbers 13 and 14. God said, "I give you the land." "Go in and possess it." All but two of the "sons of promise" who were delivered out of Egypt by God's mighty hand embraced the problem rather than God's promise. They revealed lack of true faith not by saying "we saw giants in the land" but by saying, "We be not able to go up against the people, for they are stronger than we." God said they brought up "an evil report" (Numb. 13:27-33). Persistent evil reports reveal unbelief and will keep you out of Promised Land.

Americans have created a Babylonian substitute for biblical belief. Instead of believing God despite the problem, we more often choose to deny the problem while embracing an artificially "positive" belief system. The power of positive thinking may impress men but depresses the God who made men. Positive thinking, alone, is a modern version of re-building the Tower of Babel. God desires not that you deny the problems in the wilderness but that you choose positively to believe Him, His promises and His character regardless of the "giants" that threaten to block the way.

ENFORCE THE COVENANT IN COMMUNITY

Contrary to American individualistic thinking, the journey to the Promised Land is not made alone. It is made in a "covenant community." Those who left Egypt on the way to Promised Land were referred to as "the congregation" and as "the church in the wilderness." How each person and family lived, believed, obeyed, or spoke affected and often infected the others.

Because of the power of influence one person or family has on the spiritual health of the greater "body," God expects leaders to exercise loving but firm enforcement of certain areas that are most prone to infect or affect the others so as to prevent them from reaching the Promised Land or being welcomed into it. The letters to the Corinthian church are a prime New Testament example of the Apostle Paul's emphatic conviction of the community of believers acting like a body, protecting and serving the welfare of the covenantal community as the very Body of Christ.

Biblical church discipline must be restored, reflecting God's corrective compassion for Christ's Body. "Speaking the truth in love" must not be used to frustrate speaking the truth. Concern for individual sensitivities must never trump compassion for the congregation. A little leaven still leavens the whole lump (I Cor. 5:1-8).

ENDURE TO THE END

Endurance is required in the journey through the wilderness to the Promised Land. Moses, in forsaking Egypt, "endured, as seeing him who is invisible" (Heb. 11:27). Jesus, "for the joy that was set before him endured the cross..." (Heb. 12:2). And you and I are encouraged to "consider him... lest ye be wearied and faint in your minds" (Heb. 12:3).

Each of the original disciples endured trials and tribulations as did their Master. The beloved Apostle Paul also endured problems and persecutions that make our paltry trials seem puny, yet he declared, "I have fought a good fight, I have finished my course, I have kept the faith: Henceforth there is laid up for me a crown of righteousness..." (II Tim. 4:7-8).

You and I are exhorted to "count it all joy" when we encounter trials and temptations, knowing that "the trying of our faith worketh patience" (Jam. 1:2-3). We must "press toward the mark for the prize of the high calling of God in Christ Jesus" (Phil. 3:14). We must "run, and not be weary: walk and not faint" (Is. 40:31).

The times ahead are going to become more spiritually strenuous as we approach the Second Coming of Christ and the Promised Land. Deception will be rampant. Persecution will increase dramatically. Unbelief will become the norm. Many will be offended, "And because iniquity shall abound, the love of many shall wax cold." But as Jesus, the "Captain of our salvation," having come Out of Egypt and having pressed through the wilderness declared, "he that shall endure to the end, the same shall be saved" (Matt. 24:3-13).

Let us press on, together, to Promised Land.

Endnotes

Chapter 1

1. Henri Stierlin, *The Pharaohs* (Finest S.A./ Editions Pierre Terrail: Paris, 1995), p. 119.
2. Pamela K. Stewart, *Memphis: A City Oppressed* (Pamela K. Stewart, 1991), p. 3–11.
3. Ibid., p. 18.
4. Roy Proctor, "Blockbuster," *Richmond Times Dispatch* (Richmond, Virginia), April 3, 1999, pp. A-1 and A-9.
5. Ibid., p. A-9.
6. Ezekiel 29:3.
7. Gordon Hickey, Feature: "Our River, Our City," with article entitled, "Floodwall resurrects the soul of the city," *Richmond Times Dispatch* (Richmond, Virginia), June 18, 1998, p. A- 12.
8. Ibid., p. A-1.
9. Ibid., p. A-12.
10. Ibid., p. A-12.
11. Virginius Dabney, *Richmond: The Story of a City* (University Press of Virginia: Charlottesville, VA, 1990), p. 1, 3.
12. James S. Wamsley, *Richmond: Portrait of a City* (Stockfile: Richmond, Virginia, 1989), p. 21.
13. James Shultz, *Richmond: A River City Reborn* (Windsor Publications: Chatsworth, California, 1990), front cover.
14. Ibid., p. 17.
15. Henri Stierlin, *The Pharaohs*, p. 48.
16. James J. Jeffries, *America's Seal: Its End-Time Connection*, (Battleline Publications: Mission Viejo, CA, 1994), pp. 250–257.

17. Richard Brookhizer, "Ancient, Ernest, Secret and Fraternal," *Civilization Magazine*, August/September, 1996, pp. 58–63, p. 60–61.

18. Ron Campbell, "Unearthing the Mysteries of Freemasonry", *Charisma Magazine*, November 1, 1997.

19. Jack Harris, *Freemasonry: The Invisible Cult in Our Midst* (Jack Harris, 1983), p. 35.

20. Richard Brookhiser, "Ancient, Ernest, Secret and Fraternal", *Civilization Magazine*, August/September 1996, pp. 58–63, p. 63.

21. Ibid., p. 63.

22. Mark Edmundson, "Las Vegas Rising", *Civilization Magazine*, August/September 1996, pp. 37-43, p.42.

23. Ibid., p.41.

24. Ibid., p. 41.

25. Ibid., p. 43.

26. Mark Lerner, *The Complete Pyramids* (Thames and Hudson: New York, NY, 1997), p. 242–243.

27. Barbara Kantrowitz, et al., "In Search of the Sacred," *Newsweek Magazine*, November 28, 1994, pp. 52–58, p. 54.

28. Christopher Dickey, "The Oldest Pyramid Scheme," *Newsweek Magazine*, November 28, 1994, p. 59.

29. Mark Edmundson, "Las Vegas Rising," *Civilization Magazine*, August/September, 1996, p. 43.

Chapter 2

1. Will Durant, *The Story of Civilization: Our Oriental Heritage, Egypt*, chapter 8, (Simon and Schuster: New York, 1954), p. 197.

2. Simonetta Crescimbene, *Egypt* (Smithmark Publishers: New York, 1996), p. 23.

3. Ibid., p. 198.

4. Ibid., p.199–200.

5. Ibid., p. 200.

6. Kenneth L. Woodward, "Hail Mary", *Newsweek Magazine*, August 25, 1997, pp. 49–55, (Cover Story).

7. James Paterson and Peter Kim, *The Day America Told the Truth* (New York: Prentice-Hall Inc. 1991), p. 45.

8. George Barna, "The Sad Truth About Christians and Marriage", *The Barna Report*, Premier Issue, (Word Ministry Resources: Waco, Texas), 1996.

9. "Divorced Ministers", *Ministries Today*, September/October 1995, p. 18.

10. Will Durant, *The Story of Civilization: Our Oriental Heritage, Egypt*, chapter 8, p. 204.

11. Ibid., p. 205.

12. Gaalyah Cornfeld, *Archeology of the Bible: Book by Book* (Harper and Row: New York, NY, 1976), pp. 34–36.
13. Will Durant, *The Story of Civilization: Our Oriental Heritage, Egypt*, chapter 8, p. 214.
14. Ibid., p. 214.
15. Ibid., p. 215.
16. Ibid., p. 215.
17. Ibid., p. 216.
18. Henri Stierlin, *The Pharaohs* (Finest S.A./ Editions Pierre Terrail: Paris, 1995), p. 146.
19. Ibid., p. 168.
20. Ibid., p. 24.
21. Will Durant, *The Story of Civilization: Our Oriental Heritage, Egypt*, chapter 8, p. 216.

A Voice to the Church

A **"MOSES FOR OUR TIME"** and "a John the Baptist for our generation," declare listeners to Chuck Crismier's passionate message to a church wandering in the American wilderness.

Raised a pastor's son, Chuck became a veteran sojourner in denominational Christianity, primarily of the evangelical brand. Lengthy exposure over thirty years in ten distinct denominations—mainline and otherwise, from coast to coast and from north to south—has provided the author with an enviable insider's view of American Christianity. Exposure to the charismatic renewal has broadened the scope. Having launched a nondenominational "cell church" ministry in 1995, Chuck's energies are continuously focused on raising up men and women to do the work of the ministry.

A frequent speaker, the author has a bold yet persuasive way of translating Kingdom principles. Twenty years as a trial lawyer and ten years in public education have provided "wilderness" training for the current call, while he also has served twenty years as a shepherd of God's sheep.

In his own "burning bush" experience, Chuck felt a profound call to woo and warn those who call themselves by the name of the Lord in America. And so Charles Crismier III left his lucrative law practice, forming SAVE AMERICA Ministries in 1992, to "Rebuild the Foundations of Faith and Freedom." God's 1978 call to Chuck to "Speak to My church at large, whether they will hear or whether they will forbear" was becoming reality.

Chuck moved his family by divine mandate from Southern California to the birthplace of America—Richmond, Virginia—from where he launched a daily live radio broadcast, *VIEWPOINT*: "Confronting the Issues of America's Heart and Home." Speaking provocatively and prophetically, Chuck has become "a voice to the church," declaring "vision for the nation" in America's greatest crisis hour on the near edge of the Second Coming.

For Further Contact

The Author: Charles Crismier III   c/o SAVE AMERICA Ministries
- Speaking
- Orders
- Letters
- Prayer

PO Box 70879
Richmond, VA 23255
(804) 754-1822
crismier@saveus.org

The Broadcast: *Viewpoint*
- Via Internet (live with streaming audio)
- www.saveus.org

Website: Save America Ministries
- www.saveus.org
- www.reviveus.org

Other Publications
- *Preserve Us a Nation* (1993), Vision House
- *Renewing the Soul of America* (2002), Elijah Books
- *The Power of Hospitality* (2005), Elijah Books

For additional copies of

send $16.99 + $3.95 S&H to

Elijah Books
PO Box 70879
Richmond, VA 23255

or have your credit card ready and call

(800) 728-3872